Group Analysis

Working with Staff, Teams and Organizations

Edited by
Aleksandra Novakovic and
David Vincent

Routledge
Taylor & Francis Group

LONDON AND NEW YORK

First published 2019
by Routledge
2 Park Square, Milton Park, Abingdon, Oxon OX14 4RN

and by Routledge
52 Vanderbilt Avenue, New York, NY 10017

Routledge is an imprint of the Taylor & Francis Group, an informa business

British Library Cataloguing-in-Publication Data
A catalogue record for this book is available from the British Library

Library of Congress Cataloging-in-Publication Data
A catalog record has been requested for this book

ISBN: 978-0-367-11206-6 (hbk)
ISBN: 978-0-367-11207-3 (pbk)
ISBN: 978-0-429-02531-0 (ebk)

Typeset in Times New Roman
by Apex CoVantage, LLC

Group Analysis: Working with Staff, Teams and Organizations

Featuring contributions from a range of organizational contexts, *Group Analysis: Working with Staff, Teams and Organizations* identifies the key features to group analytic practice as well as how different theoretical orientations, such as Systemic and Tavistock Consultancy approaches, can be incorporated into the process.

The book addresses two essential features of group analysis: the exploration of unconscious dynamics in groups, and the shifts of observational attention between the group as a whole, the individual in the group, and the group in the individual. Including perspectives from both organizational consultancy and reflective practice, chapters feature analysis with groups and subgroups in a range of settings, including a forensic psychiatric hospital, a children's hospice, an Anglican religious community and the management team of a global organization.

Group Analysis: Working with Staff, Teams and Organizations is a major contribution to the developing literature on group analysis. It will be of great interest to psychotherapists, organizational consultants, facilitators of reflective practice groups, coaches, trainees in these disciplines, and any professionals who work with staff, teams, and organizations.

Aleksandra Novakovic is a psychoanalyst and group analyst. She was a Consultant Clinical Psychologist in the Adult Psychology Service, and Joint Head of the Inpatient & Community Psychology Service, Barnet, Enfield & Haringey Mental Health Trust. She has worked at Tavistock Relationships and on the IGA Diploma Course in Reflective Practice in Organisations. Currently she teaches for the British Psychoanalytic Association and is a Consultant Visiting Lecturer and supervisor at Tavistock Relationships. She edited *Couple Dynamics* (Karnac, 2015), and co-edited *Couple Stories* with Marguerite Reid (Routledge, 2018).

David Vincent trained as a group analyst at the Institute of Group Analysis, and as a psychoanalytic psychotherapist at the British Association of Psychotherapists. He is an IPT therapist and supervisor, and worked for many years in the NHS, retiring as a Consultant Adult Psychotherapist from Forest House Psychotherapy Clinic. He has also worked for University College Hospital Drug Dependence Unit, MEDNET and Camden Psychotherapy Unit, and in private practice. He was Chair of the IGA from 2000–2005, and Chair of Ethics for the British Psychoanalytic Council from 2012–2016, and is now a retired member of the IGA and the BPF.

The New International Library of Group Analysis (NILGA)
Series Editor: Earl Hopper

Drawing on the seminal ideas of British, European and American group analysts, psychoanalysts, social psychologists and social scientists, the books in this series focus on the study of small and large groups, organisations and other social systems, and on the study of the transpersonal and transgenerational sociality of human nature. NILGA books will be required reading for the members of professional organisations in the field of group analysis, psychoanalysis, and related social sciences. They will be indispensable for the "formation" of students of psychotherapy, whether they are mainly interested in clinical work with patients or in consultancy to teams and organisational clients within the private and public sectors.

Recent titles in the series include:

The Art and Science of Working Together
Practising Group Analysis in Teams and Organisations
Edited by Christine Thornton

Dream Telling, Relations, and Large Groups
New Developments in Group Analysis
By Robi Friedman

Group Analysis
Working with Staff, Teams and Organizations
Edited by David Vincent and Aleksandra Novakovic

The Social Unconscious in Persons, Groups, and Societies
Volume 3: The Foundation Matrix Extended and Re-configured
Edited by Earl Hopper

Fairy Tales and the Social Unconscious
The Hidden Language
By Ravit Raufman and Haim Weinberg

For more information about this series, please visit www.routledge.com

To Zoja, Mihailo, Samuel, Laura, and Florence

Contents

PART III

Series editor's preface
Group Analysis: Working with Staff, Teams and Organizations

The clinical discipline of Group Analysis, based on psychoanalysis, sociology and the study of group dynamics, is both broad and deep. Although born in England, its conception can be traced to a configuration of ideas and consultative interventions which seem to have come alive in the years following World War I in Germany.

The scope of Group Analysis can be realized especially in its applications to the task of understanding the parameters and processes of social systems other than small groups who meet for the purpose of providing psychotherapy for the participants in them. Such understanding can be used in order to help organizations of various kinds become more effective and efficient in reaching their formal goals, the specification of which is a political process. Moreover, learning through experience in the context of organizations and their constituent committees and staff teams provides insight into unconscious life, including the restraints and constraints of the socio-cultural arrangements of which people are largely, and perhaps resolutely, unaware.

It is essential to gain insight into the social defences against anxieties associated with knowing and understanding more about the parameters and processes of a particular organization and its location in its contextual society. Group analytic consultation to organizations involves the provision of opportunities for reflective practice within those settings in which problems and difficulties are thought to have arisen. It also provides opportunities for people to learn more about themselves in the context of their work roles. It is inevitable that such knowledge will seep into other contexts, such as more personal and domestic life.

Group Analytic reflective practice is closely related to intervention based on other ways of thinking about organizations and their constituent groupings, such as more abstract 'systemic' schools of thought, and the group relations tradition associated with the Tavistock. The interpenetrations and overlaps among these orientations are not generally acknowledged and appreciated. This is an unfortunate function of the politics of organizations and training in the fields of psychoanalysis, group analysis and sociology, both inside our universities and their regulatory bodies. More reflective practice would facilitate the interpretation of these networks and ideas.

I am particularly impressed by the willing and honest acknowledgement by the authors of the chapters in this volume of the extent to which reflective practice is fraught with problems, challenges and tough resistance towards gaining insight into the world of work, especially into the dynamics of power and authority behind those of leadership and management, which are, of course, different activities. These experienced and senior practitioners no longer assume that their work will always go well and achieve favourable outcomes. However, they are most often guided by the dictum that in the first instance they should do no harm. Although questions about the cost and benefits of acquiring insight into systems of work and their roles are often ignored, the authors of these chapters are sensitive to them.

Still, it can readily be seen that the application of group analysis to the study of organizations has given rise to a body of knowledge which has yet to be appreciated fully. Learning though experience, which includes reflective practice, is rewarding throughout the dynamic matrix of an organization, the foundation matrix of its contextual society, and ultimately within the personal matrices of us all.

I know of no other book which seeks to compare and perhaps to integrate different but closely related ways of consulting to organizations whose leaders have requested help with the difficulties of working and living in their organizations, especially larger ones whose ownership and lines of responsibility are ambiguous. Well-written and well-referenced, this text will be useful for general and specialist students and colleagues, as well as those of us whose lives are structured by organizations on which we depend for remuneration and for goods and services. Aleksandra Novakovic and David Vincent are to be congratulated for encouraging and fostering these contributions, and for integrating them into a most useful addition to the sub-series of NILGA concerning the dynamic matrices of organizations.

Earl Hopper
Series Editor

Notes on editors and contributors

Sue Einhorn, BA (Hons), CQSW, Member Institute of Group Analysis (IGA), Registered UKCP Member GAN London. Sue has worked as a literary agent, a detached youth worker, a community worker, and a Senior Lecturer in social work. She has also worked clinically at the Women's Therapy Centre and at the Medical Foundation for the Care of Victims of Torture (MFVT). She is currently a Training Group Analyst for the Institute of Group Analysis (IGA) and has a private clinical practice. She convened the training of group analysts in St Petersburg and currently supervises group analysts in Russia and Norway. She lectures widely and writes occasionally.

Ray Haddock, MBChB, M.MedSc, FRCPsych, Member Institute of Group Analysis (IGA), Licensed Systems-Centered® Practitioner. He is a psychiatrist and group analyst, and worked as a medical psychotherapist for 25 years, including in a number of medical management roles. He has extensive experience applying Theory of Living Human Systems and Systems-Centered methods in leadership, organizations, individual, and group therapy. He is also deeply involved in developing SCT theory, practice, and SCT training groups in UK, Europe, and the USA. SCT® and Systems-Centered® are registered trademarks of Dr Yvonne M. Agazarian and the Systems-Centered Training and Research Institute, Inc., a non-profit organization.

David Kennard is a retired clinical psychologist and group analyst. He has worked in a wide range of mental health settings and has a particular interest in therapeutic communities and in psychosis. He was the editor of the journal, *Therapeutic Communities*, from 1992–1998, and Chair of ISPS UK (UK network of the International Society for Psychological and Social Approaches to Psychosis) from 2004–2009. He is the co-author/co-editor of books, including *An Introduction to Therapeutic Communities*, *A Workbook of Group Analytic Interventions*, *Experiences of Mental Health Inpatient Care* and *Staff Support Groups in the Helping Professions*.

Julian Lousada is a psychoanalyst (BPA), former Clinical Director of the Adult Department, Tavistock and Portman NHS Foundation Trust, former Chair of the British Psychoanalytic Council, and current Chair of the British Psycho-therapy Foundation. He has directed Group Relations conferences nationally and internationally and is an organizational consultant and founding partner of 'Peopleinsystems'. He has lectured and taught widely. He has written, together with Professor Andrew Cooper, *Borderline Welfare – Feeling and the fear of feeling in modern welfare* (Karnac, 2015), and 'The shock of the real: psycho-analysis, modernity, survival' in *Off the Couch*, edited by A. Lemma and P. Matthew (Routledge, 2010).

Martin Miksits works as a systemic therapist, executive coach, organizational consultant, and teacher. He is interested in dialogic approaches to organi-zational emergence, effectiveness, and ethical practice. He is Co-director of the Systemic Development Partnership in the UK and Director of his consulting practice in Austria. His consulting experience is in facilitating development of organizational processes, performance, strategy, and cul-ture. Martin also draws on his extensive international experience as Manager in Europe and Latin America, leading strategic change and organizational transitions. He has a doctorate in Systemic Practice and master's degrees in Business Administration, Systemic Organizational Practice, and Systemic Therapy.

Richard Morgan-Jones' original graduate and post-graduate education was at Cambridge, Oxford, and Exeter Universities in anthropology, theology and education. He has a 45-year-long career in group relations, organizational consulting and executive coaching; and a 35-year career as Supervising and Training Psychoanalytic Psychotherapist with the British Psychotherapy Foun-dation. He is a Registered Member of the British Psychoanalytic Council, and Elected Board Member of the International Society for Psychoanalytic Society of Organizations (ISPSO). He is Director of Work Force Health: Consulting and Research, and author of *The Body of the Organisation and its Health*.

Morris Nitsun is Consultant Psychologist in Group Psychotherapy in Camden and Islington NHS Trust, a Training Group Analyst at the Institute of Group Analysis, and a member of the Fitzrovia Group Analytic Practice. He was pre-viously the Head of Psychological Services in the North East London NHS Foundation Trust for almost 30 years, playing a significant role in initiating and developing clinical services and gaining considerable managerial experience in the NHS organizational setting. He is widely published and has presented his work at many international events. In 2015 he was awarded the President of the Royal College of Psychiatrists' medal for services to mental health.

Aleksandra Novakovic is a psychoanalyst and group analyst. She was a Con-sultant Clinical Psychologist in the Adult Psychology Service, and Joint Head of the Inpatient & Community Psychology Service. She worked at Tavistock Relationships, supervised on couple psychoanalytic psychotherapy train-ing and on the IGA Diploma Course in Reflective Practice in Organisations.

Currently she teaches for the British Psychoanalytic Association, and is a Consultant Visiting Lecturer at Tavistock Relationships. She edited *Couple Dynamics* (Karnac, 2015), and co-edited with Marguerite Reid, *Couple Stories: Application of Psychoanalytic Ideas in Thinking about Couple Interaction* (Routledge, 2018).

Christine Oliver, PhD, is Consultant Family Therapist and Group Analyst for East London Foundation Trust and a psychotherapist, supervisor, and organizational consultant in private practice. She also co-directs Systemic Leadership and Consulting Training, a one-year programme organized by the Systemic Development Partnership. A special interest is in the design and facilitation of dialogue to engender reflexive and coherent practice in the work place. She has contributed to the development of systemic theory and practice through many published papers and through two books: *Reflexive Inquiry* (Karnac, 2005), and *Complexity, Relationships and Strange Loops* (MHA Institute, Canada, 2003).

Cynthia Rogers is an experienced Training Group Analyst, organizational consultant, author, researcher, and company director. Cynthia is a staff member of the Institute of Group Analysis course, 'Diploma in Reflective Organisational Practice', and was a key speaker at the first international congress on Median Groups, in Bolzano, Italy. She is the author of *Psychotherapy and Counselling: A Professional Business* (Wiley, 2004), which describes the dynamics associated with earning and sustaining a living as a therapist. A research interest in professional identity informs her organizational work. She has consulted to the voluntary and public services, the business community, and individuals.

Ian Simpson is a group analyst. He was Head of Psychotherapy Services at a major London teaching hospital for 20 years. He retired from the NHS six years ago and continues to have a small private practice, offering individual and group psychotherapy, supervision, reflective practice for staff teams, organizational consultancy, and large group facilitation. He supervises on the IGA Diploma Course, 'Reflective Practice in Organisations'. He has written papers and book chapters on group dynamics, reflective practice, and contextual safety in the workplace. His special interest is on the impact of political and economic policy on social care systems.

David Vincent trained as a group analyst at the Institute of Group Analysis, and as a psychoanalytic psychotherapist at the British Association of Psychotherapists; he has a Professional Doctorate from the Centre for Psychoanalytic Studies at the University of Essex. He is an IPT therapist and supervisor, and worked for many years in the NHS, retiring as a Consultant Adult Psychotherapist from Forest House Psychotherapy Clinic. He has also worked for University College Hospital Drug Dependence Unit, MEDNET, and Camden Psychotherapy Unit, and in private practice. He was Chair of the IGA from 2000–2005, and Chair of Ethics for the British Psychoanalytic Council from 2012–2016.

Gerhard Wilke, MA Cantab., Dip. FHE, London University. Gerhard is a group analytic organizational consultant. He is an Associate of Ashridge Business School and an Honorary Fellow of the Royal College of General Practitioners and the International Association of Group Therapists. He is the author of *The Art of Group Analysis in Organisations* (Routledge, 2014), *How to be a Good Enough GP* (BMJ, 2001), and *Ordnung und Chaos in Gruppen* (LIT Verlag, 2017). Gerhard co-authored the influential book, *Living Leadership: A Practical Guide for Ordinary Heroes*, and co-wrote *Breaking Free of Bonkers: How to Lead in Today's Crazy World of Organizations*. Gerhard is also a renowned Large Group Conductor.

Peter Wilson is a Training Group Analyst and Supervisor with the Institute of Group Analysis. He is a highly experienced clinician and trainer who has taught and published papers both in the UK and internationally. As UK Director of Training for 10 years, Peter introduced the innovative training, 'Reflective Practice in Organisations', as part of a successful wider project to provide a broader range of trainings in applied group analysis. A founder member of the Fitzrovia Group Analytic practice, Peter currently works in private practice and as a supervisor in the NHS.

Introduction

This volume is a contribution to the developing literature on psychoanalytic and group analytic work with staff groups and organizations. We hope that this book will be of interest to psychotherapists, organizational consultants, facilitators of reflective practice groups, coaches, trainees in these disciplines, and any professionals who work with staff, teams, and organizations. The purpose of this book is to explore the application of group analysis to organizational consultancy and reflective practice. The contributors present their work in different settings, ranging from staff and reflective practice groups with GPs, a forensic psychiatric hospital, an Anglican religious community, a children's hospice, a long-stay psychiatric unit, an acute psychiatric ward, a palliative care unit, a student group on a Diploma Course in Group analysis, to a Large Group with psychotherapists and group analysts, and consultancy to the management team of a global organization.

The book is divided into three parts. In the first part, the contributors provide an overview of the Tavistock Consultancy approaches, systemic, and group analytic models of working with staff teams and organizations, and an opportunity to compare the group analytic approach with the theory and practice of these two established models in organizational consultancy. We hope that contributions in this section will facilitate a more comprehensive understanding about the application of group analysis in organizational contexts and how the group analytic approach differs from, but also relates to, other modalities of organizational consultancy.

The second part of the book presents group analysts' thinking and ways of working with staff teams and organizations. The contributors discuss their work with individuals, subgroups, and groups. The groups they present range from small to medium and large groups. Although most group analysts would probably identify themselves primarily as group analysts, at the same time, many acknowledge the important influence of other approaches. The authors discuss their model of applied group analysis, as well as the common group analytic 'ground' in working with the unconscious processes, transference, and countertransference, and the manifestations of these processes in the interactions and the verbal and non-verbal communications in the group.

One of the questions that this book asks is, what is it that group analysts do when they work with staff teams and organizations that is distinctively 'group analytic' in their practice, even when they have different theoretical orientations and incorporate other modalities in their practice?

The contribution in the last section of this book addresses the two essential features of the group analytic approach: the exploration of unconscious dynamics in groups and the group analytic practice of shifting attention between the foreground and the background, that is, the changes in the level of observation between the group as a whole, the individual in the group, and the group in the individual.

The foundation and development of group analysis was bound up with the establishment and growth of the National Health Service (NHS) from 1948. The early work in group psychotherapy and social milieu therapy grew out of the work of the rehabilitation services, like Dartford, and military hospitals, like Northfield. Foulkes, the founder of group analysis, worked at Northfield as a military psychiatrist after Bion and Rickman had left (Harrison, 2000), along with Tom Main, who went on after the Second World War to found the Cassel Hospital (Main, 1946; Barnes, 1968). Maxwell Jones, after Dartford, set up the Henderson Hospital (Dolan, 1996). Bion worked for the War Office Selection Boards after Northfield and then took this interest into his early work at the Tavistock Clinic (Bion, 1961; Pines, 1985; Trist and Murray, 1990). Foulkes worked at the Maudsley after the war, and then set up the Group Analytic Society and the Group Analytic Practice, and out of these grew the Institute of Group Analysis (IGA), the training organization where most of the contributors to this book trained. The training at the IGA is described in a recent article (Hopper, Vincent and Wilson, 2010).

Group analysis, both as a therapeutic practice, and as a body of theory, has developed out of this complex matrix of influences from the therapeutic hospitals of the Second World War, the NHS, and the powerful and creative combination of psychoanalysis and sociology. By the time that the IGA was founded, there was a growing interest in various kinds of social and community therapy as well as group therapy in the NHS and in private practice. The majority of IGA trainees conducted their training groups in NHS settings, and many went on to work in NHS hospitals and clinics, developing experience and expertise in outpatient and inpatient group psychotherapy, day hospitals, and therapeutic communities.

Over time, group analysts found that they could also be helpful to staff teams and could work with organizational issues. This approach was strongly influenced at first by group analytic psychotherapy in both residential and outpatient therapeutic communities, where, as part of the work, the staff carried, and often acted out, the projections of the patients. Almost from the beginning of the IGA training, group analysts were therefore expected to be involved with small groups of staff who worked with troubled patients. This has been the principal legacy of the early years, and some of the papers in this book deal precisely with that range of work. However, over time, group analysts have extended their field of expertise and now work with a variety of organizations and staff teams. Group analytic theory, which can be pragmatic and diffuse, incorporating ideas from a number of different psychoanalytic schools of thought, has had to develop alongside this.

Group analysts working with teams and organizations are now influenced by many different theories, among them Bion and post-Kleinian psychoanalysis, the Tavistock Institute of Human Relations, systems theory, and complexity theory (Stacey, 2003).

Foulkes trained as a psychoanalyst in Vienna, and his training analyst was Helene Deutsch. Arriving in Britain in 1933, he joined Anna Freud's group. It is important to note that Foulkes (1990) was always committed to psychoanalysis, as well as to group analysis. Yet, over time, the relationship between psychoanalysis and group analysis was regarded by some practitioners to be complex and often conflicted. Group analysts, like psychoanalysts, belong to different schools of thought, and have a range of different theoretical paradigms. It may be the case that these disagreements are in fact more indicative of a difference in theory and the context of work, that is, 'work' with an individual versus 'work' with a group, than in psychoanalytic or group analytic practice, and the analytic stance of working with unconscious processes, transference, and countertransference.

The complex issue of group analytic theory has always been its relationship with psychoanalysis. How true to the psychoanalytic project is group analysis? Is it a branch of psychoanalysis or a breakaway? Is it a reformation or a heresy? Group analysts have always struggled with this in various ways (Dalal, 1998). If we are influenced by psychoanalysis, are we somehow less group analytic? And if we depart from the psychoanalytic frame of reference, for example, by introducing structure and agenda in staff groups, are we less 'psychoanalytic' in our work with groups. It is also important to note that group analysts are trained to develop a capacity to perceive and conceptualize a 'larger whole': for example, the observation of the 'group as a whole' phenomena, but also awareness of the larger social context that impacts on the members of any group. This applies not only to the manifest cultural, ethnic, racial, and other differences and identifications, but to Foulkes' concepts of the dynamic and foundation matrix, and to the different levels of complexity and unconscious in the life in any group. Hopper (2003) points out that 'psychoanalytic models neglect the constraints of the social unconscious and the diversity and variety of social systems (p.21)', and develops ideas about the social unconscious:

> . . . the 'social unconscious' refers both to the fact that people can be and often are unconscious of social factors and forces, and to the social factors and forces of which they are unconscious . . . Specifically, the 'social unconscious' refers to the constraints of social objects that have been internalised, and to the restraints of those that have not.
>
> (Hopper, 2007, pp.285–86)

Another question for group analysts, perhaps most prominent in organizational work, is can we be 'true' to group analysis and at the same time be influenced by systemic, Tavistock Consultancy approaches, or complexity theory models? It can also be argued that the flexibility and openness to the new ideas and points of view in the practice of group analytic approach is in fact its most valuable feature. Just as the therapy group and the group analyst in clinical work always adapt to new and different patients, so can the body of group analysis adapt to new demands in consultancy with staff teams and organizations. This argument would support the idea that perhaps the strength of group analysis lies more in its practice than in the theory. It is a 'here and now' approach that takes into consideration the individual, the group, the organization, and the wider cultural and socio-political context, as they are all available in the present moment in the group. The group analyst's position in relation to both patient and group is always based on this essential question: 'Who is saying what to whom and why?'

The group-analytic authors in this book take a variety of positions in regard both to group analysis and organizational consultancy, and each contributor in their own particular way references different aspects of group analytic work. What unites them is a commitment to the process whereby the unconscious is made conscious in the group. The group analytic unconscious is fluid, ever-changing, and imbued with internalized social relations (the social unconscious), while the personal internal group is imbued with the rich constellation of internal objects and the relations between them. From the first moment of any group, these two complex internal sets are in a continuous dynamic interaction, they are projected into the other members of the group, the group analyst, and the group as a whole, and likewise the experiences at these different levels are taken in, or introjected. They then become available for scrutiny, understanding, and change, through 'free-floating conversation', which for Foulkes was a central idea and group equivalent of individual free association. This central process is the heart of all group analytic work, with patients, teams, and organizations: people in a room together, bearing the experience of not understanding, speaking and silence, passing thoughts in their mind and shifting feelings, and trying to understand what is happening to them and between them at this moment in time and why.

While teaching reflective practice and in discussion with colleagues, we found that some important questions were raised by students and colleagues alike: What are the similarities and differences between the group analytic, systemic and the Tavistock Consultancy approaches in working with organizations? Is there a scope for incorporating new techniques from systemic and Tavistock methods into the group analytic approach to work with organizations, while retaining the quintessential features of a group analyst approach? What is the quintessential characteristic in the group analytic approach?

Within the well-established New International Library of Group Analysis, this volume is part of a developing sub-series concerned with consultancy to work teams and organizations (Hopper, 2012; Wilke, 2014). We hope that this book will stimulate interest in, and further exploration and development of the application of group analysis in the field of reflective practice and organizational consultancy. We also hope that this book will stimulate a dialogue between organizational consultants working in various modalities, concerning their various ways of working and conceptualizing organizational dynamics.

References

Barnes, E. (Ed.) (1968). *Psychosocial Nursing*. London: Tavistock.

Bion, W.R. (1961). *Experiences in Groups*. London: Tavistock.

Dalal, F. (1998). *Taking the Group Seriously*. London: Jessica Kingsley.

Dolan, B. (1996). *Perspectives on Henderson Hospital*. Surrey: Henderson Hospital.

Foulkes, E. (1990). *Selected Papers of S.H. Foulkes: Psychoanalysis and Group Analysis*. London: Karnac.

Harrison, T. (2000). *Bion, Rickman, Foulkes and the Northfield Experiment*. London: Jessica Kingsley.

Hopper, E. (2003). Introduction. In: *Traumatic Experience in the Unconscious Life of Groups: The Fourth Basic Assumption: Incohesion: Aggregation/Massification or (ba) I:A/M* (pp.17–28). London: Jessica Kingsley.

Hopper, E. (2007). Theoretical and conceptual notes concerning transference and countertransference processes in groups and by groups, and the social unconscious: Part III. *Group Analysis, 40* (2): 285–300.

Hopper, E. (2012). Introduction: The theory of incohesion: aggregation/massification as the fourth basic assumption in the unconscious life of groups and group-like social systems. In: E. Hopper (Ed.), *Trauma and Organisations*. New International Library of Group Analysis Series. London: Karnac.

Hopper, E., Vincent, D. and Wilson, P. (2010). Training in group analysis in the United Kingdom: The Institute of Group Analysis. *Group, 34* (4): 373–80.

Main, T. (1946). The hospital as a therapeutic institution. In: E. Barnes (Ed.) *Psychosocial Nursing* (1968). London: Tavistock.

Pines, M. (Ed.) (1985). *Bion and Group Psychotherapy*. London: Routledge.

Stacey, R. (2003). *Complexity and Group Processes*. Hove: Brunner-Routledge.

Trist, E. and Murray, H. (Eds) (1990). *The Social Engagement of Social Science, Vol. 1: A Tavistock Anthology: The Socio-Psychological Perspective*. London: Free Association Books.

Wilke, G. (2014). *The Art of Group Analysis in Organisations: The Use of Intuitive and Experiential Knowledge*. London: Karnac.

Part 1

Tavistock consultancy approaches, systemic practice and the group analytic approach in work with staff, staff teams and organizations

Introduction

Group analysis developed first as a method of psychotherapeutic treatment. The classic model is the small heterogeneous stranger group, meeting once or twice a week for several years, and both theory and technique are well founded. Over time the applications of group analysis have widened and diversified, and there have been many attempts to extend group analysis into consultation with work teams and organizations beyond the scope of the small group.

Group analysts have turned to other theoretical models to help them formulate a new Group Analytic method. Hopper (2011, 2012, 2016), has directed group analysis both into psychoanalysis and sociology and has emphasized Foulkes' concept of the 'social unconscious' and the centrality of trauma in the life of organizations, while Stacey (2003) has emphasized the uses of complexity theory. The other influential theories for group analysts have been those arising from systems theory, particularly through systemic family therapy, and those from the Tavistock Institute of Human Relations and the Tavistock Consultancy.

This first chapter lays out three theoretical approaches to organizational consultancy: from a consultant experienced in and working with the Tavistock traditions and approaches, Richard Morgan-Jones; a systemic consultant, Martin Miksits; and a group analyst, Christine Oliver.

Tavistock Approaches to Consulting with Teams and Organizations

Richard Morgan-Jones

Introduction

This chapter begins with key theories in Tavistock consulting approaches, along with a worked example from the author's consulting practice. Tavistock approaches have attracted a variety of titles for different kinds of contract: organizational/team development consultant, socio-therapist, socio-analyst, group relations consultant, executive coach, human systems analyst, mentor, action researcher, evaluator, or leadership development consultant, while the activity is also described as systems psychoanalysis, socio-analysis, role-analysis, coaching, consultancy, or applied social science. Additionally, the approaches can include a *consultancy stance* in using consulting skills within other leadership, management, or training roles.

The chapter next outlines the historical development of these approaches and their institutional context, including their vision and scope. Finally, there is a brief overview of some contemporary developments in application.

Central to Tavistock approaches are the links between learning from experience in engaging with conscious and unconscious psychodynamics, and the social and technical aspects of organization tasks.

It would require a book to cover all such resources, so inevitably there will be some omissions favoured by particular consultants in this diverse and well-established community of practice. The range of history, approaches, theoretical concepts and applications through action research, organizational development and consultancy, across what this chapter describes as 'Tavistock Approaches', is vast. In consequence, any writer influenced by or having access to such approaches will always have a partial view. This chapter is no exception. It will therefore leave out many aspects of Tavistock approaches that colleagues who have been employed at one of the Tavistock institutions or been shaped by association, training, conferences, or studentships, will carry deeply felt emotional attachments to alternative perspectives. In short, this contribution is partial and for those wishing to pursue wider and deeper applications there is a wealth of history, of which perhaps the two best examples are Sher (2013) and Abraham (2013). A clear time-line history of the Tavistock is to be found on the Tavistock and Portman NHS Foundation Trust website along with many other invaluable resources.

Key theories in use developed from Tavistock traditions and influences

a) Mannie Sher (2013) defines the range of Tavistock approaches as follows: "Open socio-technical systems informed by psychoanalytical perspectives that illuminate unconscious processes in individuals, in the organisations with which they work, and in the physical and social environments in which these organisations are located".

b) The Grubb Institute, led by successive directors Bruce Reed and Bruce Irvine, have worked over decades with many faith-based and community organizations. Their 'Transforming Experience Framework' (TEF) develops a set of three overlapping circles of being a *person,* signified by yearning; within a *system*, signified by accountability; and being in a *context*, signified by 'connectedness'. These three circles overlap in an expression of the forces that impinge upon and underpin *Role*, signified by 'vocation' and 'leadership vision'. This whole model exists within a deeper framework of connectedness to *source values and beliefs* (Long, 2016). Their emphasis on *purpose* is shaped by an ecological perspective that perceives organizations as open systems inter-dependent upon their environment for which they perform delegated tasks, both consciously and unconsciously. Thus, both individuals and organizations each carry part of a larger whole to which humanity belongs.

c) The primary *task* of an organization is elaborated into:

Normative Primary Task, describes what an organization has to do to survive (Miller and Rice, 1967).
Existential Primary Task describes the reason to exist.
A *Phenomenal Primary Task* describes task performance as it is experienced (Lawrence, 2003)
The *Hermeneutic Primary Task* (Mathur, 2006) outlines seeking the search for meaning and purpose across a group or organization.

d) *Boundaries* relate to management tasks, including the supply of both human and technical resources and the demand of services and goods in an economic supply chain, emphasizing open systems theory. Leadership is seen as essentially an activity at the boundary of an organization interfacing with its environment. For the consultant, activity at the boundaries of role, task, group, and organizations are key resources for consultation and enquiry.

e) *Role exploration and description* include both formal organizational roles as well as informal *organizational role psycho-dynamics*, involving the squeeze between conscious and unconscious organizational dynamics and the *valency* (Bion, 1961) of personal emotional issues that attract people to given roles. *Valency* describes the way an individual or group may be *mobilized* into taking up a particular role, fulfilling some collectively held and hidden unconscious phantasy (Newton et al., 2006, Long and Sievers, 2006, Brunning, 2006).

f) *Authority* attracts a range of sources for understanding, from institutional authority to personal and experience-based authority, including the psychodynamics of projected authority. Such dynamics emphasize how authority for leaders needs to be earned and is never static. It can be exploited, gained, or lost and then regained. Bruce Reed (Grubb Institute, 1998) differentiated it from power. Power conveys access to resources. Authority is characterized by a context, where a task is agreed and stakeholders are free to contribute their different resources and roles. This leads to an understanding developed by Ed Shapiro (2016) that the boundary of authority relations is characterized by the mutual reciprocity of inter-dependence and the possibility of recognition of mutual vulnerability. Such dynamics can also explore problematic leader–follower relations, empowerment, delegation, sexual, age, gender, financial means, and racial politics. Sources of authorization include self and other authorization, which are essential elements in leadership.[1] (See Sher, 2013 for contemporary examples of Tavistock approaches.)

g) Resistance is key to understanding the Change Process. Lewin's Action Research idea (1946) is that the way to understand an organization is to seek to change it, and that here and now events in meetings reveal organizational truths about dynamic functioning that foster both research and change. This also links to his idea of force field analysis as a means to map forces for and against change, still actively used in the Tavistock by Jean Neuman among others. Resistance also relates to Isabel Menzies Lyth's work ([1959]1988) on 'The Functioning of Social Systems as a Defence Against Anxiety', that resulted from a study of why so many nurses left the profession early.

h) *Relatedness* describes the way an agreed task across different roles shapes the way people in a working context relate emotionally and the quality of collaboration.

i) *Systems management* maps the range of resources, roles, and technology required to perform a task. The range of tasks competing for given resources shapes the culture of the organization and its balance of job satisfaction with efficiency (Miller and Rice, 1967). However, this does not just require the management of demand. It also involves the management of supply and output of services and goods required in a given market. This is where an organization risks limiting its capacity for innovation in aligning services to the pace of demand or the preferred silos of supply (Boxer, 2017).

j) *Systems psychodynamics:* Bion's exploration of group dynamics (1961) focused on the distinction between the effective work group and the emotionality of shared basic assumptions (dependency, fight–flight, pairing) that pattern group belonging. Application of such dynamics and inter-group tensions are seen as central to understanding what goes on beneath the surface in organizational life. (Obholzer and Roberts, 1994, Gould et al., 2004; 2006 Huffington et al., 2004). The Tavistock Institute has also developed contemporary approaches to organizations that incorporate the dynamics of complexity and chaos theories (Stacey, 2003).

k) Analysis of *leadership and followership* in the organization is shaped by *sentience* and by the dynamics of *sentient groups*, meaning, the particular affiliations and emotional bonding and history attached to their morale, collective cooperation, and ethos. Matching sentience to task groups may produce an impassioned work force and yet one too rigid to change from established working practices (Miller and Rice, 1967). Sentience involves the emotional patterning of a work group's psycho-dynamics, and the desire of valency for a particular work group reveals the need to belong to a work group that makes up for emotional deficits in the life of the individual (Morgan-Jones, 2010a).

l) *Social defences* as a concept was introduced by Isabel Menzies Lyth ([1959]1988) in her groundbreaking action research project, 'The Functioning of a Social Systems as a Defence against Anxiety'. This approach has been taken forward in a clear introduction to the Tavistock approach by Larry Hirschorn (1990, 1994) and is reviewed by Armstrong and Rustin (2015) in the light of contemporary experience.

m) Eliot Jaques (1998) pointed to the limitations of the psychodynamic approach in asserting the need for *requisite organization and management* to "provide both for optimum organizational efficiency and trust" in the design of organizational structures and management. This developed out of his influential focus on organisational culture epitomised by reports on work with the Glacier Metal Company (Abraham, 2013, pp.160–62).

n) Having worked at the Grubb Institute and TCS, David Armstrong (2005) is well placed to develop a key idea (Hutton et al., 2000, Reed 1988, *the organisation–in–the–mind*, to describe the shared conscious and unconscious aspects of relatedness within organizational systems. This is discoverable in the mental images and patterns of behaviour within systems.

Brief account of consulting using a Tavistock approach

I am asked by a colleague working in a different modality to take over their role in consulting to the rehabilitation team in a forensic psychiatric hospital. In crossing the *boundary* of the organization, my first task is to clarify the task of the team within the functioning of the organization as a whole. For this, I must seek *authorization*, both initially and after a contracting procedure, first, from the line manager and second, in meeting the team themselves. This forms the beginning of an agreement about a shared and agreed task, method of working, and payments, in a written contract, together with review terms. The task of the consultation is initially to explore the dynamics of interactions at different levels of organizational experience with the patients, other units, tribunals and meetings where the future of patients is decided and with the wider local and national context for forensic psychiatry and the community in which the unit is set.

My colleague has provided emotional support and deeper understanding, through emerging group dynamics, of their working relationships with a challenging client group who have attracted diagnoses of borderline, sometimes deluded or psychopathic, personality disorders, and may have criminal records. Additionally, my Tavistock approach brings a focus on the *task* of the team, namely rehabilitation within a larger unit where they receive referrals from more secure units on a campus of secure and semi-secure 'ward units'. Beyond keeping patients, staff, and the community safe from further harm, the overall task is hitherto unclear to me. The Tavistock approach insists that it will have to emerge. My focus is not just on using the group meetings to surface hidden emotionally charged themes, but also to explore key social and emotional aspects of relating across a typical day. This is informed by the democratization and social regime aspects of the therapeutic community movement informed by pioneering experiments at the Northfield Hospital in 1946–47 (see below). This informs me and them in an action research approach into the range of roles and tasks they engage with in working with the patients in their unit across unit activities.

My authorized *role* as an organizational systems consultant is consistently tested by attempts to recruit me as a psychotherapist for assaulted staff and for challenging patients, both of which it is urgent to resist in order to retain my boundaried role and authority as an organizational consultant.

A key theme that emerges is that previously priority had been given to intense emotional engagements, insight development, and capacity to encourage insight for behaviour that may be irrational in the unit. Now in thinking about the rehabilitation tasks, these kinds of relating are seen as only one task in engaging with a fuller range of assisting in recovery of social identities that crime and mental breakdown have destroyed. The *task* the team is performing on behalf of the wider *system* of forensic units comes into focus and with it a range of challenging situations with intense dilemmas for team consultation. One focus is on a painting group that has a social learning and pocket-money contract through decorating the administration block and managing social events, trips out, and work placements.

In supporting the team in its work and in its emotional demands, my aim is to keep distinct tasks in mind and how they might be part of an overall task. As this work progresses, both team members and the team leader become more adept at moving between different roles and negotiating with each other and with the clients how each role creates specific expectations and re-socialization. We seem to be moving to a more social skills model and yet the psychodynamic perspective is not lost. Rather, it comes into its own in reviewing violent and aggressive incidents in being able to comprehend how the behaviour of staff might have provoked the particular vulnerabilities of a client. This develops critical incident supervision in which I frame the developmental task as how to learn in the consultations, how to be effective supervisors for each other on the job, and where staff are working together 'on the front line'.

A number of critical incidents over the eight years that I consult to this team reveal that staff sickness relates closely, but not always, with 'catching' the mental illness, or secondary re-traumatization, of individual clients or groups of them. This suggested that a *primary risk* (Hirschorn, 1994) and therefore developmental task of the unit is to manage the mental health of staff who are vulnerable, both to the individual dynamics that had attracted them to this work as well as to the tensions within the community. This function relates to the tasks given to the forensic units by society as a whole, to keep patients, the community, and staff safe from harm. In other words, they are encouraged to develop their inner and peer consultancy stance with each other, as a key outcome of the interaction.

A review of all this work after two years and some envy of the fortnightly consultation of the team by other unit managers lead to a request for similar work to be done in two other units, one semi-secure, the other secure. Merely applying a 'scaling-up' approach of doing the same thing in other units risks being undermined by the more complex systemic issues of how such work might be authorized, supported, or undermined by the wider system. First, there is a new authorization task to accomplish, and not just within management but with wider inter-disciplinary teams. This is a needs and resources exercise to respect and build on current practice.

What follows is a mix of developing practice and policies. These include time and skills for supervision from management, while also offering nomination from the bottom up for staff to train in supervision skills. The next task is to design a supervision development and authorization process in small groups where people across disciplines could learn how to give the mix of attention, support, feedback, challenge, and empathy needed for analyzing the roles, task, and dynamics functioning in the part of the system a given supervision incident was occurring.

Needless to say this work was not all plain sailing and some of its ups and downs can be explored further in Morgan-Jones (2005 and 2006).

History and scope

Brief history of Tavistock approaches: collaborations between clinicians and social scientists

During the years after the First World War, the Tavistock Clinic pioneered the application of Freud's psychoanalytic theories and clinical approach to the bereavement of many families and in treating traumatized soldiers. This work echoed the vision of the founder of the Tavistock clinic in 1920, Hugh

Crighton-Miller, that ". . . the healer's function should be interpreted in the broadest way and . . . consideration be given not only to the body but to the mind, not only to the patient, but if necessary to his environment" (Dicks 1970, p.19).

This foundational work in applied psychoanalysis received a further boost during the Second World War from officers and psychiatrists working with the War Office Selection Boards, through using observation of behaviour in leaderless groups and encouraging a nomination system for promotion from the ranks rather than just from officers. This led to the development of therapeutic community attempts to treat and rehabilitate war traumatized soldiers, pioneered at the Northfield Hospital, initially by Bion and his collaborator, John Rickman. The idea was to use all the relationships and activities in the unit to aid the therapeutic task. Rickman had earlier experimented with a more egalitarian role for the doctor/psychiatrist/officer, which could not be easily tolerated in the army Emergency Medical Service (EMS) at the Wharncliffe Hospital.

Despite Bion and Rickman's experiment closing after six weeks, later attempts to develop these ideas by Sutherland, Bridger, de Mare, Main, and Foulkes at the Northfield (Harrison, 1999, Pines, 1985) had huge influence on later developments at the Tavistock and on the therapeutic community movement, not to mention on the development of group analysis. Key was whether the role of a therapeutic hospital in war time was bent on the survival of humanity beyond Nazi fascism, and which supported the war effort in producing men who could return to being soldiers, or whether the task was to facilitate individuals into civilian life. This latter task became the model for social rehabilitation of the Civil Resettlement Units after the war.

Harold Bridger (1990a; 1990b)), following Bion's and Rickman's experiment at Northfield, took a different stance that was to have great impact on the field. Bridger took a view of the therapeutic community as a system that needed to be related to its wider environment, in order to manage the disruptive regressions that Bion's experiment had fostered, which were beyond what the Army could tolerate. He described his role as a 'social therapist', seeking rehabilitation through social engagement. As an educator, he borrowed from the idea of learning by doing from John Dewey and emphasized healthy activities that placed the task of monitoring group processes, developing insight, and learning to a secondary task.

This differentiation of these double tasks initiated an approach to conferences and consulting to organizations where conscious themes and issues were identified by *search groups,* leaving the examination of how tasks were tackled to a later agenda, when doing business was suspended for process review. The focus of Bridger's work created a bridge between the socio-technical and ecological approaches of Eric Trist and others at the Tavistock and those of the social-psychological approach epitomized by Kleinian influenced approaches to group dynamics led by Bion. It also provided space for integration of group analytic forms of therapy, such as those Foulkes had pioneered at Northfield within Bridger's regime (Pines, 1985).

Bridger's pioneering work enabled his later assistants, Tom Main and S.H. Foulkes to develop understandings of the democratic processes of self-organizing teamwork that could be effective in the rehabilitation task, and which required the psychiatrist and officer to relinquish his role for one that shared responsibility with patients and staff alike. Main was later to develop his psychoanalytic approach to the therapeutic community at the Cassell Hospital. Foulkes went on to develop group analysis in a format that was both social and intrapsychic therapy and which led to developing an understanding of the *social unconscious*. Robert Hinshelwood (1987) and Ed Shapiro (Shapiro and Carr, 1991) have made considerable contributions to developing therapeutic community work from either side of the Atlantic.

Following these earlier developments after the Second World War, the Tavistock's work was shaped by the wider *context*, in attempts to restore civil society with a new social contract in the post-war years in the UK. The creation of a new Welfare State with its National Health Service (NHS) and welfare provision paid for by a National Insurance scheme and free at the point of delivery was framed by the dream of a peaceful development of a society whose institutions cared for the mental health alongside other needs of its members. This was the world view alongside which Tavistock thinking and practice developed.

The Tavistock Institute for Human Relations and the Tavistock Clinic Consultancy Service and Training

With the advent of the National Health Service, from 1947 the Tavistock Institute for Human Relations (TIHR) formed a distinct unit within the Tavistock. This enabled cross-fertilisation between social scientists and psychoanalysts. Subsequently TIHR recruited researchers and applied social scientists across the fields of industrial psychology, sociology, and anthropology and began a series of Government funded projects of action research, in order to shape the rebuilding of post-war institutions in Britain. While some TIHR teams developed contributions to society by addressing the psychodynamics of institutional systems, others were more influenced by other social and management sciences. However, all sought to serve the wider community with the clear aim of improving the quality of societal and working life and in order to improve mental health in the community. Key figures in this research included Menzies Lyth ([1959]1988), Emery (Trist, Emery and Murray, 1997), Jacques (1998), Trist and Murray (1990, 1993, 1997), Turquet (1974, 1975), Miller and Rice (1967). There were several thrusts to this work. Sher describes the

> most important theories and practices of the 'Tavistock tradition' over the past eighty to ninety years: psychoanalysis (the role of thought); social technical systems (the interaction between people and technology in workplaces);

theories of leadership, research and evaluation-methodologies; participant design and greater democratisation of the work place.

(Sher, 2013)

Later the Tavistock Consultancy Service (TCS), formed in 1996, developed out of 'Consulting to Institutions Workshop' for experienced practitioners led by Anton Obholzer, CEO of the Tavistock Clinic 1980–2003 (Obholzer and Roberts, 1994 and Huffington et al., 2004). TCS was initiated and led by Jon Stokes who invited David Armstrong, Michael Rustin, and Claire Huffington to join him. This work developed alongside an effective training, Consulting to Organizations Masters Course (D10), now run on a modular basis across a year.

The action research and psychodynamic systems approach to organizational consulting was developed through training at the TCS's and TIHR's Consulting to Organizations courses, and master's level similar courses can be found in Chile (Santiago), Denmark (Roskilde), Israel (Tel Aviv), South Africa (Johannesburg), Australia (Melbourne), US (New York) and the Netherlands (Utrecht).

Group Relations Conferences (GRCs)

The psychodynamics approach to organizations was informed by theories of working group and inter-group dynamics. From 1957, Ken Rice and Eric Miller initiated the first of what were to become the annual Tavistock 'Leicester' GRCs (Rice, 1965). These working conferences provide a learning experience in which people can discover their unconscious way of relating in groups and organizational systems. Within conferences, specific events offer experiential learning in small, large, and inter-group events and application of experience to current organizational and social roles (Rice, 1965, Fraher, 2004, 2005, 2011; Miller, 1989, 2004). Organizations across the world now run such events.

Key ideas included close interpretation of transference and counter-transference relatedness as a source of information about what anxieties organizations leave uncontained, including anxieties both from within and external to the organization. These interventions develop Bion's exploration of shared *basic assumptions* and a tendency to focus on group-as-a-whole interventions, rather than linking the individual to the emerging group matrix (1961).[2]

An alternative track of Tavistock conferencing founded by Harold Bridger focuses on activity groups whose processes could be reviewed in a *suspended business* session. These groups were greatly influenced by the action research approaches of Kurt Lewin (1951), whose field theory provided an approach to monitoring forces and resistances to change. They we also influenced by the USA's National Training Laboratories (NTL) approach to T-groups, as have been a number of global approaches to organizational consultancy beyond the Tavistock traditions and institutions.

Bridger's work continues through the Bayswater Institute, whose annual Working Conference on '*Managing Complexity in Organisations*' seeks to link group dynamics and leadership to the practical tasks facing managers. Bridger's (2001) *dual task* methodology involved what he believed to be a more manageable approach to applying learning to the work place than the focus on here and now group experience emphasized in Tavistock GRCs. This work, along with his development of an understanding of the need to recognize and manage organizational transformations, drew largely on Winnicott's theory of transitional processes in development, and resulted in an approach furthered by Liesl Klein (2005) at the Bayswater Institute (Amado and Ambrose, 2001).

Tavistock GRCs have also been used as training and consultation within organizations (Gould, et al., 2004, 2006) and even with psychoanalytic institutes (Lohmer, 2004). Among many significant developments have been the Nazareth Conferences set up jointly by staff from the Berlin and Israeli Psychoanalytic Institutes to explore the representative experience of those affected by the atrocities of war. Such events have progressed from membership of Germans and Israelis to include Palestinians and others traumatized by war across generations (Erlich et al., 2009).

GRCs were developed by Ken Rice in the USA, leading to the establishment of the A.K. Rice Institute (AKRI), with both national and regional US GRCs that continue to this day. AKRI provides a mentoring and accreditation scheme for new consultants. Its series of three Group Relations Readers provide a vital resource for training in the GR approach and applying it to organizational contexts (Colman and Bexton, 1983, Colman and Geller, 1985, Cytrynbaum and Noumair, 2004), while the Tavistock approach to GRCs is well represented through the writings inspired by the triennial Belgirate conferences (Brunner et al., 2006; Aram et al., 2009, 2012, 2015).

Resulting from GRCs, contemporary developments have included a host of approaches to experience-based learning, consulting, and research. These include *listening posts* (Opus); *social dreaming and social sensing matrices* (Lawrence, 1998), *social dream drawing, photo matrix (thinking organizations through photographs); role analysis, biography, history, and reflection groups.* Collectively such designs are described as 'socioanalytic methods' and designs (Long, 2016), additionally there are skills ability and experience in designing experience-based learning events that involve regression in the service of learning and demand safety in managing task, time, and territory within a given framework and contract (Mersky, 2012).

Socio-technical systems, industrial democracy, and evaluation of organizational functioning

An alternate direction at the Tavistock Institute was led by Eric Trist, Fred Emery, and Ken Bamforth through socio-technical systems thinking and the application of democratic sharing of tasks across a team to create emotional bonds around their independence and 'sentience'. Their action-research methodology built on the observation of the self-organizing capacity of teams in the coal mining industry with the vision of industrial democracy not just by worker representation on boards but in control over work tasks and organization. Three core texts derive from the Tavistock's war and post-war history from 1941–87 under the common title, 'The Social Engagement of Social Science'. Each deals with developing shifts in understanding and engaging with social systems, ranging from the socio-psychological to socio-technical systems and the socio-ecological (Trist et al., 1990, 1993, 1997). In 1966 Trist moved away from the group relations approach, so focused on Bion's work, to develop the adaptability of the working group in relation to its wider and highly turbulent environment and took up a post as Professor of Organizational Behaviour and Social Ecology at the University of Pennsylvania.

Eric Miller and Ken Rice had developed some integration of the psychodynamic and socio-technical approaches through their roles as external and internal consultants to the Ahmedabad Manufacturing and Calico Printing Company in India (Rice, 1958). This developed a conceptualization of social systems as both productive work task *and* social organizations. Their Open Systems Theory from biology and computer science explores what is exchanged by a system across its managed boundaries and transformed internally by simple, complex, or unthought/unnoticed dynamics and processes in how people, technology, and tasks interrelate (Miller and Rice, 1967).

At the TIHR some work focused on the design and effectiveness as well as job satisfaction in effective organizational and team design, and sought to integrate quality of working life with technical and human aspects of getting a job done. This thrust was led initially by Elliot Stern, but as Sher reports in his book, *The Dynamics of Change* (2013) this has developed into contemporary training and evaluation of the role of board members and boards in the financial sector post the 2007/8 credit crisis. Other projects engaged with community issues like the nursing role, models of residential and community care for the elderly, or culture change in organizations. Other work developed participative approaches to innovation, and exploration of the relationship across boundaries of an organization with its environment. This range of work and beyond it continues currently at the Tavistock Institute (formerly TIHR). Sher also points to the significance of the technological and economic aspects of organizational life that inter-relate around shaping human systems in organizations.

Contemporary developments that have shaped my own practice of Tavistock approaches

The proceedings of annual and regional meetings of the International Society for the Psychoanalytic Study of Organizations (ISPSO), and the annual conference of the Organization for Promoting Study of Society (OPUS), along with the range of professional development programmes, topics, publications, and events organized by the Tavistock Institute of Human Relations, provide a glimpse of the vast range of application of Tavistock approaches to contemporary organizational systems psychodynamics.

Given the longevity of Tavistock approaches and the shifting nature of contemporary organizational life, there is a host of new developments in the field. Here are some emerging themes:

1   Tim Dartington (2010) integrates his long career as a consultant and manager with and experience as a user of the Care System in a moving account that explores the depth of the denials of dependency in society expressed in such systems in their task of 'Managing Vulnerability'.

2   Organizational and social observation and research – an approach to research that develops the skill and evidence from the emotional responses and associations of the observer as clues to organizational hidden dynamics and as a means of training people to be patient with their responses for effective consulting and interventions (Neumann, 1997). This approach is developed at the University of the West of England as a psycho-social research methodology (Clarke and Hoggett, 2009). A further development comes from the application of the Tavistock child psychotherapy training's infant observation methodology to organizations, initiated by Ross Lazar under the title, 'From Baby to Boardroom' (Lazar, 2008).

3   Halina Brunning (2006, 2012, 2014), in a trilogy of books, edits a highly original collection of papers by experienced research practitioners in the field, applied to contemporary societal issues. These volumes of essays provide reflections and perspectives on a changing and turbulent world and explore the dynamics of power and vulnerability. Terrorism, political leadership, financial crash, warfare dynamics, mergers, fashion, insurance, celebrities, cities, pandemics, European politics, vulnerable social identities, and national identity are all covered among other contemporary issues.

4   Amy Fraher develops her experience as a naval and civil aviator and instructor to research air, maritime, and other 'accidents', where failures in teamwork between different parts of teams or organizations contributed to failures in life threatening situations. Her work on the capacity to think through leadership in high risk fields provides a platform to approach a whole range of team and inter-organizational contexts. (Fraher, 2004, 2005, 2011).

5   Susan Long (2016) elaborates the 'perverse organization' in describing the ethical failures and abuses of commercial and institutional leadership, using psychoanalytic and socioanalytic interpretations of perversion.

6   Richard Morgan-Jones explores organizational health in *The Body of the Organization and its Health* (2010b). He develops an understanding of the emerging primitive proto mental dynamics (Bion, 1961) of what he terms *socio-somatics,* to account for the three-way meeting point between organizational risk dynamics, the individual capacity for mind in the system, and

the body that enacts organizational ailments. He develops Anzieu's work on the skin (1989) to explore organizational skin ailments and allergies and the development of a team's sensing skin to understand systemic dynamics (Morgan-Jones, 2017, Morgan-Jones and Torres, 2010). He links these risks to organizational strategic positioning in wider ecological environments, a risk carried by the work force. A key idea is the definition of *Retainment* as "development of emotional containment for the work task" (Morgan-Jones and Torres, 2010, Chapter 5).

7   Robert French and Peter Simpson (2014) develop an approach to group dynamics that interprets Bion's shared group basic assumptions not as some kind of pathology, but rather a dynamic towards which a group needs to regress in the service of its development before it can move forward to recruit such emotions for emotionally demanding tasks.

8   Simon Western (2008, 2012) develops a methodology using critical thinking to apply psychosocial studies to deconstruct the discourses surrounding leadership, coaching, and mentoring. He also develops an ecological approach to these fields that addresses the networked nature of contemporary organizational life.

9   Wendy Hollway (Hollway and Jefferson, 2000) develops an approach to psychosocial research using emotional experience of researchers and informants as data for understanding organizational and societal issues in an approach that elicits socially imbued depth, complexity, and biographical uniqueness.

10   Paul Hoggett (Hoggett et al., 2009), through his work as Professor of Politics at the University of the West of England, extends the Tavistock approach into the political arena in exploring contested community dynamics, the dynamics of politics, identity, and emotion and the ethical dilemmas of development work. He analyses the way organizations, like politics, often export the burden of strategic dilemmas to the work force, creating under-resourced 'dilemmatic space'.

11   Long and Sievers (2012) have created a collection of essays from a systems psychoanalytic frame, analysing some of the causes and consequences of the 2007/8 world banking crisis under the title, *Towards a Socioanalysis of Money, Finance and Capitalism*.

12   Increasingly Lawrence's innovation of Social Dreaming is being developed as an approach to dream up understanding of organizational experience and meaning and is being applied to organizational consulting (Long and Manley, 2017).

In conclusion, I hope this brief overview of Tavistock approaches and applications may generate an opportunity to link group analytic approaches in a way that enhances both fields in ameliorating and humanizing community, social, and organizational systems with their many current challenges.

Author's Note

I am grateful to a number of senior colleagues who have generously commented on aspects of this contribution, although opinions expressed are my own. They include Frances Abraham, David Armstrong, Tim Dartington, William Halton, Olya Khaleelee, Gerard van Reekum, Mannie Sher, Jon Stokes, and Simon Western.

Systemic Practice to Work with Staff, Teams, and Organizations

Martin Miksits

Contemporary systemic practice is informed by second order systems theory and social constructionist theory, and views communication as the primary process to knowing. My contribution here introduces and explores the relevance of a systemic constructionist stance for organizational sense-making, for constructions of power, agency, and choice in teams and organizations, and for a systemic approach to facilitate development and change.

I portray here systemic practice with organisations taking three perspectives

(i) The planned and emergent process of a systemic consultation.
(ii) The purpose and approaches of systemic inquiry as interventive practice.
(iii) The reflexive sensibilities required in the conduct of a systemic consultation.

The presented practical theory is illustrated with a practice vignette.

The relevance of systemic practice for organizational development

The traditions and approaches of systemic family therapy practice have over the past fifty years been of significant influence for the practical theory of organizational development, consulting, and coaching. This has given rise to a field of systemic practice that is oriented to work not only with systems in private but also in professional and organizational contexts. Depending on the contexts and commission for work, systemic practitioners are psychotherapists, consultants, coaches, or leaders; I will here interchangeably use the terms consultant and practitioner.

Central to the development of contemporary systemic practice are two paradigm shifts that challenge linear, mechanistic, and medical change models:

First, *Second order cybernetics*, the theory of observing systems, positions the individual observers as connected to and part of the system that is observed. Practitioners hence are not only working with a system, with relationships, and with communication processes, but they do this uniquely positioned within the system, being in relationships and in communication processes (Maturana, 1991; von Foerster, 1990; Keeney and Keeney, 2012).

Second, *social constructionist theory*, a paradigm shift frequently related to as the *narrative turn*. Social constructionist thinkers place relatedness, communication, and coordination as primary epistemological processes and invite us to appreciate how from within communication processes we come to understand the world as we know it (Shotter, 1993, 1994; Pearce, 1995; Burr, 2003; Gergen and Gergen, 2004; Shotter, 2008).

I propose such a second order, social constructionist, systemic approach (shortened to: systemic approach) has three major implications for working with organizations and teams:

First, an epistemological shift: It is in relationship with others in specific, local and contextualized conversations that meanings of terms such as 'the team', 'the organization', or any other object of the social world, are negotiated, so that we then can continue to coordinate and communicate in relation to this world and from within it (Campbell, 2000). Consequently, we can also understand problems and dilemmas as relational rather than individual phenomena – forms of coordination in a system, discursive achievements, i.e. descriptions and storylines (Anderson et al., 1986; Anderson and Goolishian, 1988; White and Epston, 1990).

Second, there are implications for individual agency from within a system: Participants in conversation are not free to make just any distinctions or conversational moves, but, being part of a system, part of a culture, being in relationships, are also bound to what is meaningful, intelligible, and morally possible from within the discourses and practice repertoires available in these contexts (Pearce and Cronen, 1980; Pearce, 1989, 2004; Miksits, 2014). In thinking and talking we operate within the realm of conversational and cultural resources available, and consequently we must be responsive to the power structures that are immanent and expressed in the practices and discourses we are participating in (Foucault, 1981).

Third, we need to conceptualize change differently: Not having access to an objective vantage point in making observations or forming judgments, nor being able to offer truth or certainty based on theories or methods, has vast implications for approaching change in organizations. Coherent with a social constructionist approach, the communication process and the forms and qualities of interrelatedness become the primary site for intervention and change. Systemic practitioners therefore are concerned with their ways of joining and coordinating with a system, with approaches to moving conversational patterns, and with the co-creation of meaning from within conversations.

Tasks and processes in systemic practice with organizations

Commissions for systemic work with organizations can be for facilitation of communication processes, consulting to achieve particular aims, and training in systemic approaches, to leadership and consulting. I will here relate to what is involved in systemic consulting practices oriented to a particular organizational development task. Specifically, I will attend to the *consultation process*, to *systemic inquiry*, and to *systemic sensibilities* for practising.

I will also illustrate the presented ideas using a case vignette from my work with a leadership team in a global industrial concern and in relation to the organizational task of preventing work related accidents, injuries, and loss of life. Notably the management of hazards and risk, in relation to people or assets, is a topic that spans across all sectors, be it private financial, industrial or services, or the public sector, including healthcare and social services. My invitation for reading this vignette is to relate its potential relevance to your sector or professional field.

As we shall see, the way systemic practice with and in organizations unfolds and how tasks and processes are structured vary to meet the needs of the organization or team, the consultants, and the task at hand. My illustration of presented ideas through practice is, therefore, not to be understood as an expression of any archetypical way of working but just one illustration of how systemic practice can 'play out', so to speak.

A planned and emergent consultation process

We have said that systemic practice relates to the situated, local, and contextual, hence there is a strong commitment to the uniqueness of both, the situation and the system involved. A consultation process, whilst deliberately *designed and planned* to meet local circumstances, to be responsive has also to be *emergent and attentive* to unfolding conversations and group processes. It is therefore neither possible nor desirable to settle on a generic approach for systemic consultations. Nevertheless, frameworks and scaffoldings for the tasks involved in systemic consultation processes offer useful orientations. Campbell and Huffington (2008, p.3), for instance, present us with a framework of six stages to a systemic consultation:

1   Developing an understanding of the consultant's relationship to the client.
2   Identifying a problem and making a contract for work.
3   Designing a consultation.
4   Working directly with the participants.
5   Using continuous feedback.
6   Evaluation.

These stages are probably not followed through in strict order: interrelated tasks may overlap, contextualize each other, or collapse into one. It is perhaps useful to see the tasks present in every single conversation: For instance, in a first conversation engaging with a client, a systemic practitioner will be mindful of the relationship with the client and its development (1), learn about the dilemmas and hopes involved (2), perhaps already engage in an inquiry that expands how the problem can be talked about and facilitates insight and agency (4, 5). The conversation probably closes with some shared sense-making of what emerged in it (6) and an agreement on useful next steps (3). In the next conversation all these six dimensions will continue to be of relevance, their meaning will continue to emerge. So in a series of conversations, the contexts for work, such as relationship, problem, and process design, are clarified, but every single conversation involves also working with participants, processing of feedback, and evaluation.

Practice illustration

The consultant's emergent relationship to the client (1)

I was working with a leadership team of general managers (GMs) responsible for managing the operations of a global industrial concern. The responsibilities of the different GMs was either regional (Latin America, Europe, etc.) or functional (human resources, safety, finance, etc.). The organization had just gone through a restructure. My relationship at the beginning of the work was that of an executive coach to one of the GMs, the Safety Manager. From this initial coaching relationship emerged a wider commission to support the delivery of safety targets in the organization. This required me to also establish a working relationship with the whole leadership team.

Identifying a problem and making a contract for work (2)

The role and responsibilities of the Safety Manager included providing governance and leadership to prevent work related accidents, injuries, and loss of life in the operation of the organization. The whole leadership team had committed to a target of zero safety incidents, such as, injuries or fatalities, for the years to come, a target that the newly established safety function would have to meet in collaboration with the regionally responsible GMs; a target also that seemed unrealistic if not impossible in the light of sector benchmarks and the organization's historic safety record.

My emergent hypothesis was that the Safety Manager's dilemma had multiple dimensions, one of which was the unattainability of the goal as such. Another consequence of the rather radical safety target was that ideas and programmes for improving work safety were liable to be critiqued as insufficient: proposals were scrutinized for the difference they could make and criticized for not being radical or innovative enough. A third dimension was that due to the reorganization responsibilities for safety, initiatives were now centralized in the new Safety Manager's role, which perhaps disenfranchised the regional GMs to develop and co-own initiatives to improve safety themselves.

Designing a consultation and working directly with the participants (3, 4)

The proposal for an initial intervention was developed in close collaboration with the Safety Manager, and in ongoing alignment with the Organizational

Development Manager and the CEO. The work conducted can be portrayed in three stages:

In a first stage, I conducted individual interviews with all GMs, inquiring into their experiences of excellence in safety management or safety operation. This included their own experiences and observations but also stories and evidence they had heard of. The inquiry was into the specifics of what constituted excellence, what facilitated and sustained it.

In a second stage, I consolidated each of these inputs into a format for presentation of exemplars of excellence in safety operation and the factors that seemingly supported or constituted such excellence. Each of these summaries were sent back to the respective GM so they could make final changes and own these narratives and findings.

A third stage was to facilitate a process with the leadership team, where all these insights were shared and the leadership team would collectively develop an action plan or road map to achieve the safety goal.

Continuous feedback and evaluation (5, 6)

Ongoing formal feedback and evaluation of this work was through the Safety Manager and the Organizational Development Manager sharing with me their observations about the process and the feedback they had received from others. Then the process of inquiry with each of the GMs also generated feedback. My observation was that the whole intervention from the very first stage unleashed significant tacit agency of the GMs who developed a well-grounded understanding of how they could see the organization respond to its safety target.

Reflections on practice and outcomes

The consultation held the potential to invite a difference in relation to those contexts that seemed to be limiting initiative:

First, it grounded the safety target and related initiatives in benchmarks and practices of excellence valid to the participants.

Second, it legitimated and facilitated the agency, competence, and voice of all team members, which was a counter dynamic to the concentration of agency in only the Safety Manager.

Third, it invited a co-ownership of the action plan or road map through co-authorship and grounding it in lived experience of all involved.

The meaning of the zero incidents target shifted in the process of consultation: rather than a reified and institutionalized measure of success, it became a metaphoric expression of the collective wisdom and commitment to improved safety. The evaluation of the process, its findings, and the experience of it led also to a wider appreciation of the generative qualities of systemic inquiry. This was reflected in the action plan to improve safety, which included further inquiry into the insights and wisdom of other managers with responsibilities for work safety in the different countries the organization was operating in.

The task of planning a consultation is a form of conversation design, often with an emphasis on systemic inquiry in relation to the hopes and dilemmas expressed in the commission. In consulting and teaching, my colleague, Christine Oliver, and I have developed the concept of *systemic domains of practice* (Lang et al., 1990; Oliver, 2005) in a way that facilitates orientation for this design activity:

- The domain of aesthetics invites an attention to values, ethics, purpose, and beauty of what will be created in a consultation. From an aesthetic sensibility we reflect, for instance, on how participants are positioned in the process of the consultation, how their sense of purpose in and of the system will become evident in the consultation, how to value contributions, validate voices, and create choices for all involved.
- The domain of production is about contract, clarity, structure, decision, and task. The domain is important to coordinate action, to plan, manage resources, time, and expectations. It serves to reduce uncertainty, manage safety, and provide orientation in the group process.
- The domain of explanation is about meaning making, opening up multiple views and perspectives, open dialogue and exploration. Systemic inquiry, reflecting, and reflexive conversations are used to facilitate insight, choice, and agency in this domain.

Practice illustration (continued): The Systemic Domains

The commission to facilitate the development of an action plan to improve safety can be seen placed dominantly in the domain of production. It is a contracted, scoped, and planned time and resource bound intervention, relating to a specific organizational target. The commission is also coherent with the organization's domain of aesthetics, with dimensions of team-functioning, inclusiveness, and the aim to improve safety reflecting ethical, and aesthetic concerns.

The intervention starts with an inquiry exploring multiple exemplars and contributing factors to safety. Narratives that may add to each other but may also contradict each other in terms of values and what matters become emphasized and expressed. This inquiry is in the domain of explanation, with a commitment to a multiverse of insights and truths.

The final part of the intervention, however, is agreeing on an action plan or road map for safety. Here decisions have to be made on what specific ideas and reality will be acted upon and how. This part of the inquiry emphasizes the domain of production and facilitates specific accountability, ownership, and coordinated action in the team.

The domains model offers orientation to consider what kind of discourse needs foregrounding in a particular phase of the consultation and what is most relevant to achieve in a particular moment in a conversation. It also helps consultants to be vigilant in moving the conversation from one domain to another when needed. Most practitioners think of systemic inquiry in the domain of explanation as the central instrument for facilitating change. It is, however, important to attend to practice coherent in all three domains. Consultations conducted with an explicit orientation to ethics and aesthetics, and with clarity of processes, tasks, and agreements not only serve their immediate purpose, they also become part of a shared lived experience of participants in a system, and hence are resources to further conversations.

Systemic Inquiry – engagement with possibility and choice

Methods for systemic inquiry include questions, but also other forms of dialogue, reflections, group processes, performances, and other participative practices. They have in common the aim to invite differences in coordinating, meaning-making, and acting from within the conversational process. A range of principal approaches, or schools of practice, conceptualize systemic approaches to invite change – here is a brief orientation to a few selected approaches:

*   Through Reflexive Inquiry (Tomm, 1987, 1988; Oliver, 2005; Oliver, 2013) participants are invited to attend to how current communication and coordination processes operate, what stories and positions are validated, and who is contributing how to meaning making and acting in the system. It is in a detailed attending to the emergent process of communication and co-creation that the implicit choices and influencing contexts, such as task, role, relationships, or professional scripts, are rendered visible and other choices can be considered by those involved.
*   Narrative Practice (White, 1989; White and Epson, 1990) invites participants to step by step challenge self-limiting stories and accounts from experiences: Consultants lead to disentangle stories of identity (of self, team, organization) from the story of the problem – and in this process facilitate new stories to emerge, expressive of agency, resources, and abilities that otherwise are overshadowed by perceived failure or internalized limitations.
*   Solution Focused Inquiry (De Shazer, 1985; Berg and Szabó, 2005; De Jong and Berg, 2008) invites a repositioning and re-storying of clients' meaning making and acting in the past, present, and possible future as an emergent pathway to desired outcomes. Client resources, agency, values, determination, and learning are foregrounded. Different from narrative practice, solution-oriented inquiry is not interested in an affirmative understanding of the

problem or its emergence, instead problem talk is reframed as a form of orientation to the desired solution.

- Appreciative Inquiry (Cooperrider et al., 1995; Cooperrider and Whitney, 1999, 2005) is an inquiry framework engaging participants in a staged process oriented to a generative metaphor or goal. The group process aims to discover resources and practices available in the organization, its participants, its practices and achievements, to facilitate an unrestricted engagement with developmental possibilities, to design a way forward in relation to the generative metaphor or goal, and to facilitate its delivery.

Whilst systemic inquiry can also lead to new instrumental knowledge, a knowing how, the emphasis of the change invited is a shift in orientation: a change in the story we share about the situation we are participating in, ideas about the person or team that we are or can be, and the relationships we have. This emergent difference of participants' knowing from within (Shotter, 1994, 2008) the situation, their orientation to the world and they in it, gives rise to different coordination, sense making, and acting in a system.

Practice illustration (continued): Systemic Inquiry

As mentioned before, the commission developed out of my work as a coach to the Safety Manager. In these coaching conversations, which can be referred to as *Reflexive Inquiry*, we explored the relational dynamics and positioning of the GMs in relation to each other, the Safety Manager, the CEO, and the safety target. This included to reflexively making sense of the Safety Manager's position in the process and the way she was relating to her peers and the safety target; it also included attending to the contextualized relational dynamics that brought about the dilemmas and difficulties that I have portrayed earlier in my emergent hypothesis.

The actual intervention with the leadership team can be seen as a form of *Appreciative Inquiry* into experiences of exceptionally safe operational practice. I was hoping to co-create accounts of outstanding achievements and practices that serve as insights and resources for constructing new ways of working with safety challenges. The inquiry can also be related to as a form of *Solution focused* practice, positioning GMs in a meta narrative of their continued resourceful orientation towards opportunities to improve safety; a lived narrative that starts in the past (experiences) and extends into the future (action plans).

Practitioner sensibilities and orientation in relation to the emerging process and the present moment

Systemic practitioners cannot rise above the process of being in conversation, however, they can aim to reflexively consider how conversational contexts and processes inform their feelings, meaning making, and acting, and they can take charge of choices involved in conducting consultations. The following are sensibilities for practitioners in relation to their own practising:

Taking control of own sense making

To open up possibilities in the domain of explanation, consultants aim to stay curious about what is and what might be, and not fall in love with singular explanations or prejudices. In this spirit, practices of hypothesizing (Selvini et al., 1980; Cecchin, 1987; Lang and McAdam, 1995) have been proposed for practitioners to reflect on and utilize in their sense making: hypotheses are treated as stories that facilitate coherence and orientation; the formulation of multiple hypotheses and hypothesizing from different positions and perspectives is advocated to facilitate irreverence to any single way of making sense. Similarly, curiosity and positions of 'not knowing' are stances that help promote discursive openness and agility over accepting a particular explanation or description, however compelling.

Practice example (continued): Control of own sense making

It was my hypothesis earlier that in light of the target of zero incidents, proposals to improve work safety were liable to be scrutinized and rejected as not radical or different enough. This hypothesis was informed by reflections and narratives in the organization; however, I also experienced myself levels of scrutiny, intervention, and challenge from the CEO from the very moment I moved from being a coach to the Safety Manager to the position of a consultant to the leadership team. I then felt that my proposal and practice was challenged as not good enough, perhaps that I was not good enough as a consultant. I felt drawn into a defensive position.

To move from such a defensive and perhaps singular way of orienting in the situation to a more open and explorative position, I reflected on the sense making and acting of the CEO and other members of the leadership team. Specifically I attended to the meaning of my proposal for the CEO and other GMs in relation to their significant contexts, their accountability to stakeholders, and their personal and professional risk. With this thinking I could acknowledge the positions of others better and appreciated differently how the CEO related to me and my contributions. I further suggest that taking up some of these reflections in communication with the CEO enhanced my credibility and facilitated coherence of decision making in favour of the proposal I was making.

A strong emotional response of the practitioner can be informative of how other participants in a system may feel, as they are perhaps participating in patterns of communication similar to the one the practitioner is experiencing. For instance,

I had a sense of understanding the Safety Manager's position better when I felt my proposals being criticized. Strong emotions also can orient practitioners to re-examine the stories they are holding and point to the possibility of alternative stories and positions that legitimize or explain better what perhaps seems problematic or deficient (Oliver and Miksits, 2016). In this case an active engagement and hypothesizing in relation to the positioning and meaning making of the CEO has facilitated my practice of validation and inclusion of such positions, and a way of overcoming a potential impasse in the consultation.

Forging and enabling relationships

Systemic consultants are mindful of how through listening, expressing empathy and validation, and more generally their use of language, they can facilitate relationships that are uniquely enabling for clients (Flaskas, 1997). Inquiry is informed by the notion of circularity (Selvini et al., 1980; Penn, 1982; Cecchin, 1987; Tomm, 1988), which means the consultation is framed and conducted making use of the commission, concerns, language, and resources of the client system. This concept is not to the exclusion of other discourses and resources that may be helpful, however, it foregrounds a sensibility to a relational affirmative practice and an attending to the construction and use of power in the relationship. Forging enabling relationships also includes rigour in attending to all three domains of systemic practice introduced earlier.

Practice example (continued): Forging and enabling relationships

I was concerned to develop relationships with the GMs that were safe enough for them to take generative risks, such as making proposals that perhaps are not popular with peers. At the same time, I wanted the dialogue in the leadership team to facilitate constructive ways of relating between all GMs and the CEO. My hypothesis was that giving voice and fostering participation of all team members would facilitate forward movement. The interviews I conducted with the GMs were therefore not only to access ideas about contexts, resources, and learning processes to improve safe work practices, but also to validate their experiences and their agency in relation to safety.

Validation and fostering of agency of all GMs was a central element of the intervention. In a facilitated workshop with the leadership team, all GMs shared their experiences of excellence and what they felt was most important to learn from them. Notably, the whole inquiry was not to take information from the interviewees but to develop with them stories of insight and agency. Following on from the sharing of experiences, resources, and ideas, I facilitated a participatory process for the GMs to consolidate this input, to decide on the major themes and approaches to improve safety, and to collectively develop a work programme.

I propose the whole of the consultation served as an enactment inviting a way of relating with each other in the context of improving work safety: it positioned the central safety function in the GM for safety, as a process owner for safety management without taking away from the ownership, experience, and voice of the other GMs.

In processes such as the above, useful questions to ask are "what positions are participants afforded", "what control do participants have", "what forms of relating are invited", and "to what extent is the consultation process useful as a blueprint for relating in this system". In my example I tried to facilitate validation and agency of all involved and to make everybody's contribution to the organization's ethical goals visible and relevant.

For participants to relate safely with each other and with the consultant it is important to be clear and transparent about what will happen with the information that is contributed by the participants in the process and about how decisions will be made to inform coordinated action. In the practice example, this clarity of process in the domain of production made it safe to entertain ideas and articulate fully experiences of good safety practice in an environment where proposals to improve work safety have been prone to be criticized or rejected.

Aiming for an ethical critical distance to discourse

Critical sensibility (Cunliffe, 2004; Oliver, 2005) marks the practitioner's awareness to what is privileged and what is marginalized, an attention to how power is created and used (Carr, 1991), and how markers of social differences (Burnham, 1992, 2012), such as gender, race, abilities, age, culture, ethnicity, and education, to name a few, are of relevance to participation, voice, and discursive practice. This reflexive attention is directed to the system in focus of the conversation as well as the relationship between the consultant and the client and the discourses the consultant contributes to the situation.

A critical sensibility in relation to discourse invites a practitioner to attend to what can and can't be created by one way of talking, relating, and use of language, as opposed to other possible ways of communicating and being with each other. Such a *discursive reflexivity* is also a forward looking imaginative achievement informed by the practitioner's accumulated experience and repertoires for practising (Miksits, 2014).

Practice example (continued): An ethical, critical distance to discourse

The organization in my practice example could be described as operating with an engineering discourse privileging linear ideas and reasoning. In such a discourse participants relate to the organization as if it were a machine, a metaphor that justifies order and power in sustaining its functioning (Morgan, 1996). Power was particularly vested in the CEO and a few persons close to him.

In relation to the task of facilitating the development of a work programme to improve safety, power was expressed in significant contexts, such as the organizational structure and the goal of no incidents. The implications of these contexts were that it was difficult to deliver satisfactory work or even to make valid proposals for improvement of work safety. The centralization of responsibilities for safety also disenfranchized those holding relevant skills and knowledge to contribute.

Being critical about how power seemed to limit the organization, I planned a consultation that invited a counter discourse. I imagined an intervention that privileged everybody's insights, experience, and resources and facilitated agency and dialogue across boundaries. I also treated the safety goal metaphorically rather than literally: I gave it the meaning of 'not leaving any stone unturned to improve safety', which invited permission for all to contribute.

Aiming for an ethical, critical distance to discourse also means to be aware of and be prepared to challenge the ideas, values, practices, and experiences informing one's practice. My practice in the example was informed by experiences of working with and in large organizations that operate and organize using conventional and mechanistic ideas, experiences in change management and governance of strategic processes, and systemic consulting practice repertoires. I also hold personal aesthetic preferences for how teams should work and coordinate and no doubt these have also been of influence in the design of the consultation.

Conclusion

Systemic practice with teams and organizations takes communication processes as the primary site for change. The practitioner is strategic in participating in the unfolding conversational frame throughout a consultation, inviting what is aesthetically meaningful and appealing (domain of aesthetics), facilitating coordination and participation with clear and safe processes, tasks, and relationships (domain of production), and engaging in systemic inquiry as a generative practice in relation to the commission, the problem, or dilemma and relevant local circumstances (domain of explanation).

Practitioners use systemic inquiry methods to facilitate participants' changes in their orientating in and acting into their world. This may include a reorientation to the process of coordination they are part of, their sense of self, their relationships, and the objects of their social world, such as roles, goals, or problems. To conduct this work, next to technical abilities in systemic inquiry, practitioners draw on reflexive sensibilities in relation to their sense-making, being in relationship, and participating in the unfolding conversation.

Through this contribution, I have shared theoretical concepts informing systemic practice, which I then illustrated with a case example. Whilst theories are informing practice, it should also be clear that such theories and approaches for systemic practice have to a great extent been developed and validated through processes of practising; it is also often through practising that theories are enriched in meaning and relevance. In that sense, systemic lived practice and systemic theory are informing each other in a continuous unfolding pattern.

Systemic practice skills and abilities are learned and developed in communities of practitioners. Whilst practice research and practical theory are essential elements to developing as a practitioner, the sensibilities, methods, and techniques are significantly conveyed through the practising itself. There are a number of consulting centres and communities offering trainings in systemic leadership and consulting practice across Europe.

Inquiries regarding the above, systemic organizational practice, communities of practice, and training possibilities can be directed to the author (martin.miks its@syde.org).

A Group Analytic Approach to Work with Staff Teams and Organizations: A Contextual Framework

Christine Oliver

I examine here the contribution group analysis has made, and can make, to consulting work with organizations, suggesting that a coherent paradigm has been slow in its articulation, yielding limited training and practice opportunities. In tracing a range of group analytic contributions to the field, I attempt to build a coherent framework.

I propose that a contextual framing of communication can provide orientation, a tool for sense making in the communicative matrix, and a guide to action within the complex, intersubjective world of organizational work, widening the scope and linkage between theory, method, and intervention for the group analytic organizational consultant. Conceptualization will be linked to a case vignette of work with a monastery.

The organizational group analytic contribution

Many authors have contributed to and critiqued the narrative for organizational group analysis (Rance, 1998, Curnow, 2000, Roberts, 1983, Spero, 1998, Nitsun, 1998a, 1998b, Stacey, 2000, 2005 Kapur, 2009, Blackwell, 2000, Binney et al., 2005, Thornton, 2017). Nitsun (1998a), for instance, proposes that "group analysis is essentially a clinical theory . . . (and) has no organizational equivalent" (p.250).

One feature of the literature historically is the limited scope of vision and focus, group analysts tending to focus either on the techniques that can be drawn from small stranger groups or from large 'taskless' groups (Curnow, 2000). While this contribution is significant, a problem is highlighted if group analysis aspires to represent itself as relevant to organizations more broadly.

For Rance (1998), the consultant's responsibilities are to recognize unconscious processes, those of others and one's own, and to create conditions for understanding the psycho-social origins of organizational behaviour through identifying processes of transference and counter transference, resonance, and mirroring. He advocates that the consultant enables conditions for "creative conversation" and does, importantly, emphasize the significance of context and the matrix as subject and object in organizational work, though he does not make explicit what "creative conversation" might look like. Others, for instance, Blackwell (2000), emphasize the value of dialogue in the context of change and uncertainty, the consultant facilitating constructive rather than destructive expression of fear and anxiety.

However, it is apparent that prior to Nitsun's work (1998a, 1998b), the group analytic contribution lacked some theoretical and practical specificity. Nitsun's model primarily focuses on *making sense* of organizational dysfunction, though he does also provide some insights about *intervention* into organizational processes. He suggests:

> the aim of the consultation is to recognize and clarify dysfunctional mirroring so as to strengthen boundary differentiation amongst groups and individuals and hence their capacity for adaptation to the organizational task (245).

Nitsun offers insight into organizational communication processes with his development of the concept of mirroring. He also highlights the concept of the group matrix. I will return to his ideas in the section on *making sense of the organization*.

Sue Einhorn's endorsement of Wilke's recent book enthuses: "finally a book about working with organizations that demonstrates the value of group analytic thinking from an experienced, theoretically agile practitioner" (2014). Wilke applies group analytic concepts to the conscious and unconscious processes of contemporary organizational life, focusing on "interlinked minds, emotions, and social defences", in processes of working together (p.xvi). Wilke also acknowledges that "the group analytic study of organizations is much less well developed and consulting to small, median, and large groups in situ is relatively rare" (p.x).

Wilke's creative thinking can be applied to the many sizes of group comprising the organization. He talks of how the group analyst invites a shared communication process where current organizational realities can be explored and developed, emphasizing the importance of working with emotional defences against anxiety and fear. He helpfully connects the reality of contemporary organizational life – the world of targets, strategic change, open space offices, permanent transition – to the work of the consultant, suggesting that the state of continuous transition in organizational life means that organizational members resort to protecting themselves destructively through disturbance, searching for organizational parents.

Thornton (2017) has also argued that detailed analysis of the application of group analysis in work settings "is relatively sparse" (p.2). She suggests that a core characteristic of group analysis is the ability to stay connected to the individual in the group and to the group as a whole – a basis for both conceptualization and intervention. She argues that the group analyst has a significant grasp of the unconscious nuances of communication; an appreciation of context and difference; and has skills in the management of projections in relation to leaders and organizational members, including projection onto the consultant.

Inspired by many of these contributions, in attempting to develop a coherent model, I will foreground communication as a core focus at different levels of abstraction – communication theory, the communication matrix, the reflexive communicative role of the consultant, and communicative intervention.

Theory related to communication

The basic construct of group analysis is that individual and social are not separable: "the individual is conditioned to the core by his community even before he is born (Foulkes and Anthony, 1957: 23).
Foulkes identifies the communicative matrix as:

> the hypothetical web of communication and relationship in a given group, the common shared ground which ultimately determines the meaning and significance of all events and upon which all communication, verbal and non-verbal rests.
>
> (1948: 292)

For Nitsun, the matrix is the most significant group analytic concept for organizational consulting, comprising: "the totality of the group as an experiential process that has spatial, historical, contemporary, and developmental aspects" (Nitsun, 1998a, p.251).

Stacey (2000), too, invites the consultant to encounter the group matrix, through treating mind and society as the same process of communication – the former is private and silent (talking to oneself), the latter public and vocal. He sees the 'I' and the 'me' as dimensions of one act: the self becomes repeated iterations of 'I' responding to 'me' through communicative interaction. The organizational matrix becomes: "moment by moment iterations of patterns of interaction in which we are perpetually constructing the future of the organization in the present" (Stacey, 2000 p.485).

In processes of co-construction, narratives of self (personal), relationship (interpersonal), and culture (trans-personal) are developed (Oliver, 2005, Pearce 2007). This *construction* communication approach can be distinguished from what I am calling a *transmission* approach: "Communication . . . is everything sent out and received with response, whether consciously or unconsciously" (Foulkes and Anthony, 1957).

Transmission manifests in the form of unconscious mechanisms of transference, projection, introjections, and projective identification. Both *construction* and *transmission* approaches are relevant to the consultant interested in what is sent and received, consciously and unconsciously, historically, and in ongoing communication; and in how communication exchanges shape or construct organizational possibilities and constraints, "through the actions" of its members (Frosh and Barraitser, 2008).

We can think of the organization as a matrix of conscious and unconscious communication comprising: communication exchanges occurring within communication episodes, building patterns of self, relationship, and culture, which, in the form of narrative, shape communication episodes. Consultants experience, observe, highlight, make sense of, and intervene in conscious and unconscious processes of communication, encouraging the development of new patterns more fitting to organizational purposes and task(s), through communication episodes designed and facilitated to enrich the matrix.

In the next section, I will explore how the concept of the matrix might be developed to help the consultant make sense of the network of communications they are relating to, offering vocabulary for how to make sense of and link narratives and patterns of communication of which the consultant may be a part (Foulkes, 1964, Nitsun, 1998a, Nitzgen and Hopper, 2017).

First, I will introduce the case vignette.

Vignette

I have been working with a male Anglican religious community[3] for some years, having been initially approached as a consultant, to facilitate improved communication and relationship. The community elected a group of six, representing a diversity of perspectives, to meet me and a colleague and to present the concerns of the community. The language employed was characterized by conflict, demoralization, and communication breakdown:

- It is hard to experience hope.
- There is envy and competition, but we don't talk about it.
- There is a lack of charity in our talk about others.
- We don't recognize each other.
- We need to drop our masks.
- We are shrinking daily.
- I ask myself, "Has my life had meaning?"
- We need to face the truth about ourselves as a community (Oliver, 2005).

This breakdown in community functioning both transmitted and constructed high levels of distress, as the behaviours, thoughts, and feelings experienced were incongruent with the community's religious values and faith. The breakdown had been triggered by a series of communicative episodes that had occurred two years previously when a personnel decision had been made that split the group into two 'camps'. The community had employed a woman to run an outreach centre on their behalf in the grounds of the site. However, not long before the end of her probationary year, she was sacked for behaving disloyally to the community in making public a document that expressed critical views of the community. Although they had attempted to engage consultants in the past, the split had only become more entrenched. One camp comprised the leader of the community (superior) who had instigated the sacking, and his followers, who believed that due process had occurred, and the other camp comprised some leading voices in their theological college, who believed that both the decision and the process of decision making were unjust.

The initial meeting with the group of six revealed a preoccupation with the death of the community, pessimistic and stuck experiences of conflicted relationship, and a depressed and fearful paralysis for individual members.

The next section will propose and explore the micro-detail of the matrix for facilitating sense making, and following this, the narrative of the vignette will continue.

Making sense of the organization as a communicative matrix

For Foulkes and Anthony (1957), "every event in the group is considered as having its meaning within the total communicational network – the matrix . . . this constitutes a 'figure-ground' relationship . . ." (p.256).

This frame of communicative *figure and ground* is both a context for making sense in relation to past history, and a resource for shaping the future. Conversational *figurations* (Elias, 1994) are the site where transformation can occur through the moment by moment discernments that we make about our patterned interaction.

To regard organizations as patterns of communication is . . . to take a group-analytic view of organizations (Stacey, 2005, p.479).

The group analytic consultant could be said to harness the creative and collaborative power of groups so that destructive patterns are minimized (Thornton, 2010). Schlapobersky and Pines (2009), describe destructive group behaviour as disturbance of patterns of reciprocity, encouraging forms of relatedness that are "marked by understanding, fairness, mutuality, and reciprocity" (p.4).

Foulkes' concepts of *resonance* and *mirroring* express the largely unconscious processes whereby group members relate to each other. *Resonance* involves unconsciously connecting, in a way specific to one's own history, to the communication act(s) of another. Nitsun (1998a) explains *mirroring* as the process whereby narratives of self are developed through the conscious and unconscious responses of others, often predicated on *resonance*. *Dysfunctional mirroring* reduces the capacity of the individual or group to discern appropriate and effective decision and action, penetrating "the system from the widest external preoccupations of the organization to the innermost and deepest levels of experience" (pp.247–48).

The concepts of *resonance* and *mirroring* facilitate explanation for how *individual* patterns can become *collective* organizational patterns through *transmission* mechanisms of identification, projection, and introjection within communicative exchanges.

Wilke (2014), notes:

> The collectively shared habits and ways of feeling and of acting and thinking do not exist in some abstract social world, but are part of us and are internalized through socialization and adopted through identification and attachment processes.

> (p.xxii)

For Nitzgen and Hopper (2017), the tripartite matrix, comprising foundation, personal, and dynamic dimensions, is imbued by the social unconscious. Adapting their model, I propose that we think of *patterns of figuration* as inter-subjective communication acts, comprised of *feeling*, *thinking*, and *action* responses, taking place within communication episodes that repeat over time and become embedded in the dynamic matrix (Nitzgen and Hopper, 2017) as conscious and unconscious narratives of organizational *culture, relationship*, and *self* (Oliver, 2005). These contextual narratives become the *ground* that shapes future *figurations* of *feeling, thinking*, and *action*. The structure of *culture, relationship*, and *self* can provide a basic template for contextualizing patterns within the matrix, but, where relevant, other narratives might be hypothesized, e.g. foundation myths (Wilke, 2014), or wider societal narratives of power and identity.

To make sense making manageable, I suggest three patterns, *reactive, paradoxical*, and *reflexive*, for framing a contextual analysis, holding sufficient complexity for the consultant to intervene strategically and creatively (Oliver, 2005, 2016). Reactive and *paradoxical* patterns represent forms of anti-group behaviour, but as Nitsun (1996) points out, generativity can emerge from anti-group forces. Wilke (2014) highlights the challenge of key organizational themes manifested in patterned form, such as belonging and exclusion; equality and inequality; the legitimization of authority; struggles with mourning.

Reactive patterns are repeated linkages between *feeling, thinking*, and *action*, characterized by unconscious defence, mistrust, paranoia, hate, simplification of complexity through polarization, and poor reflective capacity. A *culture* of dysfunctional mirroring contextualizes competitive/defensive *relationships* where the position of the other is delegitimized, further contextualizing *self* narratives of exclusive legitimation, difficulty in tolerating difference, uncertainty, ambivalence, and poor discernment for decision and action.

Paradoxical patterns are in a form, inspired by Hopper's 'non dialectical oscillation' (1991) and the notion of strange loops (Cronen et al, 1982), of a figure of eight, where patterns of *feeling, thinking*, and *action* stimulate the opposite meaning at each level, contextualized by processes of splitting and fragmentation, so that when an individual or group are connected to one experience of *feeling, thinking*, and *action*, they become disconnected from awareness of its opposite. *Cultural, relational*, and *self* narratives are contradictory, ambivalent, or polarized.

Reflexive patterns are those characterized by the relational qualities described by Schlapobersky and Pines (2009) – mutuality, fairness, understanding, and

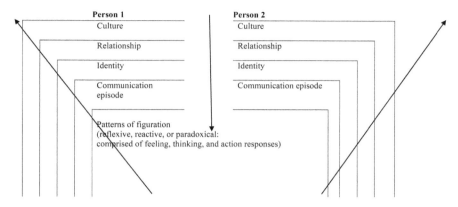

Figure 1.1 Matrix of contextual narratives and patterns of figuration

reciprocity, but also by reflexive abilities, whereby individuals and groups show preparedness to reflect on and evaluate the ways their own *narratives* and *feeling, thinking,* and *action patterns* contribute to the organization. A *culture* of functional mirroring and reflective learning contextualizes *relationships* of self/other legitimation and empathy, linked to *self* narratives of partial legitimation, i.e., the person takes a position of humility in relation to their own views and experiences and is curious about those of the other. Tolerance of difference, ambivalence, and uncertainty becomes possible at cultural, relational, and personal levels.

Figure 1.1 shows these patterns in abstract form, contextualized by the reactive, reflexive, or paradoxical narratives described above.

Vignette

The consultants learnt of a long community history of discomfort with relational engagement, predicated partly on fear that differences of status, class, and education would be exposed, leading to fragmentation. In private communication, individuals shared their despair that nothing could be done, and their determination for their own position to dominate, demonizing the other; in public forum, the consultants observed that whenever a difficult discussion or painful expression of thought or feeling was anticipated, community members behaved as if they feared a relational and emotional encounter, defensively avoiding connection, and creating a pseudo-safety, never directly addressing the conflicted pattern and its contextual narratives, thus concerns would not get named, with the consequence of withdrawal of engagement. However, the context of disengagement would stimulate such emotional intensity of righteous anger, that community members would feel obliged to critique or challenge the other camp and would then enact anger. This would stimulate a fear of destructive consequence, and withdrawal would occur.

The consultants hypothesized that a paradoxical *pattern of figuration* constructed the *figure* for the *ground* of *cultural, relational,* and *self* narratives which, in their turn, shaped paradoxical *figuration,* mediated by transmission mechanisms of resonance, projection, and mirroring.

The role and participation of the consultants in the pattern will be explored when we return to the vignette. First, I show below the relationship between unconscious narratives and the *paradoxical pattern of figuration.* Note that although the two camps experience themselves as in opposition, their narratives are shared.

The monks' matrix of contextual narratives and paradoxical pattern of figuration

Culture: dysfunctional mirroring characterized by poor reflexive and reflective abilities; splitting and polarization; fear that exposing differences would lead to fragmentation.

    Relationship: conflicted and competitive; a belief in the justice of one's own position and the illegitimacy of the other who is positioned projectively as unethical.

    Self: individual feelings of failure and paralysis while at the same time believing that one's own position is exclusively legitimate.

    Communication episode: paradoxical pattern of figuration.

Reflexive communication: management of the consultant's role, relationship, and task

In this section, I will explore the role of the consultant as a contributing participant to organizational *figurations.*

    An emphasis on self, relational, and cultural reflexivity can orient the consultant to her contribution to the matrix, and help others to do the same (Oliver, 2005). The aim of consultancy in these terms is to facilitate the powers of *location* and *translation* (Thornton, 2010) for organizational members as well as for the

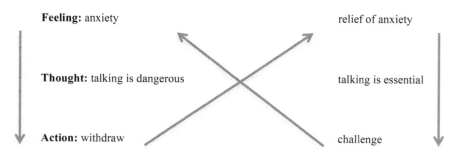

Feeling: anxiety   relief of anxiety

Thought: talking is dangerous   talking is essential

Action: withdraw   challenge

Figure 1.2

consultant herself. Frosh and Barraitser (2008) define reflexivity as: "an inter-actively critical practice that is constantly reflected back on itself and is always suspicious of the productions of its own knowledge" (p.350).

Foulkes himself advocates stepping back and examining the patterns he is par-ticipating in. The group analyst: "has to be both a member of his group, . . . as well as its leader, who stands in a sense outside of it, sees beyond its immediate affairs, keeps his head above water" (Foulkes, 1948, p.36).

The consultant pays conscious attention to her own unconscious responses, moving her focus from individual to pattern, to the group as a whole – an actor, in *patterns of figuration*. In this way she mediates knowledge through her own subjective experience, on the boundary of conscious and unconscious, not only facilitating expression but contextualizing, and then recontextualizing, patterns of *feeling, thinking, and action, with* organizational members.

The reflexive consultant focuses not only on her own counter-transference responses as information about narratives and patterns but also on what she *con-structs* through her participation in those patterns. Further, the consultant needs to participate within the organizational conversation in a way that enables a shift-ing of conversational patterning, enhancing the conditions whereby the reflexive and reflective capacities of organizational members are encouraged, so that their agentic abilities to make conscious choices in the context of collective account-ability are developed.

Vignette

The consultants developed an understanding of the paradoxical pattern partly through their counter transference experience. When in the public forum, they felt a constraining tentativeness, predicated on fear about opening up the sub-ject of conflict yet also of the consequences of not addressing it, as both pos-sibilities invited damage. If they addressed the conflict head on, they would create a defensive reaction; if they did not, they would not be doing their job. In order to enable them to take a third position, the consultants realized the need to meta-communicate about the dilemma that they and the community were in. They did this, explaining that the paradoxical behaviour of the com-munity (and temporarily of the consultants) was making the feared destruc-tive consequences more likely.

The consultants made the decision to interview all 25 monks individually, before working in the group as a whole, suggesting that this process would constructively protect and strengthen the fragile heart and mind of the com-munity that the current pattern was protecting destructively. Following the interviews, they would present the themes back to the community, with ideas about intervention. The community responded with relief that they could move forward gently. Schein (1992) has shown how small steps in consul-tancy design can facilitate the psychological safety necessary to maximize the conditions for organizational change.

Intervention: generating conscious communication

Group analysts advocate *extending* the range of communication of group members, encouraging putting into words troubling experiences, thoughts, and feelings. The consultant also needs to *develop* conversational forms to enable new intersubjective patterns: changes in conversation make for changes in organization.

Intervention is perhaps the aspect of organizational group analysis that is least described in the literature. I suggest that free floating discussion alone is not always sufficient as a conversational form in facilitating new organizational patterns. Often it needs to be purposefully combined with proactive design of processes, where participants are positioned purposefully to encounter themselves, each other, and the organization in more creative ways.

Nitsun (1998a) argues that it is not possible: "to be prescriptive about the exact method of intervention, other than to suggest that it should help identify and explore the mirroring process with a view towards boundary regulation and realistic problem solving" (p.516).

He advocates that "communication in a relatively structured way with individuals, groups, or a combination" (p.509) is appropriate in an organizational context.

For Foulkes (1948), dynamic administration is a significant task of the group analyst, creating the contextual conditions for the group to thrive, facilitating the analyst's ability to hold the boundaries of the group. On these terms, the consultant needs to employ sensitivity to the management of communication contexts and the ways in which participants are positioned in those contexts, through how she designs, structures, and facilitates conversation.

An organization that is characterized by *reflexive patterns* will be more curious and open about painful or uncomfortable experiences than an organization caught up in *reactive* or paradoxical patterns. Binney et al. (2005) point out that in much consultancy theory, the trend for developing a "positive forward looking mentality could leave people feeling compliant, resentful, and paralysed" (p.15). They advocate embracing the negative: for instance, feelings of loss, anger, and fear. I propose that uncomfortable feelings are best not thought of as negative but more as of significance for learning about organizational life. While they may be experienced as uncomfortable, if they are treated as of value, recognized, explored, accepted, and contextualized, their meaning can be reframed and incorporated as necessary for individual agency and organizational integrity.

Positioning organizational members as responsible for the part they play in making the *organization as a whole*, reflecting on the ways their behaviour contributes to *cultural, relational* and *self narratives* and *patterns*, encourages them to explore those themes that play a key role in shaping their organizational experience.

In considering *boundary regulation*, the boundaries that are significant in design are those related to tasks, roles, relationships, rights and responsibilities, and the different structures for conversation that are created. Organizational patterns can undermine the consultancy process, unless conversational structures are created for reflecting on rather than enacting of such patterns.

Consultancy processes usually need to include a series of conversations of some kind. An important aspect of dynamic administration is to consider with those commissioning the consultancy work how the meaning of engagement should be framed for organizational members; how the conversations are to be linked meaningfully together; how they link with daily organizational life, in particular, organizational decision making; and the powers that consultancy participants have in processes of decision making relating to the consultancy.

Vignette

Following the individual interviews, the consultants designed an exercise for the whole group, to facilitate a change from *reactive* and *paradoxical* patterns to greater reflective and reflexive capacity, hoping to enrich the communicative matrix. They framed the purpose of the exercise as enabling the community to speak with each other and with the consultants about what had been – and still was – difficult, in a different way than they had previously encountered. The consultants shared how, in their listening, they had heard about the destructive and painful effects of the split in community, and had heard the desire for change, but appreciated that people needed to learn how to change. The exercise was framed as facilitating new ways of relating to self, other, and community, through purposeful, structured conversation, enabling a greater sense of safety than had previously been felt.

All participants were asked to work with one other person with whom they felt they could work. All participants remained in the room.

Stage 1: Write a statement about how you feel you have contributed to misunderstanding, distancing, and mistrust in community life, particularly in relation to the conflict that has contributed to so much unhappiness.

Stage 2: Read each other's statements and take it in turns to explore, from a position of curiosity, the feelings, meanings, and actions described.

Stage 3: Write a response in the form of a letter, saying how you have been affected by the conversation; what you have understood about the other's feelings and thoughts; what you wish for the other now.

Stage 4: Share letters and make verbal responses.

Stage 5: Reflect in the large group about the experience and how it has affected your narratives of self, relationship, and community.

In this free-floating reflection, some of the comments included:

"The exercise fitted with our valuing of confession and helped things to begin to come out into the light."

"It is the first time I have been challenged to take responsibility for my contribution to the malaise. Previously I have tried to analyse what went wrong or tried to put it right; this is a new position to be in."

"Focusing on one's own vulnerability makes one more attractive to the other and paradoxically helps to build strength."

In conclusion

The organization represents a complexity of contexts, and unless one has a robust frame, the consultant can feel overwhelmed by contextual juggling: negotiating a contract; developing processes of inquiry to make sense of organizational predicaments; and structuring organizational conversation in ways that enable new *patterns of figuration*. I hope that I have shown through my development of a contextual framework that group analysis has a great deal to offer the organizational consultant, through integrating *transmission* and *construction* discourses of communication, building a notion of communicative matrix made up of *contextual narratives* and *patterns of figuration*, proposing reflexivity for consultant and organizational members, and enabling contextual analysis and intervention into organizational life in ways that both employ and extend group analytic processes.

There is a sense in which Nitsun (1998b) is right when he says that it is not possible to be prescriptive about consultancy intervention. By this I mean that each intervention needs to be tailor made for the specific organizational context, linked to hypotheses about *contextual narratives*, and designed to intervene in specific *patterns of figuration*. It is possible, however, to work within a framework of group analytic principles about the design and facilitation of conversation.

The work with the monastery represents such a framework involving careful analysis, reflexive reflection on consultant experience, and specified exercises that link *free* floating *discussion* with task centred exercises that enable the development of meaning, the expression of emotion, the challenging of *contextual narratives* and the creation, through the experience, of new *patterns of figuration*.

Commentary on Systemic, Tavistock, and Group Analytic Approaches

Christine Oliver

Nitsun (1998a) celebrates how group analysis has been informed by many theoretical traditions: psychoanalysis, systems theory, social psychology, and sociology, suggesting that a multi-perspective frame, fitting to the challenges of organizational complexity, can enrich the possibilities for building a robust approach to organizational consultancy. It is in this spirit that I share some reflections about the three approaches outlined in this chapter, exploring some similarities and differences relating to theoretical assumptions; ideas about organizational sense making; consultant role, relationship and task; and intervention.

Theoretical assumptions

I start with a basic tenet of what Dalal (1998, p.34) calls "radical Foulkes", "a systemic and multi-dimensional theory" that supports a meta-theoretical belief in the "interconnected nature of existence itself", conceiving of the individual and social as abstractions that may, for certain purposes, be useful to differentiate in language, but, by implication, should be treated as narratives not entities and as "two sides of the same coin" (Foulkes and Anthony, 1957, p.26).

As early as 1948, Foulkes spoke to the importance of not treating individual and social as separate entities, saying: "They can at no stage be separated from each other, except by artificial isolation" (Foulkes, 1948, pp.10–11).

What I see as a fundamental distinction to make in commenting on the three approaches is that, unlike Foulkes, the Tavistock approach, a "well established community of practice" (Morgan-Jones in this chapter) offering a large range of application of a systems psychodynamics approach to organization, appears to treat individual and social as separate ontological elements of the organizational system, de-emphasizing the question of narrative. Influenced by open systems theory, Bion's basic assumptions (1961) and group relations theory, the Tavistock focus is on part/whole relationships – on 'whole systems' and 'group as a whole' phenomena, the significance of the individual underplayed to these purposes.

A systemic focus, on the other hand, influenced by social constructionism, is more on how the living process of construction, through individual and group storylines/narratives and patterns of communication, comprises the system through the behaviour of interacting persons. Personal and social become dimensions of patterns and storylines; organizations are discursive phenomena – contextual, relational, local, negotiated, and emergent within specific conversations. In this sense it shares a meta-theoretical assumption with group analysis.

I imagine that systemic practitioners would agree with Dalal (1998), who proposes that "essence is partly the property of an object but is also a function of context" (p.172). He speaks of the importance of not objectifying context, fitting with the systemic language of contextual storylines. Dalal points out that our ways of seeing significantly shape how we think about context and how we think about the objects of our social worlds.

It is in these terms that I want to explore the use of *systemic domains of practice* for group analysis (Miksits in this chapter, Oliver, 2005). This model represents a meta-communicative orientation for the consultant, enabling analysis of the system in a way that embraces productive, aesthetic, and narrative dimensions of organizational life. Group analysis, in its "half way land" (Dalal, 1998) between orthodox Foulkes and radical Foulkes has possibly not taken radical Foulkes sufficiently by the horns, with the consequence that group analysis is in danger of representing one pole of a binary in organizational work, e.g., as expressed by the language of group analytic *or* corporate thinking. I would like to suggest that group analysis, if adopting the *systemic domains of practice* model, and treating all descriptions as discourses rather than entities, can embrace *and* critique the language of targets, appraisals, tasks, hierarchy, and production. We might call this frame for thinking and positioning of the consultant in organizational conversation, the *discursive matrix*. The organizational group analyst thus acknowledges the significance of discourse in organizational life, foregrounding discourses of production or narrative when contextually appropriate, though not losing sight of the other, and helped by the third space of the *domain of aesthetics*, which foregrounds higher level contexts shaping action, such as purpose and morality.

Miksits values discursive openness in hypothesizing about systemic storylines and patterns, and similarly group analysts treat the matrix as a hypothesis about a complex process of meaning making. The focus for hypothesizing for Tavistock approaches relates to "the importance of unconscious factors in the life and destiny of our social and economic institutions . . . the emotional dimensions of institutional functioning", particularly those that remain "unspoken and unaddressed" (Obholzer, 1994, p.xvi) or "hidden" (Morgan-Jones in this chapter).

The tendency of organizational members to build defences against feelings of aggression and anxiety, through processes of splitting, projection, introjections, and identification is foregrounded. For Armstrong (2005), for instance, the primary focus of the consultant is the emotional exchange between consultant and client, be it individual, group, or whole organization. This emotional experience is informative of the relationship between task, structure, culture, environment, or "context" and the "personality structure", role and position of individuals, manifested as the "organization in the mind" (p.6).

While group analysis also has a core interest in the unconscious, its curiosity, I have postulated, is focused on how organizational distress *and* creativity is located in narratives and patterns of figuration in the matrix, and not just in how organizational structure, culture, and boundaries shape the possibilities for individual behaviour but also how, in specific episodes of communication, dynamic patterns can change and influence higher level contexts. For the systemic practitioner, the unconscious is more implicit than explicit, with a focus on the detail of the emerging process of communication patterns and how they are shaped by implicit (conscious and unconscious) contexts that construct storylines of obligation. The use of context is broader here than in the Tavistock tradition, treating culture, structure, task, relationship, identity – or any other narrative – as contexts that shape organizational behaviour consciously and unconsciously. Miksits, in his case vignette, shared how he felt drawn into a defensive position and used this observation of his own response as information of narratives and patterns in the organization but did not explicitly reference the unconscious. His focus was on ensuring he did not enact a defensive position and this was enabled by hypothesizing about perceived obligations and pressures shaping anxiety in the system.

Making sense

All three approaches focus on experience as a primary source for sense making: group analytic and Tavistock approaches using language of transference, counter-transference, and projection, and systemic using the language of positioning: Miksits speaking of feeling drawn into a position by a specific dynamic and concerned to change the form and direction of that pattern through his own reflexive action.

Tavistock approaches' notion of the system relates to socio-psychological, socio-technical, and social–ecological systems, whereas the group analytic focus on the matrix and the systemic focus are more related to a system of conscious and unconscious meaning making, the matrix/system providing resources and constraints for action.

The Tavistock approaches highlight organizational hierarchy, clarity of roles and responsibility, and alignment with the primary task; on the one hand, there is an interest in the unconscious and on the other on 'rational' processes. A systemic approach treats these phenomena as narratives within which emotion and hierarchies of power and task all have a place in meaning making – they are not separate processes. These narratives may also be part of wider narratives and, in exploring these, the meaning of storylines can change. The *systemic domains of practice* model does not separate out the rational and emotional but treats these as ways of talking/discourses that create particular, temporary work worlds.

I propose that it is congruent for a group analytic approach to not split so-called rationality and 'emotionality' but to treat them as in a contextual relationship, not assuming that clarity, for instance, is preferable, but more concerned with how clarity, or the lack of it, has meaning within a network of relationships and conversations (Oliver, 2016).

For the Tavistock, there is an interest in role theory, using language like "the organization in the mind" (Armstrong, 2005). The systemic practitioner might think more in terms of "the organizational mind" – with its sense of the system/mind comprised of patterns and storylines. Systems dynamics for the Tavistock consultant relate to the resources, roles, and technology needed to perform organizational tasks. The context of the task is paramount, whereas for the systemic practitioner, there are a number of contexts that relate to tasks, and this hierarchy of contexts will vary in its order of influence on accounts of obligation, depending on the unique circumstances of a given communication episode; this is the material for systemic contextual analysis. The *systemic domains of practice* model enables *task* to be thought about in three dimensions: the aesthetics of task, the narratives relating to task, and the production of task.

Group analysts, with their interest in the group in the individual and the individual in the group might think both in terms of "organization in the mind" and the "mind in the organization", although the notion of 'mind' is also contested as it is important not to create a Cartesian split (Nitzgen and Hopper, 2017).

Consultant role, relationship, task

While all approaches think of consultants as participant observers, developing hypotheses, valuing reflective abilities, the role of the consultant using Tavistock approaches involves a deliberate encouragement of the articulation of aggression and regression, working with boundaries, authorities, role, and task in its focus on emotional exchange, as shown by Morgan-Jones' case vignette. The systemic approach emphasizes relatedness, communication and coordination, the consultant designing and facilitating conversational patterns and the coordination and enrichment of meaning, and conscious connections between storylines and patterns. The task of the consultant is to explicitly foreground questions of power, choice, agency, and purpose. Miksits emphasizes the value of a critical sensibility or discursive reflexivity – examining discourse from a lens of what is privileged and marginalized. In his case vignette he shows us how he deliberately invited a counter-discourse of power.

A group analytic approach looks for themes and patterns that enable the anti-group to become generative and the difficult topics to become explicit through their experience and ability in identifying, exploring, expressing, and interpreting the nuances of communication.

Intervention

Stacey (2000) suggests that the Tavistock model privileges pathology as a focus for intervention, potentially deflecting from organizational creativity. The tendency of systemic approaches to frame communication, not as pathological but as meaningful information, whatever its form, can facilitate openness and diminish defensiveness for participants in consultancy processes. Also, systemic designs of interventions that bypass destructive patterns can help organizational participants feel 'safer' and less 'lost' in unconscious dynamics.

Wilke (2014), a group analyst, underlines how interpretation of unconscious defences is not enough, creating spaces for development in communication in the context of the network of organizational relationships. He uses different conversational forms in small and large groups, including the organization's 'normal' meetings, punctuated by spaces for reflection, to enable "exchange through storytelling" (p.8), facilitating a different conversational flow that gives permission for difficult topics to be addressed, the implicit made explicit, and organizational members held to account in face to face interaction.

Tavistock approaches pay attention to design of conversational structures, for instance, with methods of social dreaming and role analysis, while design has often been underplayed in group analysis, focusing more on the development of insight and the ability to mentalize. I would say that role and task might not historically have been so centred for group analysts, but they are potentially treated as contextually meaningful and integrated dimensions of narrative: the *systemic domains of practice* model facilitates this.

For the systemic practitioner, similarly, the system of relationships and communication processes becomes the site for intervention and development. Interventions are deliberately designed but also responsive and emergent, attentive to "unfolding conversations and group processes". Miksits uses the term "systemic inquiry" to contain a range of conversational structures and patterns. The emphasis in interventive processes is in changing the shared story of a situation and one's part in it with others.

In conclusion

Tavistock and systemic approaches offer group analysis resources – in particular, the Tavistock emphasis on task as a key context and the systemic, discursive emphasis on a multiplicity of contextual storylines (Campbell et al., 1989) and the *systemic domains of practice* model. While Tavistock, systemic, and group analytic approaches work with some fundamentally different theoretical assumptions, including different views about what counts as a system, and what counts as appropriate intervention, ultimately all are interested in enabling organizational members to feel safe enough to be vulnerable and open to learning.

I would propose that historically organizational group analysis has been limited by its narrative of scope for what might count as appropriate group analytic intervention of the consultant. I argue here that the *systemic domains of practice* model can help to widen the scope in a way that offers coherence, alongside group analytic expertise, in the exploration and expression of communication and relationship.

Notes

1 Note these first four concepts are sometimes defined as the BART approach = Boundary, Authority, Role, Task.
2 Although in practice some consultants can be observed gathering and making available evidence for specific hypotheses, while others seek to engage with the hidden aggressive dynamics of groups by being withholding and opaque. Additionally, many GR consultants have a therapeutic or group analytic background.
3 The community and individuals within it are anonymized.
4 These are a collation of all references for all authored sections within Chapter 1.

References[4]

Abraham, F. (2013). The Tavistock Group. In: M. Witzel and M. Warner (2013). *The Oxford Handbook of Management Theorists.* Oxford: Oxford University Press.

Amado, G. and Ambrose, A. (2001). *The Transitional Approach to Change.* London: Karnac.

Amado, G. and Vansina, L. (2003). *The Transitional Approach in Action.* London: Karnac.

Anderson, H., Goolishian, H.A. and Windermand, L. (1986). Problem determined systems: towards transformation in family therapy. *Journal of Strategic and Systemic Therapies, 5* (4): 1–14.

Anderson, H. and Goolishian, H.A. (1988). Human systems as linguistic systems: preliminary and evolving ideas about the implications for clinical theory. *Family Process, 27* (4): 371–93.

Anzieu, D. (1989). *The Skin Ego.* New Haven, CT: Yale University Press.

Aram, E., Baxter, R. and Nutkevitch, A. (Eds) (2009). *Group Relations Conferences II: Adaptation and Innovation: Theory, Design and Role-Taking in Group Relations Conferences and their Application.* London: Karnac.

Aram, E., Baxter, R. and Nutkevitch, A. (Eds) (2012). *Group Relations Conferences III: Tradition, Creativity and Succession in the Global Group Relations Network.* London: Karnac.

Aram, E., Baxter, R. and Nutkevitch, A. (Eds) (2015). *Group Relations Work IV: Exploring the Impact and Relevance Within and Beyond its Network.* London: Karnac.

Armstrong, D. (2005). *Organisation in the Mind: Psychoanalysis, Group Relations and Organisational Consultancy.* London: Karnac.

Armstrong, D. (2016). (Unpublished paper). Psychoanalytic study and the ethical imagination: the making, finding and losing of a tradition. Presented at 34th ISPSO Annual Conference 2016. Granada, Spain: 'Ethical Dilemmas in our Global Era – Challenging Psychoanalytic Understanding of Organizations'.

Armstrong, D. and Rustin, M. (2015). *Social Defences against Anxiety: Explorations in a Paradigm.* London: Karnac.

Berg, I.K. and Szabó, P. (2005). *Brief Coaching for Lasting Solutions.* New York: W.W. Norton & Co.

Bick, E. (2002). Collected Papers. In: A. Briggs (Ed.), *Surviving Space: Papers on Infant Observation.* London: Tavistock.

Binney, G., Wilke, G. and Williams, C. (2005). *Living Leadership: A Practical Guide for Ordinary Heroes.* Harlow: Pearson/Financial Times.

Bion, W.R. (1948–1952, collected and republished 1961). *Experiences in Groups and Other Papers*. London: Routledge.

Bion, W.R. (1961). *Experiences in Groups and Other Papers*. London: Tavistock.

Blackwell, D. (2000). The psyche and the system. In: D. Brown and L. Zinkin (Eds), *The Psyche and the Social World*. London: JKP.

Boxer, P. (2017). Working with defences against innovation: the forensic challenge. *Organisational and Social Dynamics Journal, 17* (1). London: Karnac.

Bridger, H. (1990a). Courses and working conferences as transitional learning institutions. In: E. Trist and H. Murray (1990), *The Social Engagement of Social Science: A Tavistock Anthology – The Socio-Psychological Perspective*. Philadelphia: University of Pennsylvania Press.

Bridger, H. (1990b). The discovery of the therapeutic community: the Northfield experiments. In: E. Trist and H. Murray (1990), *The Social Engagement of Social Science: A Tavistock Anthology – The Socio-Psychological Perspective*. Philadelphia: University of Pennsylvania Press.

Bridger, H. (2001). The working conference design. In: G. Amado and L. Vansina (2001). *The Transitional Approach to Change*. London: Karnac.

Brunner, L., Nutkevitch, A. and Sher, M. (Eds) (2006). *Group Relations Conferences I: Reviewing and Exploring Theory, Design, Role-taking and Application*. London: Karnac.

Brunning, H. (Ed.) (2006) *Executive Coaching – Systems-psychodynamic Perspective*. London: Karnac.

Brunning, H. (Ed.) (2012). *Psychoanalytic Reflections on a Changing World*. London: Karnac.

Brunning, H. (Ed.) (2014). *Psychoanalytic Essays on Power and Vulnerability*. London: Karnac.

Brunning, H. and Perini, M. (Eds) (2010). *Psychoanalytic Perspectives on a Turbulent World*. London: Karnac.

Burnham, J. (1992). Approach – method – technique: making distinctions and creating connections. *Human Systems, 3* (1): 3–26.

Burnham, J. (2012). Developments in Social GGRRAAACCEEESSS: visible-invisible, voiced-unvoiced. In: I. Krause (Ed.), *Culture and Reflexivity in Systemic Psychotherapy: Mutual Perspectives* (pp.139–60). London: Karnac.

Burr, V. (2003). *Social Constructionism* (2nd edn). Hove, East Sussex: Routledge.

Campbell, D., Draper, R. and Huffington, C. (1989). *A Systemic Approach to Consultation*. London: Karnac.

Campbell, D. (2000). *The Socially Constructed Organization*. London: Karnac.

Campbell, D. and Huffington, C. (2008). Six stages of systemic consultation. In: D. Campbell and C. Huffington (Eds), *Organizations Connected. A Handbook of Systemic Consultation* (pp.1–14). London: Karnac.

Carr, A. (1991). Power and influence in systems consultation. *Human Systems, 2*: 15–29.

Cecchin, G. (1987). Hypothesizing, circularity, and neutrality revisited: an invitation to curiosity. *Family Process, 26* (4): 405–13.

Clarke, S. and Hoggett, P. (2009). *Researching Beneath the Surface: Psycho-Social Research Methods in Practice*. London: Karnac.

Colman, A. and Bexton, H. (1983). *Group Relations Reader 1*. Florida: A.K. Rice Institute.

Colman, A. and Geller, M. (Eds) (1985). *Group Relations Reader 2*. Florida: A.K. Rice Institute.

Cooperrider, D.L., Barrett, F. and Srivastva, S. (1995). Social construction and appreciative inquiry: a journey in organizational theory. In: D. Hosking, P. Dachler and K. Gergen (Eds), *Management and Organization: Relational Alternatives to Individualism* (pp.157–200). Aldershot: Avebury Press.

Cooperrider, L.D. and Whitney, D. ([1999]2005). *Appreciative Inquiry*. San Francisco: Berret-Koehler Communications.

Cronen, V., Johnson, K. and Lannamann, J. (1982). Paradoxes, double-binds and reflexive loops: an alternative theoretical perspective, *Family Process, 21*.

Cunliffe, A. (2004). On becoming a critically reflexive practitioner, *Journal of Management Education, 28* (4): 407–26.

Curnow, B. (2000). The Group Analyst as Consultant, IGA qualifying course paper.

Cytrynbaum, S. and Noumair, D. (Eds) (2004). *Group Dynamics, Organizational Irrationality and Social Complexity: Group Relations Reader 3*. Florida: A.K. Rice Institute.

Dalal, F. (1998). *Taking the Group Seriously: Towards a Post-Foulkesian Group Analytic Theory*. London: Jessica Kingsley.

Dartington, T. (2010). *Managing Vulnerability – The Underlying Dynamics of Systems of Care*. London: Karnac.

De Jong, P. and Berg, I.K. (2008). *Interviewing for Solutions* (4th edn). Belmont, CA: Brooks Cole Publishing.

De Shazer, S. (1985). *The Keys to Solution in Brief Therapy*. New York: W.W Norton & Co.

Dicks, H.V. (1970). *50 years of the Tavistock Clinic*. London: RKP.

Eason, K. (1998). *Information Technology and Organisational Change*. London: Taylor & Francis.

Einhorn, S. (2014). Endorsement. In: G. Wilke, *The Art of Group Analysis in Organisations*. London: Karnac.

Elias, N. (1994). *The Civilising Process*. Oxford: Blackwell.

Erlich, H.S., Erlich-Ginor, M. and Beland, H. (2009). *Fed with Tears – Poisoned with Milk: The 'Nazareth' Group-Relations Conferences. Germans and Israelis – The Past in the Present*. Giesen: Psychosozial-Verlag.

Flaskas, C. (1997). Engagement and the therapeutic relationship in systemic therapy. *Journal of Family Therapy, 19*: 263–82.

Foucault, M. (1981). The order of discourse. In: R. Young (Ed.) *Untying the Text: A Post-Structuralist Reader* (pp.48–78). London: Routledge.

Foulkes, S.H. (1948). *Introduction to Group Analysis*. London: Maresfield.

Foulkes, S.H. (1964). *Therapeutic Group Analysis*. London: Allen & Unwin.

Foulkes, S.H. and Anthony, E.J. ([1957]1975). *Group Psychotherapy: The Psychoanalytic Approach*. London: Karnac.

Fraher, A. (2004). *A History of Group Study and Psychodynamic Organizations*. London: Free Association Books.

Fraher, A. (2005). *Group Dynamics of High-Risk Teams: A 'Team Resource Management' (TRM) Primer*. Lincoln, NE: iUniverse Books.

Fraher, A. (2011). *Thinking through Crisis*. Cambridge: Cambridge University Press.

French, R. and Simpson, P. (2014) *Attention, Cooperation, Purpose: An Approach to Working in Groups Using Insights from Wilfred Bion*. London: Karnac.

Frosh, S. and Barraitser, L. (2008). Psychoanalysis and psycho-social studies. *Psychoanalysis, Culture and Society, 13*: 346–65.

Gergen, K.J. and Gergen, M. (2004). *Social Constructionism: Entering the Dialogue*. Chagrin Falls, Ohio: Taos Institute Publications.

Gould, L.J., Stapley, L.F. and Stein, M. (2004). *Experiential Learning in Organizations – Applications of The Tavistock Group Relations Approach*. London: Karnac.

Gould, L.J. et al. (Eds) (2006). *The Systems Psychodynamics of Organisations: Integrating the Group Relations Approach, Psychoanalytic and Open Systems Perspectives*. London: Karnac.

Harrison, T. (1999). *Bion, Rickman, Foulkes and the Northfield Experiments: Advancing on a Different Front*. London: Jessica Kingsley.

Hinshelwood, R.D. (1987). *What Happens in Groups – Psychoanalysis, the Individual and the Community*. London: FaB.

Hirschorn, L. (1990). *The Workplace Within. Psychodynamics of Organizational Life*. Boston: MIT.

Hirschorn, L. (1994). Transference, the primary task and the primary risk. In: P. Hoggett (2009). *Politics Identity and Emotion*. London: Paradigm.

Hoggett, P., Mayo, M. and Miller, C. (2009). *The Dilemmas of Development Work – Ethical Challenges in Regeneration*. Bristol: Policy Press.

Hollway, W. and Jefferson, T. (2000). *Doing Qualitative Research Differently – A Psychosocial Approach*. London: Sage.

Holti, R. (1997). Consulting to organisational implications of technical change. In: Neumann, et al. (Eds) (1997). *Developing Organisational Consultancy*. London: Routledge.

Hopper, E. (1991). Encapsulation as a defence against the fear of annihilation. *The International Journal of Psychoanalysis, 72* (4): 607–24.

Hopper, E. (2003). *The Social Unconscious: Selected Papers*. London: Jessica Kingsley.

Hopper, E. (2011). *The Social Unconscious in Persons, Groups and Societies Vol. 1*. London: Karnac.

Hopper, E. (2012). *Trauma and Organizations*. London: Karnac.

Hopper, E. (2016). *The Social Unconscious in Persons, Groups and Societies, Vol. 2*. London: Karnac.

Huffington, C. et al., (2004). *Working Below the Surface: The Emotional Life of Contemporary Organizations*. Tavistock Clinic Series. London: Karnac.

Hutton, J.M. (2000). *Working with the Concept of the Organisation-in-the-mind*. Grubb Institute Publications.

Hutton, J.M., Bazalgette, J.L. and Reed, B.D. (1997) *Organisation-in-the-Mind: A Tool for Leadership and Management of Institutions*. Grubb Institute Publications.

Jaques, E. (1998). *Requisite Organization: A Total System for Effective Managerial Organization and Managerial Leadership for the 21st Century*. London: Gower.

Kapur, R. (2009). *Managing Primitive Emotions in Organisations, Group Analysis, 42* (31).

Keeney, H. and Keeney, B. (2012). What is systemic about systemic therapy? Therapy models muddle embodied systemic practice. *Journal of Systemic Therapies, 31* (1): 22–37.

Klein, L. (2005). *Working across the Gap: The Practice of Social Science in Organizations*. London: Karnac.

Lang, P., Little, M. and Cronen, V. (1990). The systemic professional: domains of action and the question of neutrality. *Human Systems, 1*: 39–55.

Lang, P.W. and McAdam, E. (1995). Stories, giving accounts and systemic descriptions. *Human Systems, 6*: 71–103.

Lawrence, W.G. (1998). *Social Dreaming @ Work*. London: Karnac.

Lawrence, W.G. (2003). *Tongued with Fire*. London: Karnac.

Lazar, R (2008). From baby to boardroom. Unpublished paper, delivered to conference, *From Baby to Boardroom: The Tavistock–Bick Method of Infant Observation and its Application to Organisations and in Consultancy* (2008). Tavistock Centre, 17–18 October 2008.

Lewin, K. (1939[1951]) Experiments in social space. In: G.W. Lewin (Ed.) *Resolving Social Conflicts: Field Theory in Social Science* (pp.59–67). Washington, DC: American Psychological Association.

Lewin, K. (1946). *Resolving Social Conflicts and Field Theory in Social Science*. Washington, DC: American Psychological Association.

Lohmer, M. (2004) *Psychodynamische Organisationsberatung Konflikte und Potentiale in Veränderungsprozesse* [Psychodynamic Consultation to Organisations Conflicts and Potentials in Change Processes]. Stuttgart: Klett-Cotta.

Long, S. (2008). *The Perverse Organisation and its Deadly Sins*. London: Karnac.

Long, S. (Ed.) (2016). *Transforming Experience in Organisations*. London: Karnac.

Long, S. and Manley, J. (2017). *Social Dreaming: Philosophy, Research and Practice*. London: Karnac.

Long, S. and Sievers, B. (Eds) (2012). *Towards a Socioanalysis of Money, Finance and Capitalism*. London: Routledge.

Mann, R.D. (Eds). *Analysis of Groups*. San Francisco, CA: Jossey-Bass.

Mathur, A (Ed.). (2006). *Dare to Think the Unthought Known?* Tampere, Finland: Aivoairut Oy.

Maturana, H. (1991). Science and daily life: the ontology of scientific explanations. In: F. Steier (Ed.), *Research and Reflexivity* (pp.30–52). London: Sage.

Meltzer, D. and Harris, M. (1994). A psychoanalytic model of the child-in-the-family-in-the-world (Ch. 22). In: *Sincerity and Other Works*. London: Karnac.

Meltzer, D. and Harris, M. (2014). *The Educational Role of the Family: A Psychoanalytical Model*. London: Karnac.

Menzies Lyth, I. ([1959]1988). The functioning of social systems as a defence against anxiety. In: I. Menzies Lyth (1988), *Containing Anxiety in Institutions: Selected Essays, Vol. 1*. London: Free Association Books.

Mersky, R.R. (2012). Contemporary methodologies to surface and act on unconscious dynamics in organisations: an exploration of design, facilitation capacities, consultant paradigm and ultimate value. *Organizational and Social Dynamics, 12* (1): 19–43.

Miksits, M. (2014). *Imagining Organisational Futures. Towards a Systemic Constructionist Practice Perspective*. Professional doctorate thesis. Luton: University of Bedfordshire.

Miller, E. (1989) *The 'Leicester' Model: Experiential Study of Group and Organizational Processes*. Occasional paper no.10. London: Tavistock Institute of Human Relations.

Miller, E. (1993). *From Dependency to Autonomy: Studies in Organisational Development and Change*. London: Free Association Books.

Miller, E. (1997). Effecting organisational change in large complex systems: a collaborative consultancy approach. In: Neumann et al. (Eds), (1997), *Developing Organisational Consultancy*. London: Routledge.

Miller, E. (2004) The 'Leicester' model revisited. In: E. Miller et al. (Eds). *Experiential Learning in Organizations: Applications of the Tavistock Group Relations Approach* (pp 11–18). London: Karnac.

Miller, E. and Rice, A.K. (1967). *Systems of Organisation*. London: Tavistock.

Morgan, G. (1996). *Images of Organization*. London: Sage.

Morgan-Jones, R.J. (2005). Supervision in a forensic unit: How the re-cycled trauma in search of containment shapes the container for team supervision. In: B. Bishop, A. Dickinson, A. Foster and J. Klein (Eds) (on behalf of The London Centre for Psychotherapy), *The Practice of Psychotherapy Book Four: Difference: Avoided Topics in Practice*. London: Karnac.

Morgan-Jones, R.J. (2006). The management of risk of re-cycling trauma in the context of conflicting primary tasks: an analysis of the use of the group dynamic of incohesion basic assumption activity. *Organizational and Social Dynamics, 6* (1): 22–41.

Morgan-Jones, R.J. (2010a). The work group as an object of desire: the embodiment of protomental life. *Journal of Organisational and Social Dynamics, 10*: 79–98. London: Karnac.

Morgan-Jones, R.J. (2010b). *The Body of the Organisation and its Health*. London: Karnac.

Morgan-Jones, R.J. (2015). Developing Sociotherapy as a Resource for Organisational Health. *Socioanalysis, 2* (17): 27–42.

Morgan-Jones, R.J. (2017). The language of the group skin: how teams are shaped by the experience of belonging to a body bigger than your own. In: M. Ringer (Ed.), *Thinking in Groups and Teams*. Italian Journal ARGO.7 (2017).

Morgan-Jones, R.J. and Torres, N. (2010). Individual and collective suffering of organisational failures in containment: searching for a model to explore protomental dynamics. *Socioanalysis, 12* (10): 57–75.

Neumann, J.E. (1997). *Negotiating Entry and Contracting*. In: J.E. Neumann et al. (Eds), *Developing Organisational Consultancy*. London: Brunner Routledge.

Newton, J., Long, S. and Sievers, B. (Eds) (2006). *Coaching in Depth: The Organizational Role Analysis Approach*. London: Karnac.

Nitsun, M. (1996). *The Anti-Group: Destructive Forces in the Group and their Creative Potential*. London: Brunner-Routledge.

Nitsun, M. (1998a). The organisational mirror: a group analytic approach to organisational consultancy, part 1 – theory. *Group Analysis, 31*: 245.

Nitsun, M. (1998b). The organisational mirror: a group analytic approach to organisational consultancy, part 2 – application. *Group Analysis, 31*: 505.

Nitzgen, D. and Hopper, E. (2017). The concepts of the social unconscious and of the matrix in the work of S.H. Foulkes. In: E. Hopper and H. Weinberg (Eds), *The Social Unconscious in Persons, Groups and Societies, Vol. 3: The Foundation Matrix Extended and Re-configured* (pp.3–6). London: Karnac.

Obholzer, A. and Roberts, V (Eds), (1994). *The Unconscious at Work*. London: RKP.

Oliver, C. (2005). *Reflexive Inquiry: A Framework for Consultancy Practice*. London: Karnac.

Oliver, C. (2013). *Systemic Reflexivity. Building Theory for Organisational Consultancy*. PhD thesis: University of Bedfordshire.

Oliver, C. (2016). Response to C. Grace: Endings and loss in mergers and acquisitions: an exploration of group analytic theory. *Group Analysis, 49* (2).

Oliver, C. and Miksits, M. (2016). Leadership: putting our systemic sensibilities to work. *Context, 148*: 14–20.

Pearce, W.B. (1989). *Communication and the Human Condition*. Carbondale: University of Southern Illinois.

Pearce, W.B. (1995). A sailing guide for social constructionists. In: W. Leeds-Hurwitz (Ed.), *Social Approaches to Communication* (pp 88–113). New York: Guilford Press.

Pearce, W.B. (2004). The coordinated management of meaning (CMM). In: W.B. Gudykunst (Ed.), *Theorizing about Intercultural Communications* (pp.35–54). London: Sage.

Pearce, W.B. (2007). *Making Social Worlds: A Communication Perspective.* Oxford: Blackwell.

Pearce, W.B. and Cronen, E.V. (1980). *Communication, Action and Meaning: The Creation of Social Realities.* New York: Praeger.

Penn, P. (1982). Circular questioning. *Family Process 21* (3): 267–80.

Pines, M. (Ed.) (1985). *Bion and Group Psychotherapy.* London: RKP.

Rance, C. (1998). The art of conversation: the group analytic paradigm and organisational consultancy. *Group Analysis, 31* (519).

Reed, B.D. (1988) *Professional Management – notes.* London: Grubb Institute.

Reed, B.D. (1998). *Organisational Transformation.* Grubb Institute Publications. See also, chapter in J.E. Neumann (1997). *Developing Organisational Consultancy.* London: Routledge.

Rice, A.K. (1958). *Productivity and Social Organisation: The Ahmedabad Experiment.* London: Tavistock.

Rice, A.K. (1965). *Learning for Leadership. Interpersonal and Intergroup Relations.* London: Tavistock Publications.

Roberts, J. (1983). The group analyst as consultant to a therapeutic organisation, *Group Analysis, 16* (187).

Schein, E. (1992). How can organisations learn faster? the problem of entering the green room. *MIT Sloan School of Management, Spring 1992*: 3409–92.

Schlapobersky, J. and Pines, M. (2009). Gruppenanalyse und Analytische Gruppenpsychotherapie. In: Georg Thieme (Ed.), *Herausgegaben von Volker Tschuschke.* New York: Verlag Stuttgart.

Selvini, M.P., Boscolo, L., Cecchin, G. and Prata, G. (1980) Hypothesizing–circularity–neutrality: three guidelines for the conductor of the session. *Family Process, 19* (1): 3–12.

Shapiro, E.R. (2016). Learning from the director's role: leadership and responsibility. *Organisational and Social Dynamics, 16* (2): 225–70.

Shapiro, E.R. and Carr, A. (1991) *Lost in Familiar Places: Creating New Connections between the Individual and Society.* New Haven: Yale University Press.

Sher, M. (2013). *The Dynamics of Change: Tavistock Approaches to Improving Social Systems.* London: Karnac.

Shotter, J. (1993). *Conversational Realities: Constructing Life through Language.* London: Sage.

Shotter, J (1994). Conversational realities: from within persons to within relationships. The Discursive Construction of Knowledge Conference (Feb. 21–25, 1994). University of Adelaide.

Shotter, J (2008). *Conversational Realities Revisited: Life, Language, Body and World.* Chagrin Falls, Ohio: Taos Institute.

Spero, M. (1998). From group to organisation: engaging in organisational life, redrawing boundaries and relationships. Paper to IPSO 1998 Symposium, Jerusalem. http: www. sba.oakland.edu/ipso/html/1998/Spero.htm

Stacey, R. (2000). *Strategic Management and Organisational Dynamics: The Challenge of Complexity,* 3rd edition. London: FT Prentice-Hall.

Stacey, R. (2003) *Complexity and Group Processes: A Radically Social Understanding of Individuals*. Hove: Brunner-Routledge.

Stacey, R. (2005). Organisational identity: the paradox of continuity and potential transformation at the same time. The 29th Foulkes Annual Lecture. *Group Analysis, 38* (4): 477–94.

Thornton, C. (2010). *Group and Team Coaching*. East Sussex: Routledge.

Thornton, C. (2017). Towards a group analytic praxis for working with teams in organizations. *Group Analysis, 50* (4).

Tomm, K. (1987). Interventive interviewing: part II. Reflexive questioning as a means to enable self-healing. *Family Process, 26* (2): 167–83.

Tomm, K. (1988). Interventive interviewing: part III. Intending to ask linear, circular, or reflexive questions? *Family Process, 27*: 1–15.

Torres, N. (2003) The psychosocial field dynamics. In: N. Torres and R. Hinshelwood (Eds) *Bion's Sources*, chapter 7. London: RKP.

Trist, E. and Murray, H. (1990). *The Social Engagement of Social Science: A Tavistock Anthology – The Socio-Psychological Perspective*. London: Free Association Books.

Trist, E. and Murray, H. (1993). *The Social Engagement of Social Science: A Tavistock Anthology Vol. 2: The Socio-Technical Perspective*. Philadelphia: University of Pennsylvania Press.

Trist, E., Emery, F. and Murray, H. (1997). *The Social Engagement of Social Science: A Tavistock Anthology Vol. 3: The Socio-Ecological Perspective*. Philadelphia: University of Pennsylvania Press.

Turquet, P. (1974). Leadership: the individual in the group. In: G.S. Gabbard, J.J. Hartman and R.D. Mann (Eds), *Analysis of Groups*. San Francisco: Jossey-Bass.

Turquet, P. (1975). Threats to identity in the large group. In: L. Kreeger (Ed.), *The Large Group: Dynamics and Therapy*. London: Constable.

von Foerster, H. (1990). Ethics and second-order cybernetics. *Stanford Electronic Humanities Review, Constructions of the Mind, 1995 4* (2).

Western, S. (2008). *Leadership. A Critical Text*. London: Sage.

Western, S. (2012). *Coaching and Mentoring. A Critical Text*. London: Sage.

White, M. (1989). The externalizing of the problem and the re-authoring of lives and relationships. *Dulwich Centre Newsletter, Summer 1988/89*: 3–21.

White, M. and Epston, D. (1990). *Narrative Means to Therapeutic Ends*. Adelaide: Dulwich Centre Publications.

Wilke, G. (2014) *The Art of Group Analysis in Organisations*. London: Karnac.

Chapter 2

Tavistock consultancy, systems centred and group analytic perspectives on a community meeting on an acute psychiatric ward

Introduction

In this chapter we present an observation of a community meeting on an acute male psychiatric ward and we are very grateful to J.M. for his very detailed account.[1] This material is discussed from Tavistock Consultancy, Systems Centred and Group Analytic Consultancy perspectives.

The commentaries on the observation material provide an understanding of how consultants applying different models of consultancy think about the group and organizational dynamics when they analyze and reflect on the same observation material.

The observation of the community meetings on the acute psychiatric wards was part of a larger Observation Project (Novakovic et al., 2010, Novakovic, 2011), inspired by the work of Hinshelwood and Skogstad (2000). The aim of the project was to gain a deeper understanding of the complex issues faced by staff in this setting.

Ward observation

Upon entering the ward, I went to the nurses' office. The nurses were very busy with something and did not seem to notice my presence. After waiting for a short while, I said that I had come for the community meeting. One nurse then told me to go to the nearby large common room, where the community meeting group was about to start.

In the group room, five patients and one nurse were seated, in two circles. There was an inner circle composed of several chairs and one sofa, and an outer circle formed by several chairs scattered farther away and one sofa near the wall of the room. After a short while, a second nurse entered and then a third came in to ask for the television to be switched off: she then went out, although she returned a few minutes later. One patient left the room, and another patient shouted very loudly just outside the room. Another nurse then also left, and one of the nurses who remained in the room asked me if I wanted to introduce myself; I did so.

One of the patients agreed to write the minutes for this meeting, and a note-book was produced, but then he changed his mind and said that he did not want to do it anymore. Another patient took on this task. Looking at the notebook, he said: "From last week there was nothing, we did not have a meeting". Patient A said, "What's the point of talking?" He went on to say that he really disliked the patients spitting on the floor – but none of the culprits who were dirtying things were in the room, so what was the point of saying anything.

Patient L, who was sitting in the outer circle, started laughing as he was read-ing the newspaper. The two nurses immediately reprimanded him, and he stopped laughing. Patient A said that he would be leaving the ward soon and he planned to do some voluntary work in a patient organization. He thought that patients were not really introduced properly to the ward activities and that patients needed to know where the general office was. Patient L started laughing again, and this time nobody paid attention to him. One of the nurses continued to gently prompt one of the other patients to speak, saying to him, "Say something,", but the patient remained silent. One of the patients then said, "Oh I like the audiological depart-ment, music is played there, it's good to expose yourself to music." He then said that he would like to go swimming. The nurse said, "You can't go swimming here!" Someone said something about drowning in the swimming pool, and a few patients laughed. One patient said that this meeting should really be made com-pulsory, that everyone should attend.

By this time two more nurses had arrived. Patient A remarked that there were four nurses in the room and only three patients talking. He said that in this meeting there were more staff than patients. Another patient, B, came into the discussion saying, "Can we go anywhere; where can we go?" And again some-one said something about swimming. Another patient said, "The patients can drown, can't they?"

Patient A said, "You know what you can do if you're really bad, you can smash things." And he added with pleasure, "And I want to smash things!" Someone said that if you did that, you ended up in P Ward (Psychiatric Intensive Care Unit). Someone else (I think it might have been a nurse) said that P Ward was a very difficult ward to be in. Another patient, Z, who had come into the room when the discussion about smashing things started, said, "I want to go to P ward and I will smash my room." He loudly exclaimed, "I am bad." This did not produce any effect, and he said even more loudly, "I want room service." A nurse said to him, "You are not in a hotel." Patient Z continued to say, "We should have breakfast every morning, in bed really, I really think we should do that."

Another patient joined in the discussion, saying to no one in particular, "Look, there are a lot of people around here who are out of order." Patient A said, "Yes! A lot of intimidating people around." I think Patient B said people actually come on to the ward and can't leave because they are on a section. Someone asked what a section was. Patient A explained that someone was sectioned when they did not want to be admitted on to the ward, and he then said that he had come volun-tarily. He said that he was asked at the emergency reception if he would go into the hospital, and he said that he agreed because he knew that he was disturbed. Otherwise, if he had not wanted to go, he would have been sectioned. He said that at the time he thought that he was trying to kill the whole world. Then he laughed and said maybe it was the other way around, and that he was trying to get the others to kill him.

Then another patient said that something of his had gone missing. He was asked what had gone missing, and he said that it was a mobile phone. The nurse said, "You really should not keep personal items of value unattended." Patient A said that another patient had lost two phones. Then he quickly lifted up his phone and said loudly and provocatively, "I nicked it off him!" There was an air of some surprise, mixed with excitement, but he then said that he was joking.

Patient B said that it was actually dangerous here. He asked: "What are these bars?" and somebody suggested they were for "health and safety". Then another patient said, "But the door has been locked!", and he went on to say that a few days ago there had been a real fire on the ward, and if there had been a big fire they would have all burnt down, since the fire door was locked. The first patient said, "Look, how could you get out of this door?" He put his foot up, gave an imaginary kick with his leg in the direction of the door, and said, "Certainly, I could not break that door." He said to the nurse, "Don't tell me you can get out of it!" And the nurse said, "No, there is another fire exit." The patient contested this by saying, "No, there is a padlock on that other door, it is impossible to get out." The nurse seemed surprised about the padlock and said that they would have to see about that. There was a discussion about how they could actually all burn down and this needed to be looked into because the fire exits were locked.

Patient B said, "What about the grandeur?" Patient A explained something about a very good place where one could have a meal and can go anytime, something like a drop-in centre. He said that there was a day especially for women and there was a day for gay men, but three days per week one could drop in there. Patient Z asked, "Can you go if you are transsexual?", and everyone laughed.

Patient A said, "This is really a bad situation. Did you know that Trust X is going to take over our Trust?" One of the nurses asked how this related to this meeting. Again the discussion returned to the issue of safety. Patient Z said "Look at that corner." We all looked and saw a damp and mouldy corner, from floor all the way to the ceiling. He asked the nurses mockingly how healthy that mould was and then jokingly said that it would certainly improve his bones and his breathing. They talked about the moss growing in different places, like behind the sink and in the bathroom. One patient asked, "What about the cockroaches?" and the nurse said, "You know what, we have cockroaches because you eat in your rooms!" The patient asked the nurse if she ever had breakfast in bed. She replied, that she did not, and he said "No, you did!" She said, "No, I didn't." The patient said, "You must have eaten in the bed at some point in your life, come on, admit it, don't say that you have never ever eaten in your bed." She replied, no, she has never eaten in her bed. Somebody then said that they even had rats.

Another patient said, "Oh here is Mother Teresa, but without sandals!" I presumed that this referred to Patient O, who was just walking into the room.

Everyone then started talking at the same time; it was impossible to follow the discussion. The new patient, O, made a dramatic and loud statement: "Can a spark from my lighter blow up the whole hospital?"

There was a brief silence, no one responded to his question, and he slowly moved into the room to sit in the inner circle. He then said that he could not shower with hot water, he said it was impossible, it took only 15 seconds, and he had measured this, exactly 15 seconds before the hot water started. Somebody asked why he did not want the hot water and another patient asked him if he wanted a Jacuzzi.

Unperturbed, Patient O said no. Patient O with deliberate slowness, and it seemed as if he were teasing, said, "Lord, I did not get the name of this gentleman, he is a good friend of mine." He then looked at all with some deliberation and said slowly but clearly and loudly that the only toilet that was clean was the one he used. Another patient said to Patient O, "That is not true, your room is the dirtiest one in the ward!". And suddenly all the patients and the nurses started telling Patient O that his room was dirty, and someone added that he was dirty, and his room was dirty. Patient O did not look affected by this criticism and nonchalantly said that, yes, it was so because somebody else lived in his room on the ward.

One nurse asked if anyone had any other contribution to make and, without waiting very long for responses, she announced that this was the end of the meeting.

Commentary I: Tavistock Consultancy Perspective

Julian Lousada

The ward observation presents a vivid description of a community meeting in which the patients demonstrate their disturbance and frustration. For the most part it is only their voices that we hear. So, from the outset, I found myself wondering what was understood by the term 'community', and whether the patients or staff belonged to it in any meaningful sense. The theme of anonymity and the poverty of relatedness pervades the account from the very outset. For example, I was struck by the generic reference to 'nurse', as if the nurses could not in any way be differentiated, by gender, age, or ethnicity, or, indeed, by name. The ward manager's absence from the community meeting seemed to express something powerful about the utility of this meeting in the manager's mind. What is revealed systemically is a repeated failure of connections or communications, and an absence of relatedness between those involved.

From the outset, both the task and the activity are sabotaged. The two circles made for a confusing 'setting', perhaps indicating an inner and outer state of mind or an atmosphere in which there was no expectation that the nurses and the patients might find a way of connecting such that a community could be experienced. Certainly, the boundary and container of time was damaged by the nurses' inconsistent arrival; three were present and then, as the meeting began, two left. The coming and going of both nurses and patients has a restless pacing quality, as if checks are being made on whether or not the community has formed only to discover it hasn't, but, nevertheless, the meeting continues, with the nurses enquiring about the minutes from the previous meeting when no decisions or comments had been made.

The meaninglessness of the notebook for the minutes is raised by Patient A, who asks, "What's the point?", given the absentees. Patient L is then reprimanded for his laughter and subsequently ignored. When two further nurses arrive, now outnumbering the patients, another patient suggests that attendance should be compulsory, a comment clearly directed towards the staff 'community' members. It is as if the patients are more in tune than the nurses, not only with the lack of containment, but also, and critically, with the absence of a belief in a task that involves all in the community.

The community meeting seems like a rudderless ship battered by disturbance and lacking any capacity to navigate towards a place of purpose and safety. The atmosphere becomes progressively more disturbed, and the patients reflect this by discussing the wish to smash things and the desire for containment on P (the locked) Ward. The need for and the absence of authority, a captain, as it were, seems to be implicitly and repeatedly referred to.

There is some evidence that the patients are 'engaged', but in the context of inattentive parental objects, who are too anxious to be able to detoxify their own and the patients' disturbing thoughts. The meeting produces more, rather than less, rigidity of role. The patients are trapped in free floating association and disturbance, while the nurses are trapped in a concrete state of mind where symbolization is not available for thinking.

In the psychiatric ward in question, I am left curious about the experience of the nurses who are running the community meeting. What are we to make of their late arrival, their coming and going, the absence of the manager, and the gap between their contribution to the content of the meeting and that of the patients? In short, what can we speculate about their emotional experience and, as such, their relatedness to both the community group and the wider organization?

From the limited material we have, I would suggest that there is a sense not just of individual disconnectedness, but of two groups, each of which is unable to use the other to establish a fuller picture. Both groups seem to be trapped in a place where the 'other' is unable or, indeed, unwilling to 'venture out' for fear of entrapment or contagion. This, then, is a situation in which neither group can conceive of the possibility that the experience of the other might illuminate their own, and, indeed, without such access to the other's experience, no transformative experience is possible. At the simplest level, group activity depends on individuals bringing themselves to a collective task. The community meeting is, one supposes, intended to make connections between the experience of staff and patients, which in turn depends on the presence of individuals engaged in an activity *together* for the purpose of learning from the outset. This requirement is not met, with the result that the 'idea' that underpins the community meeting is not discovered.

David Armstrong (2005) refers to a situation of "organizations locking themselves in" in those circumstances where they are unable to entertain a new idea: whether it (*the idea*) comes from outside or inside or through the pores of sensitivity to the presence of the not known. But we can easily lose sight of the fact that any new idea requires a host through which it is disseminated, but is also made available throughout the community. . . . Ideas are precious; they do not necessarily emerge fully formed or in a way that is fully understood (p.26).

I think that what is 'locked in' is the ward's 'requirement' to have a community meeting without the understanding that the meeting needs individuals in their roles to be present and curious about each other.

The absence of task and the continuation of method

What emerges is a loss of 'task', but nonetheless a continued commitment to 'method', without an agreement about what the community meeting is meant to achieve. The commitment to 'method' without a sense of purpose is not simply a managerial failure, it is also a bewildering and alienating experience for those who are expected to work within the 'method'. In these circumstances, there can be no way of deciding how to work together or, indeed, of determining what has gone on and its quality, or lack of it, or knowing what has been achieved. The organizational mind is seriously weakened by the absence of the reality provided by the task or purpose.

The evacuation of purpose from the method is endemic in the system. Activities become bureaucratized – that is to say, they become part of a routine that has no aim. The nurses in the meeting are present but without any sense of purpose. What has seemingly been lost is the idea of what a connection between staff and staff, patients and patients, and patients and staff actually entails. Being physically present without a corresponding psychological presence is not enough. The unconscious working assumption seems to be that these patients are so disturbed that to engage with them is to run an unacceptable risk. There is no exploration of whether this assumption is right or whether just possibly the disturbance in the meeting is a product of the experience of being present within it.

Many writers have drawn attention to the vulnerability of teams and organizations to acting in with the disturbance of the patients or the activity they are required to undertake. Most famously and certainly most influentially, Isabel Menzies Lyth (1960) developed the concept of 'social defences' as a way of explaining the organized but often unconscious ways in which those providing welfare services erect defensive manoeuvres to protect themselves from their unacceptable feelings associated with their role and task. As Paul Hoggett (2010) writes:

> These defences are both adaptive, enabling workers to cope, and, usually, simultaneously dysfunctional. They can be defences against seeing and facing suffering, feeling the suffering or thinking about it.
>
> (p.203)

In the context of an acute psychiatric ward, like the one we are discussing, it is hardly surprising that well intentioned staff erect social defences. The role of nurse is a complex one, in as much as it is imbued with the maternal functions of physical and emotional care, together with a compliance with the doctor's authority. However, the role is not an automatic one: it requires a capacity for thought and judgement. Such a capacity can be undermined by the organizational dynamics and by the nature of the patients being treated. The more disturbed the patient, the more the capacity to think is put under strain:

> Patient L started laughing again, and this time nobody paid attention to him. A nurse continued to gently prompt one of the other patients to speak, saying to him, "Say something,", but the patient remained silent.

The point is not that there is an absolutely correct interpretation of the communication contained in the above material; rather, that a therapeutic benefit is derived from the clinician's attempt to give it meaning. It would be this 'attempt' that would be noticed and responded to. This is not an easy process: it requires knowledge of the psychotic state of mind, but also some knowledge of how to use oneself, and an expectation of support. Hinshelwood in discussing a similar group of staff comments:

> Hence staff working with such disturbed people need some understanding of communication processes which are not abstract or symbolic. Staff need to explore the 'Language of Action' (Hinshelwood, 1987). Relationships that occur in 'activities' are likely to be more significant in care institutions that look after people with severe mental disturbance.
>
> (Hinshelwood, Pedriali, and Brunner, 2010, p.27)

All activity requires roles to achieve its purpose. When roles become invisible or undifferentiated, development in object relating becomes increasingly difficult. It is through the exploration of the boundary of the role and the discovery of the skills associated with it that colleagues discover what they individually bring to the role, how to work together, and what they require to sustain the quality of their work. This reflective activity is an essential *part* of the work in order to protect the task and the organization from the distressing projections they are subjected to.

Implicitly in this account, there is an *idea* or *method* called 'community meeting'; however, for some reason it does not appear as an idea whose history is known and cherished, and that inhibits the ability to transform it into a valued and purposeful activity that can be explored, understood, or worked on. In effect, it has no 'contemporary' meaning. The organizational context, the primary task of the ward, and indeed the task of the community meeting are strangely absent, as if they are so obvious that they do not need to be commented upon and as such would add nothing of value to an understanding of the task and the observation. In this way, we see how the nurses' action mirrors that of the patients, who also have thoughts that they wish to act on but cannot find meaning for (swimming, making the meeting compulsory, and smashing things up).

How does the nurses' behaviour reflect the task they have in their minds, and how does the 'way' in which they worked help us understand something of what is happening? Vega Roberts (1994) writes:

> . . . it can be helpful to ask what are we behaving *as if* we were here to do? Identifying this 'as if' task can provide clues about the underlying anxieties, defences and conflicts which have given rise to the dysfunctional task definition and associated dysfunctional boundaries.
>
> (p.38)

There is little doubt that the patients in the community meeting are very disturbed and that their contact with reality is at best tenuous. The nurses' anxiety is understandable, as is the need, as they see it, to hold on to reality as far as possible. I imagine that the purpose of a community meeting is to do what can be done to put into words the relatedness between what is said and what might be the more hidden – that is to say, the unconscious communication relating to the patients' experience *as community members*. However, to engage in this communication it is necessary for the nurses themselves to accept that they also have an experience *as community members*: this is the site of potential connection, but it requires the nurses to use themselves, and it is here that the risk to their own state of mind feels most acute.

The casualty in this ward is twofold. First, curiosity and the capacity to have experience that can be made sense of are lacking. Second, there is no belief in the possibilities of connections between people, such that engagement within and across the boundary or role could be explored systemically and therapeutically, which would enable a community meeting to take place for the benefit of all concerned. This is a suffering system for all concerned.

Commentary II: Systems-Centered® Consultancy Perspective

Ray Haddock

To understand the material presented and to suggest some interventions, I will use Yvonne Agazarian's (1997) Theory of Living Human Systems and her substantial model, Systems-Centered Therapy (SCT), which is the application of the theory to any living human system.[2]

Agazarian states:

> A theory of living human systems defines a hierarchy of isomorphic systems that are energy organising, goal directed and self correcting.
>
> (Agazarian, 1997: 18)

The primary goals of any living human system are *survival*, *development*, and *transformation*; the energy for this process is information, which is taken into the system through a process of discrimination and integration. *System* refers to an individual, couple, group, or organization. Survival takes precedence over other goals. Development takes places through predictable phases of flight–fight, intimacy/cooperation, and work and play (Agazarian, 1997), which will be familiar to many already. Any living human system, whether an individual, a one-off encounter, or meetings over time, has developmental phases that relate to how members build their relationships with each other or themselves, in a particular context. SCT is distinguished by phase specific methods for reducing the restraining forces (Agazarian, 1997) in relation to system goals. The theory also hypothesizes that the dynamics of one part of a system hierarchy are isomorphic at all system levels.

Recently Agazarian (2017a and 2017b, Gantt and Agazarian, 2017) developed a detailed map of the 'person-as-a-whole' system that describes how individuals respond to context by adopting survival role repetitions or functional, context-related, "curious explorer" roles. She also defines inner person communication (me, my, I feel, I think you . . ., I should . . .) and inter-person communication (we, let's, how about you? . . .). From any individual output we can intuit whether the person is in a survivor role or a curious explorer role. Using the principle of isomorphy, because each person is in the context of the larger system and all communication is influenced by that context, individual outputs are seen as a voice for the system as a whole. This in turn enables us to diagnose the system's developmental phase.

Attuned communication is at the heart of Systems-Centered practice. In a group context, Agazarian developed a process, *Functional Subgrouping*, whereby when a member brings in information, the heart of this communication is first *reflected* by the next speaker, who then *adds a similar experience* to build the subgroup. This method is profoundly linked to the Theory of Living Human Systems concept that systems close their boundaries to difference and open them to similarity. If a boundary is closed, no information can cross and change cannot happen. Functional Subgrouping is the method by which individual voices can be developed in a subgroup and, through a process of continual exploration be integrated into the system as a whole.

Using the Theory of Living Human Systems map, the individual and group communications described in the group indicate a system in survival. I give examples that support this hypothesis and suggest Systems-Centered Therapy interventions that could enable the system to develop from survival to exploration.

I will now consider the ward observation group meeting with reference to structure, context, and function/process.

Structure

Some structure is evident in having a room with chairs in haphazard circles and a time during which the group takes place. However, boundaries are ambiguous, start and finish times are unclear, nurses and patients come and go, the observer arrives and only when he speaks is he acknowledged and directed to the meeting room. No membership roles are defined. As the boundaries are ambiguous, the sense of safety is reduced. In Systems-Centered Therapy terms, what we see is evidence of early developmental roles adopted when survival is threatened.

Context

Context defines the environment of the group and its possible goals and therefore what communication is functional. There is no information about the goals of the group, it is a 'community group' which is not defined, there is no evidence that the group addresses explicit individual, ward, or organizational goals and the recording notebook has nothing written in it. The communication in the group is for a better, safer ward environment and for recovery. This is voiced mostly by patients and mostly in complaints and various forms of acting out. The response is blame, denial, prohibition, and threat. The staff goal is to avoid the danger of blame both from patients and the hospital management, though the reality of this is not tested.

Process

Process refers to how information is managed in the system. Attuned communication is completely absent. When the observer arrives on the ward no one attempts to engage him. Staff offer no direct supportive acknowledgement of group members' contributions, which are ignored, countered, or followed by a disconnected response. For example:

> Patient A says, "What's the point in talking?" Patient L responds by laughing and attracts a reprimand. Patient A identifies further issues and steps he might take to address them; Patient L again laughs and discussion diverts via a nurse to another patient who does not speak. Another patient comes in with suggestions about productive activities, countered by "You can't . . ." from a nurse.
>
> Patient A makes an observation about the number of nurses compared with patients. Here Patient B heads off any consideration of this reality by asking what patients can do, and this time a patient voices a prohibition about swimming.
>
> Patient A is then more direct about feelings in saying he wants "to smash things up", countered this time by a patient with the threat ". . . you end up in P ward", reinforced as a bad place to be by (possibly) a nurse and Patient Z. Attempts to engage the ward staff in discussion about realities are blocked by the system – both patients and nurses.
>
> Patient Z then engages in direct communication with the ward system by demanding room service. The nurse's response, "you're not in a hotel", implies admonishment, but without voice tone, it is ambiguous. This is followed by a patient highlighting "people being out of order". Patient A adds "intimidating" and gives an account about his own avoidance of compulsory detention, ending with a joke. This is another version of the repeated pattern that keeps exploration and interaction at bay.

There are numerous similar observations, which indicate there is little exploratory curiosity and little real exchange of information. All of this indicates group members are in survival roles repeated from their own early development, in order to stabilize themselves and the wider system.

System level hypotheses

Through the Systems-Centered Therapy lens, the system exhibits the characteristics of flight, with individuals mostly in personalized survival roles. There is no engagement or attuned communication in the service of exploring and solving mutual problems. The voice of authority is to maintain safety by prohibition, blame, or threat, while the stability of the meeting is largely managed by individual survival roles. Patients express these through non-context-related (crazy) behaviours, such as Patient L's laughter, Patient A's wanting to smash things, Patient Z's wish to go to ward P, Patient Z asking for room service, and Patient B desiring grandeur. Meanwhile the nurses' survival roles, which will be isomorphic with the larger system, are expressed by holding boundaries that do not relate to the group. Their entering and leaving must relate to goals of another context. Time boundaries are ambiguous; the arrival of the observer on the ward is ignored. Nurses close down discussion by blaming, prohibiting, and changing direction and do not engage in attuned interactions with patients.

Patient O warrants particular discussion, as he demonstrates an effective if non-adaptive survival role. He maintains a coherent sense of self and of his world with his non-reality-based assertions. He is a strong voice for his own person system survival and a strong voice for the person system survival of all present. He is clear on his facts even if others do not agree. He is given a system role name, 'Mother Teresa'. He indicates no impact of the wider system and yet is seen and responded to as both a saviour and a scapegoat, uniting nurses and patients in common cause in relation to the uncaring and unsafe environment. At the same time his "Can a spark from my lighter blow up the whole hospital?" invites profound reality testing. Where, indeed, is the danger that induces survival dynamics at the expense of all else?

In the face of such powerful system dynamics it may seem foolhardy to think it possible to intervene. Our Systems-Centered diagnosis that the system is in flight and individuals in survival roles is the first step.

The principle of isomorphy tells us that the norms of the larger system are the context of its subsystems. The challenge is to establish explicit functional norms for the group, knowing that interventions that change the system dynamic at one level impact the system immediately above and below. We assume a system's goal is always to maintain homeostasis and changes that are too big will destabilize the system and generate survival reactions. Knowing this we can then test interventions to reduce system restraining forces to working towards its goals (Gantt and Agazarian, 2005).

I will now describe structural, contextual, and functional/process interventions:

Structural

Defining group and role boundaries sets structure, necessary to establish stability, which creates a context for exploration and problem solving. Managing boundaries requires authority and any interaction around them enables learning about relationships to authority.

Interventions

1   Make explicit boundaries: "We start at 2 pm and finish at 3.15 pm every Wednesday in room W". This does not mean boundaries are necessarily held to, however it enables exploration of the impact of having boundary.
2   Define the role boundary of membership using explicit criteria for staff and patients.

3   Create explicit structure within the group, including leadership roles and any differentiation of role between nurses and patients. Clarify the purpose, agenda, note taking, actions, and timekeeping.

Contextual

The environment defines what goals are realistic. The phase of this context is flight and survival. The nurses need to be clear about how the group context is similar or different to the ward context, and how the ward context is similar or different to the wider environment.

Example

"Thank you for letting us know the door is locked. We will check this out." The message is that this is a context in which we can work together to identify and find solutions to problems. It also clarifies that nurses are responsible for this aspect of the ward context. Incidentally, it also implicitly clarifies role boundaries and a group goal.

Functional

At a theoretical level, this refers to how information – content and emotion – is transferred and organized in the system. Having established boundaries, context and goal, the next step is to open boundaries to communication within the group.

Systems-Centered practice pays detailed attention to communication, as it is fundamental to the function of any human system. This group is operating in flight with predominant individual survival role communication, the patients impacted by the ward dynamic and the nurses by the organizational dynamic, which also needs to be taken into account. Functional Subgrouping is the method used in Systems-Centered practice that enables closed boundaries to become permeable.

The first step is attuned reflection of the content and emotion of the previous speaker, using words, tone of voice, and body posture (see Agazarian 2001 and Gantt and Agazarian 2017) The member reflecting then builds with a similarity and asks, "Anyone else?" and so on.

EXAMPLE

Patient A: What's the point in talking; nothing changes (with frustration)? Anyone else?

Patient B: (to Patient A looking at him) You can't see the point in talking as nothing changes and you're frustrated. Have I got it? I am frustrated

too as there are so many people out of order and no one listens to us!
Anyone else?

Patient C: reflects then adds – I am frustrated too and really wish we could
do something . . ., etc.

This is a very truncated example of Functional Subgrouping to illustrate how
creating a subgroup promotes exploration of here and now context-related issues.
What we see emerge with Patient C's last comment is a shift from frustration and
complaint to desire to do something: a new subgroup emerges with new possibilities, providing evidence of system development.

Commentary III: A Group Analytic Perspective

David Kennard

My first reaction on reading this account was to identify with what I imagined was the experience of the observer, first, on not being noticed when he went to the nurses' office, and then sitting in the room waiting for the meeting to start. It was the experience of being ignored, unrecognized, almost not existing. I was surprised at how these very disturbing ideas could be so easily aroused just by reading the opening lines of the account, which recalled some of my own experiences of ward meetings. It was a reminder of how powerful the effect can be simply of walking on to an acute psychiatric ward without a clearly defined role, of feeling excluded from the busy world of those with roles.

As the account went on, I found myself caught up in the interactions of the meeting, and my initial feelings subsided. I still experienced strong reactions, but now they were ones of interest, anxiety, irritation, or amusement at the unfolding drama of the meeting, until it came to its abrupt end. I share these initial reactions in the hope that they may be similar to some readers' reactions, and also because they may reflect some aspects of the experience of life on the ward.

The material we are presented with seems full of interpersonal and emotional meanings, which, like the patients themselves, are allowed to wander at will without attempts at understanding or interpretation, but within the boundaries set by the nursing staff. There are recurring themes. The most prominent is danger or risk of harm – from drowning, being killed, from fire, unhealthy damp, or explosions. There is a theme of escape from the ward – to go swimming, to go to the intensive care unit, to go anywhere. There is irritation with patients who are dirty or who don't come to the meeting. None of these meanings are explored with the patients.

The use made by the patients of the meeting appears to oscillate between attempts to set an agenda or raise matters of concern on the ward, such as the patients who make things dirty, how new patients might be better introduced to the ward, personal items going missing, alternating with dramatic, even melodramatic 'show stoppers', such as Patients A and Z claiming to want to smash things and later Patient O loudly asking if his lighter could blow up the hospital. The tone, at least until near the end of the meeting, remains largely good natured, with elements of humour when the nurses are challenged over the padlocked fire exit or the mould in the corner of the room. The nursing staff maintain certain boundaries. They switch the television off, invite the observer to introduce himself, end the meeting, and comment on some realities of the environment – "you can't go swimming", "you are not in a hotel", "you really should not keep personal items of value unattended"– but otherwise allow the patients a free rein.

On the positive side, this is a lively meeting. Patient A takes the lead, several patients contribute, there is some interaction between patients, and a number of direct responses are made by the nurses to what is being said. I've certainly sat through less interesting or interactive meetings.

But there also appear to be missed opportunities. At the start, there are some attempts to get things off the ground – inviting a patient to take the minutes (the account implies this); reprimanding an individual who laughs at a newspaper he is reading; prompting one patient to speak. But following this, there is little attempt by the nurses to support the healthy, socially aware capacities of the patients, by facilitating discussion in the group of issues of common concern. Neither is there any acknowledgement of the repeated expression of aggressive or fearful fantasies – at least to enquire what effect these have on the rest of the group. The staff do not interact with the patients. They restrict themselves to maintaining the boundaries of time and, occasionally, content. For example, staff question the relevance of the Trust takeover to the meeting, and they respond to requests or complaints in what comes across as quite an admonishing tone: "you are not in a hotel", "you really should not keep personal items of value unattended", "we have cockroaches because you eat in your rooms". Only on one occasion does a nurse engage at a more personal level in conversation with a patient, about whether or not the nurse has ever eaten in bed. And if the underlying, unasked question here is, "Are the staff like the patients in any way?", the answer is a resounding "No".

An important question to ask is, was this meeting successful? The 'success' of a meeting depends on its aims, which are not explained, but I shall take the liberty – and risk – of using my experience of mental health wards, therapeutic communities, and group analysis to speculate on what the aims of this meeting might be, and how far they were achieved.

At its lowest level, the aim of the meeting could be to provide a safe space for patients to meet together to 'let off steam', which is a lot better than leaving them in isolation to wander or sit without stimulation or attention. In terms of ward-based group approaches, there is no particular conceptual underpinning, although its antecedents may include the therapeutic community approach (see below), for example, Bion's attempts at conducting groups as described in *Experiences in Groups* (Bion, 1961), and Quaker meetings for worship. The patients are free and able to express their opinions, wishes, and fears to an audience of their peers and to get some recognition and response. Such an aim was successfully met.

Another 'lower level' aim could be to 'take the pulse' of the ward, so to speak, for the staff to check on the mental state of the patients and on issues or tensions that might need watching and managing by the staff in the day ahead. This aim contributes to better ward management and so, indirectly, to benefit for the patients.

A more ambitious aim, using the *therapeutic community approach* (Clark, 1965; Kennard, 1998), is to engage patients in the day-to-day running of the ward. The potential benefits of the therapeutic community have been well summarized by Haigh (1999): to provide a sense of belonging, to provide emotional containment and safety, to foster open communication within and between the staff and patients, to learn from involvement in the day-to-day problems of living together, and empowerment through shared decision-making. Arguably the meeting meets the first two of these aims, the third to a limited extent (limited by the absence of some patients and the non-communication of the nurses), but not the last two aims. There is no attempt to foster discussion between the patients on the problems of shared living or to engage the patients in thinking about how things might be improved on the ward. The references at the start of the meeting to minutes being taken and read out, to the absence of those individuals whose dirty habits need talking about, and to the need for a better introduction for new patients to ward activities, all suggest that there is some initial expectation of patient involvement in decision-making, but on this occasion, at least, none of the staff take this up and the expectation lapses.

From a group analytic perspective, the aim might be to help the group to develop more free flowing communication, overcoming the isolation of individuals, and to 'translate' the grandiose or fearful fantasies into a common meaning that can be shared and talked about. One of Foulkes's best known descriptions of this process is quoted by Pines (1983), referring to both neurotic and psychotic disturbances: "The language of the symptom, although already a form of communication, is autistic. It mumbles to itself hoping to be overheard; its equivalent meaning conveyed in words is social" (pp.276–77). In the meeting, the various fantasies about drowning, smashing things, being burnt, or affected by the damp could be translated into a common language as expressing a need to feel safe. This is a basic concern of any group, especially in its early stages, and the turnover of a ward-based group is such that it is likely to return frequently to these early stages in the life of a group. (Stock, 1962, has given a classic account of the different concerns that members have about potential harm in the early stages of a group.)

It is unrealistic to expect ward staff to use a group analytic approach unless they have had relevant training. However, the use of a community meeting as part of a therapeutic community approach in an acute psychiatric ward is more likely to be something the nursing staff are aware of. Elements of a therapeutic community approach in the meeting are visible: the attempted involvement of patients in talking and reading minutes, the invitation to the visitor to introduce himself, the wish by some patients to discuss the problems caused by those who dirty the ward, even the perfunctory request at the end for any other contributions. But beyond this, the nurses opt for a largely passive role, apart from offering occasional reality checks and admonishments. The patients do perhaps have the experience of a safe container in which to play out their fantasies and frustrations. But they do not have the experience of re-connecting with others through communication about shared concerns that is potentially available in a ward-based community meeting.

Notes

1   The observation material and commentaries by David Kennard and Julian Lousada are republished from 'A community meeting on an acute psychiatric ward: observation and commentaries', In D. Bell and A. Novakovic (Eds), *Living on the Border: Psychotic Processes and the Individual, the Couple and the Group.* Tavistock Clinic Series, Karnac, 2013.
2   SCT® and Systems-Centered® are registered trademarks of Dr Yvonne M. Agazarian and the Systems-Centered Training and Research Institute, Inc, a non-profit organization.
3   These are a collation of all references for all authored sections within Chapter 2.

References[3]

Agazarian, Y.A. (1997). *Systems-Centered Therapy for Groups.* New York: Guilford Press.
Agazarian, Y.A. (2001). *Systems-Centered Approach to Inpatient Groups.* London: Jessica Kingsley.
Agazarian, Y.A. (2017a). Use our Systems-Centered pictures as a map. *Systems-Centered News, 23* (2): 3–9.
Agazarian, Y.A. (2017b). Making invisible role-systems visible. *Systems-Centered News, 23* (2): 10–15.
Armstrong, D. (2005). Names, thoughts, and lies: the relevance of Bion's later writing for understanding experiences in groups. In: *Organization in the Mind: Psychoanalysis, Group Relations, and Organizational Consultancy* (pp.10–28). London: Karnac.
Bion, W.R. (1961). *Experiences in Groups.* London, Tavistock.
Clark, D.H. (1965). The therapeutic community–concept, practice and future. *British Journal of Psychiatry, 131*: 553–64.
Gantt, S.P. and Agazarian, Y.A. (Eds) (2005). *SCT in Action: Applying Systems-Centered Approach in Organisations.* London: Karnac Books.
Gantt, S.P. and Agazarian, Y.A. (2017). Systems-Centered group therapy. *International Journal of Group Psychotherapy, 67* (Supp. 1): S60–S70. http://doi.org10.1080/00207 284.2016.1218768
Haigh, R. (1999). The quintessence of a therapeutic environment: five universal qualities. In: P. Campling and R. Haigh (Eds). *Therapeutic Communities: Past, Present and Future.* London: Jessica Kingsley.
Hinshelwood, R.D. (1987). *What Happens in Groups: Psychoanalysis, the Individual and the Community.* London: Free Association Books.
Hinshelwood, R.D. and Skogstad, W. (2000). 'The dynamics of health care institutions'. In: R.D. Hinshelwood and W. Skogstad (Eds). *Observing Organisations: Anxiety, Defence and Culture in Health Care* (pp.13–16). London: Routledge.
Hinshelwood, R.D., Pedriali, E. and Brunner, L. (2010). Action as a vehicle of learning. *Organisational and Social Dynamics, 10*: 22–39.

Hoggett, P. (2010). Government and the perverse social defence. *British Journal of Psychotherapy*, *26* (2): 202–12.

Kennard, D. (1998). *An Introduction to Therapeutic Communities*. London: Jessica Kingsley.

Kennard, D. (2013). Commentary I: A community meeting on an acute psychiatric ward: observation and commentaries. In: D. Bell and A. Novakovic (Eds) (2013). *Living on the Border: Psychotic Processes and the Individual, the Couple and the Group* (pp.152–55). Tavistock Clinic Series, Karnac.

Lousada, J. (2013). Commentary II: A community meeting on an acute psychiatric ward: observation and commentaries. In: D. Bell and A. Novakovic (Eds) (2013). *Living on the Border: Psychotic Processes and the Individual, the Couple and the Group* (pp.156–61). Tavistock Clinic Series, Karnac.

Menzies Lyth, I. (1960). The functioning of social systems as a defence against anxiety. In: *Containing Anxiety in Institutions: Selected Essays* (pp.43–85). London: Free Association Books.

Novakovic, A. (2011). Community meetings on acute psychiatric wards: rationale for group specialist input for staff teams in the acute care services. *Group Analysis*, *44* (1): 52–67.

Novakovic, A., Francis, K., Clark, J. and Nolan, L. (2010). Therapeutic intervention or meaningless exercise? Community meetings on acute psychiatric wards. *Mental Health Review Journal*, *15* (3): 45–53.

Pines, M. (1983). The contribution of S.H. Foulkes to group therapy. In: M. Pines (Ed.) *The Evolution of Group Analysis*. London: Routledge and Kegan Paul.

Roberts, V. (1994). The organization of work. In A. Obholzer and V.Z. Roberts (Eds), *The Unconscious at Work: Individual and Organizational Stress in the Human Services* (pp.28–38). London: Routledge.

Stock, D. (1962). Interpersonal concerns during the early sessions of therapy groups. *International Journal of Group Psychotherapy, 12*: 14–26.

Part II

Chapter 3

"How did you get here from there?"

Psychosis, stigma and the counter transference

David Vincent

Introduction: ". . . this group is not working"

Psychotherapists and group analysts are often called on to help groups of staff working with psychiatric patients. These well-meaning attempts to help their colleagues often go wrong and this is one of the themes of this book. Why is this work so difficult?

Sometimes, the idea of a staff consultation is abandoned. They have changed their mind or there is an emergency. If the group does start, the group members do not all attend or quickly stop coming. The few that do attend feel guilty that they have left the patients to the others or angry at the lack of cooperation in the team. Often, group after group is concerned only with the people who don't attend. The members of staff who never attend the group can give rise, in those who do attend, to ambivalent feelings of guilt, envy and anger, and they may come to represent either the imagined and envied sane people who do not need to attend groups, or their defiant, disturbed and unreachable patients. Even if the group does manage to start and then survive, it may turn out to be a difficult and painful experience. Why should this be so? And what can group analysts, working as staff consultants, do about it?

Bion's 'Basic Assumption Theory' is an attempt to explain why the work of groups, the "work-group function", is so easily and frequently interrupted (Bion, 1961) and with everyday staff consultancy the work can go wrong in different ways at any point in the process. Perhaps the first task for the consultant is to identify and understand the strong and disabling counter-transference feeling of failure and depression in this work experienced by the group analyst, the staff, the patients and the group as a whole. The group analyst's private thought at that moment of realization might be: "I can't do this", and the group's simultaneous thought, usually spoken out loud, is: ". . . this group is not working".

Group analysts and staff groups

Group analysts have worked with staff groups for many years (Skynner, 1991, Hartley and Kennard, 2009, Thornton, 2017). This is partly because of the un-examined assumption that the general principles of work with psychotherapy groups are transferable to other types of group, and partly because of the nature of the training and employment of group analysts. The majority of group analysts conducted their training groups in NHS hospitals and clinics and many went on to work in the psychiatric services. They were then expected to offer assistance to their colleagues on the basis of an assumed competence in 'group dynamics'. The process of learning that Group Analytic clinical skills were not all immediately transferable to work with staff was often slow and painful.

This was my own experience, working in the psychotherapy department of a large Victorian psychiatric hospital. I was expected to be helpful to my colleagues in the main hospital, and I wanted to be, but it often went wrong. Gradually, over many years I began to understand this, while working with a wide variety of staff groups in admission wards; long-stay and secure hospital wards; day hospitals, out-patient clinics and community services and group homes and residential units for children, adolescents and adults. I realized that just as each clinical psychotherapy group creates the group analyst that they need at that point in time, so staff groups will call up the staff consultant that they need to solve the problem that is just now getting in the way of their "work-group function" (Bion, 1961). It is therefore important, in my view, to be both modest in aim and economical with theory in staff group work. Group analysis can be helpful with this, as overall it is a flexible and inclusive set of interlocking principles rather than a grand design.

In staff consultation and reflective practice over the years I have found four Group Analytic ideas helpful.

The first of these is the idea of the 'free-floating' discussion: ". . . the group analytic equivalent of what is known as free association in psychoanalysis" (Foulkes and Anthony, 1957, p.37). The primary task of the group analyst is always to provide a setting for open and free conversation.

The second is the 'matrix': "a psychic network of communication which is the joint property of the group and is not only interpersonal but transpersonal" (Foulkes, 1990, p.182). It is an important part of the staff consultant's task at the beginning of the work with a staff group to understand this group's particular matrix. What are the ties that bind these people together in this way?

Third, I would use the Group Analytic principle of 'trusting the group'. This is, of course, not a theory, more an exhortation to the group analyst to adopt a particular state of mind, one of assuming that the group has it in them to find a way forward if they can learn from one another to use themselves as a group.

And fourth, in staff work, it is important to hold onto the idea of 'dynamic administration'. It is very common in my experience that even over the course of a long consultation there will be periods when the administration of the sessions breaks down: a room is double booked or changed, the chairs are piled up or missing. Disorganization like this in a staff group is often an angry communication of the staff's feeling of being bullied or ignored by their own managers. It is always important to experience this as a communication of the group's state of mind, and possibly to interpret that, but only when the group is sitting back down. The staff group consultant might need to actually put the chairs in a circle, a behaviour which models taking responsibility for the problem at hand.

I also find it helpful in staff consultation to think about Bion's basic assumption theory in general, and in particular in the face of rigid institutional defences, his injunction to "shake oneself out of the numbing feeling of reality" (Bion, 1961, p.149).

Finally, I try to follow Ezriel's bracing advice to stay firmly in the here and now of the "common group tension" by asking myself about the group: "What makes this patient (group) behave (speak or act) toward me in this particular way at this moment?" (Ezriel, 1950, p.114).

Beginning a staff consultation: the three stages

A consultation, in my experience, passes through three stages and can fall away at any point. Complex dynamics may emerge immediately, albeit in a disguised form, in the initial request for a consultation, which is almost always uninformative or awkward. This may be a factor of the staff's initial depressive sense of failure and is a reminder that from the first moment of contact the staff group's problem is being communicated to the consultant, consciously and unconsciously. Usually, a manager or a senior clinician will ask for a meeting to discuss the possibility of a staff group or one-off meeting. There is usually a series of missed calls, cancellations and misunderstandings, and the consultant can then become irritable and uncooperative, getting caught up in this vivid counter-transference feeling, hidden from immediate awareness of the actual difficulties being experienced at that moment by the team in the person of the enquiring member of staff. Sometimes the request for help then disappears into the confusion of ambivalent miscommunication: both parties feel aggrieved and nothing changes.

That is the first stage of the consultation, when the work can come to grief. If the consultant can tolerate the confusion and not act on the irritation and can begin to understand what is being communicated, then the consultation process may reach the second stage, in which an opening meeting is organized. This stage is subject to the same difficulties as the first, cancellations and miscommunications, and the same potential for the consultant's disabling confusion and frustration. Often, if the consultation gets this far, then a further dynamic needs to be considered, the possibly problem solving function of the request. Asking for help from outside the team may be an end in itself, a change promoting motivation of the organizing structure and interpersonal relationships within the team. Once the team have worked through the need for help in the form of a concrete request to a consultant, they may have actually begun to work on the problem themselves. The consultant should try to be aware of this possibility and withdraw gracefully. Some teams will let go of the request at the first stage, after a useful delay, and will have done their necessary work without a meeting.

What is perhaps more common is that they get as far as the second stage and an initial meeting. The key indicator that the team have been working together help-fully without the consultant during the initial delays is that the whole team will be present at the first meeting and there will be a positive and energetic tone. Often this is explicit and the team will make it clear in the course of the meeting, perhaps with some humour, that they have had to wait for so long for this consultation that they have started to sort things out themselves. If there are further meetings they will usually have poor attendance and be pleasant, but desultory. The consultant will need to watch for this and take the responsibility for bringing the consulta-tion to an end. If, on the other hand, there is a difficult, depressed and angry tone to the first meeting and attendance is poor and interrupted, or there are problems with rooms and chairs, then the work is only starting. The team will have done no preparatory work together and their treatment of the consultant at that point is a vivid counter-transference guide to both the team's shared state of mind and the work that lies ahead in the group. One variation of the second stage of the consul-tation is that the problem solving actually arises directly in the first meeting and the consultation is then over.

An example of this is a request from an in-patient ward for a consultation about the expectation that the ward staff should provide group therapy for their patients and the nurses' dislike and discomfort with this. I arranged a time to meet. I expected that this was a disguised complaint about over directive man-agers, excessive workload and inter-professional rivalry. The meeting was at first edgy and tense and then the nurses began to talk. It turned out that the request for help was to do with their anxiety about the patients' madness. One more confident nurse began to say how much he hated the groups at which he had to help. It is always important, at this point in the consultation, to note who is the nominal initial spokesperson and to try to understand why they in particu-lar have been thrown up by the group to speak the problem, just as a clinical group will often throw up one patient to speak at transitional points in group therapy. In other words, when the 'problem speaker' emerges in the staff group, the consultant may need to be aware that this is the point when the consultation work begins in earnest. The problem speaker will often be angry and critical, but it will almost certainly be on behalf of the other non-speaking group mem-bers, whether they are a consciously chosen spokesperson or an unconscious vehicle for the staff group's projections, and the consultant's engagement with the 'problem speaker' has to be careful and protective and may require individ-ual attention. The consultant's counter-transference danger at this point is the temptation to engage in individual interpretation, even with some understanding of the representative role of the problem speaker, and they will need to remind themselves that this is a group process.

What this nurse went on to say was how much the nurses hated these groups, how badly the patients behaved in them and how unhelpful they were. I encour-aged them to say more and actively sought the views of the other group members about what he was saying. Gradually, as the staff group relaxed, they all began to talk about these groups, and a vivid picture arose of what happened in them, and their bewildered feelings about the mad patients. In staff groups, just as in psychotherapy groups, there is often a point, roughly in the middle of the session, that acts as a kind of fulcrum. The first part of the group leads up to this point where something important is said, or happens, which is a key to the whole of the session, and the session then balances on the tip of this fulcrum. If this point is negotiated well enough, then the session slowly tips down towards a natural end. In this particular staff group the fulcrum was a description by the first problem speaker of the behaviour of a disturbed patient in a ward group. He gave a lively account, to which the rest of the staff group contributed, of how this particular unwell psychotic patient would get up from his chair and turn cartwheels across the group room, back and forth, during the course of the group. This gave rise then to what seemed to me to be a life affirming account by the nurses of the incomprehensible, frightening and exciting madness of their psychotic patients.

After a while the emotional atmosphere in the staff group began to change and wind down, over the fulcrum, as it were, and there was a more accepting, depressed feeling in the room. It is helpful to think of Melanie Klein's positions at this point (Klein, 1998). The paranoid-schizoid preoccupations move over into depressive position thinking across the group fulcrum in the course of the meeting. It is important for consultants at this stage in a staff group to keep it simple and let the group do the work. I limited myself to one question: "The patient who does the cartwheels across the group, what is he like outside the group, on the ward?" The staff all looked at me incredulously, as though I should see that it was obvious, and then they all shrugged and said he was fine, "no problem at all". It is important to leave some things where they fall in a staff group and I did not comment on this, or open it up or interpret. What needed to be said had now been said by the group. At the end I asked them to let me know if they wanted to meet again. They did not, but I heard that the group therapy continued on the ward.

One of the many interesting things about this one consultation was that it expressed in a lively and human way one of the central and commonly held dilemmas about group psychotherapy: is the group a means of expressing, containing and learning from madness, or does group therapy drive people mad? This same question applies to staff groups and is part of the anxiety that staff bring to the group. Will the group make things worse between them, or for them as a whole? This is often a loudly voiced anxiety in staff groups and consultations, as though they can only survive as a team by keeping their troubles secret.

If the first stage of a consultation is the initial negotiation of the request, and the second stage is the initial meeting, then the third stage is the process of consultation itself, with which the remainder of this chapter is concerned.

In particular, this is about staff groups who care for psychotic and other very unwell patients who create unusual demands both on the staff and on staff group consultants.

Caring for patients with psychotic illness

Why should this be so difficult? I will try to approach this complex question by discussing some aspects of the counter-transference in work with psychotic patients. Perhaps the most important fear, which is difficult to talk about, as it seems naïve, is that of contamination, a fear that the madness will infect the staff, or, worse, that they have already been driven mad and don't know it. More generally, these and other counter-transference feelings evoked in staff working with psychosis can be confusing and frightening and are urgently defended against as a matter of basic psychic survival.

Some of these defences, particularly those that belong to the institution or the staff group as a whole, can themselves be harmful and counterproductive and they serve to make things worse for individual staff, the team, and the patients. They are often intricately constructed, difficult to see, experience and understand, and can form a barrier to helpful work in the organization or group. In its most developed form this defence constitutes the "Total Institution" described by Erving Goffman (Goffman, 1998). The effect on the patients in the large psychiatric hospitals is now better understood and less taken for granted, than it was when the problem was first urgently described in the UK as "Institutional Neurosis" by Russell Barton in 1960 (Barton, 1959). This made clear that long-term patients had two illnesses, their psychosis and a neurosis caused by impoverished institutional care.

The staff consultant needs to be ready for this, to be baffled by the complex group and institutional defences and to sit in the meeting with the feeling of not knowing and not understanding. They should try to be aware that their own counter-transference experience at that moment in the group, of feeling utterly bewildered and panicky, is a vivid unconscious communication of the state of mind of the individual staff members and of the group as a whole. The closer that the free-floating discussion gets to this group anxiety, the more strongly it will be denied, often by cruel humour and a rather brittle kind of cynicism. This anxiety in turn, of course, arises from the bewildered and panicky internal world of the psychotic patient and it can arrive suddenly and unbidden in the group consultant's mind in the course of the group.

In a consultation with a group of young women nurses in their last year of training, they spoke movingly of their attachment to the older schizophrenic patients. They liked them and understood them and did not feel threatened. By this stage in their training, they could identify with and take a full part in the hospital's entrenched social defence systems, which were fostered by training, supervision, and, above all, the example and informal guidance from experienced colleagues, with whom they could identify. In addition, the older schizophrenic patients were all institutionalized and subdued on large doses of anti-psychotic medication. They already knew how to play their part in the long-running drama of hospital life, and the young nurses were learning theirs, coached by their experienced colleagues. Where they were let down, was in their work with a different group of patients, the young women admitted to hospital after a suicide attempt. All the young female nurses in the staff group talked about how they hated these patients with a passion. They were the same age and from a similar background to these patients and they felt hopelessly identified and frightened by being put so vividly in touch with their own potential for anger and despair. This then turned so easily into hatred for the patients and pessimism about helping them, as the institutional defences broke down.

Another group of more experienced nurses, working in a very well-run therapeutic community, talked in group supervision about a very particular countertransference reaction that they gradually realized they had all experienced in their group work with psychotic patients. This was an unexpected, vivid and frightening feeling of levitating while the patients were talking and rising up a few inches in the air above their seats. They were embarrassed at having such a peculiar hallucinatory experience and it took some time for them to speak of it in the supervision meeting. This made sense to me, and I recalled a moment in a long-term psychotherapy group when a young woman patient, who was breaking down, told the group that sometimes, when she was walking along the street, that she felt that she was actually floating 18 inches above the pavement. The group and I became disoriented by this and an odd, floaty conversation followed. I suspect that we all began to identify, even if only for a moment, with this patient's sensation of levitating. Perhaps this feeling is a kind of somatization of the frightening experience of losing touch with reality. After all, we often talk of 'coming down to earth', which is a recovery from the feeling of floating away, losing touch or "falling forever" (Winnicott, 1965).

The concept of "social systems as a defence against anxiety", developed by Menzies Lyth (Menzies Lyth, 1988), is helpful here, and the staff consultant will often be up against a harshly interpersonal version of this in an angry and deprived staff group and will be accused of trying to make their life more difficult: ". . . it just can't be done", "you're making things worse", "we tried that five years ago and it didn't help" and, hopelessly, "it's alright for you . . .". Part of the difficulty here is the set of taken for granted views about psychosis taken on without much thought by the staff group as a whole and their management, but not necessarily by the individual members of staff. Lucas describes vividly the difficulty in accepting the reality of psychosis and how hard it is to get onto to what he calls "the psychotic wavelength" (Lucas, 2009). This is all in the setting of what can become a 'psychotic climate': "a driving-and-being-driven-crazy type of relatedness" (Searles, 1959, p.277). In this 'psychotic climate' the three parties involved, patients, staff and management can use up all their energy driving one another crazy, and the staff consultant can fall down into the middle of this madness, like Alice down the rabbit hole.

It can however be a rich and consoling experience for staff consultants to talk with a team who are trying their best to overcome these difficulties: working together to talk to the patients and make contact, to understand the nature of the psychotic illness, to throw off the institutional defences pushed onto them by the hospital culture, and to maintain as far as possible a sane world on the ward, while recognizing the individual humanity of the patients.

Currently in the NHS, staff find themselves under the normal pressures from patients and, at the same time, under even greater pressure from the management cuts and changes that feel to the clinical staff as mad as the maddest patients. The obvious consequence of the changes is the loss of long-term services to patients with psychotic illness. The closure of hospitals and community units affects many psychotic patients who may be least likely to complain. Long-term psychotic patients have therefore, by displacement, become the scapegoats for long-term services, which are now universally disliked by health service managers. The pressure to close and sell NHS property falls heavily on this patient group and they are as a result, both consciously and unconsciously, blamed for holding up 'modernization' and then stigmatized and rejected as 'untreatable'. Alongside this, the staff who care for them are therefore also blamed and stigmatized, as 'uncooperative', particularly if they work actively to protect the patients and the service. Finally, the staff caring for long-term patients tend to be largely BAME (Black, Asian and Minority Ethnic), and they will already be vulnerable to 'Institutional Racism' (Macpherson, 1999). They can therefore be doubly stigmatized by being associated, in the view of management, with the already stigmatized, deprived and troublesome psychotic patients.

A consultation with the staff of a long-stay unit: the background

This took place several years ago. A large psychiatric hospital was in the process of closing down. There were many elderly patients on the long-stay wards, most of them suffering from schizophrenia and highly dependent on the hospital. A number of them were offered accommodation in group homes and were given, in recognition of their many years in the care of the hospital, a firm promise that this was for life. This promise, and its later consequences, encapsulated the maddening changes in policy. It was a caring and thoughtful commitment when it was made, but very quickly it became an unwanted burden to the changing management. Group homes and day units, often in suburban areas with rising property prices, occupied a lot of land, which could be sold, under the hypocritical guise of the 'modernization' process. The promise was protected by the staff of the unit and by the families of the patients and the management found this intolerable: unwanted patients, all untreatable by the desirable short-term manualized therapies, and protected by unwanted staff, in unwanted buildings. All management failure could be projected into this stigmatized and hated pair: the psychotic patients and their nurses.

I was invited to come to the unit and talk to the team manager about starting a staff group for the staff of the several group homes and the attached day hospital. I was only vaguely aware at the referral of the problems outlined above and I was told that they were having some problems as a staff group.

The consultation: how did you get here from there?

I arranged to meet the team manager at the day unit. I was told at the desk that he was a few minutes delayed and was asked to wait in the waiting room. I looked around at the old, shabby and very clean building. In the distance I could hear voices and there was a faint smell of boiled cabbage and disinfectant. In the waiting room every chair was old and battered, and all different. The linoleum was worn but polished. There was a sense of warmth and comfort in spite of the tiredness and institutional poverty. The chairs were arranged in small groups and I sat down and looked around the room.

After a few minutes a very tall, elderly man came into the waiting room, carrying a large pair of workman's boots in one hand. He walked slowly over and sat down in a chair facing me. He had the unmistakeable look of a long-term psychiatric patient: ill-fitting clothes, a bad haircut and a preoccupied air. He nodded at me in a friendly way, got himself comfortably settled and then asked me why I was there. I said I had come for a meeting. He nodded and thought about this and then asked me: "An attendant?" This, of course, was the former term for a male nurse at a psychiatric hospital. I realized that this man must have been a patient for at least 40 years. I thought about this for a moment and said: "No, a psychotherapist". He nodded sagaciously and said: "Aah, yes". His expression then changed and he looked confused for a moment and then anxious. He leaned forward and scrutinized me. "Have you come far?" he asked me, looking more worried. I felt the need to reassure him and told him the name of the hospital where I worked, which was just a few miles away. He leaned forward again with a furrowed brow and an expression of great concern. In a much louder voice, full of tragic anxiety, he asked: "How did you get here from there?"

This is such an important question, the most important, perhaps. It is what we ask our patients in an assessment and it is what our patients ask us about our comments and interpretations. We ask ourselves this, hopefully, all the time in our work. How did this come about? Why am I here? Where did it all go wrong? And staff groups ask this, in various ways, wondering how their youthful idealism led them to be here, in this group, full of anger and anxiety about their patients and the future of their work.

I did not try to answer the man in the waiting room and merely nodded. He did not pursue it. I wondered if he was prompted by my saying that I was a psychotherapist to ask in this mournful way how *his* life had happened the way it did, all those years in the asylum. What could I have said? I became depressed, full of an overwhelming sense of the tragedy and waste of psychosis, and of his loss.

I met the team manager and his deputy, both serious, calm, responsible men in middle age. They told me a little about the difficulties and we set a starting date for the group.

The staff group: "that old colonialist attitude"

The room for the meeting was packed and every comfortable seat was taken. A young member of staff, from Eastern Europe, jumped up immediately I came in, called me 'boss' and insisted that I take his seat. He and I were the only white people in the room, the two managers and all the rest of the staff were BAME, from India, Pakistan, Malaysia, Africa and the Caribbean. Almost all the patients were elderly working class white British, and yet, as far as I could understand, this was never an issue between staff and patients and their families. The staff's devotion to the care of patients, guided by the team managers, was admirable. They banded together against the illness and against the new common enemy of the health service managers. One of the many problems here for me was, as a white, middle class, middle-aged, psychotherapist, my anxiety about being identified with the management, and not with them, and I did not know how to deal with my embarrassment at being called 'boss' by the young man and given his seat. We somehow found a way to work together and the meetings continued.

At one early meeting they talked at length about the death of a patient and how difficult this was. Some of the patients had no contact with any family and the team manager felt that it was his responsibility to arrange and attend the funeral, where he would be the only mourner. It was the team's final duty to the patient.

This kind of work was regarded as a waste of time by the senior managers and at the start of one meeting the group described an angry telephone conversation the deputy manager had just had with a young white manager who was aggressive and insulting in the way that he issued rebukes and instructions. The deputy manager gave an account of this and I became so enraged that I did not know what to say, as I could have easily slipped into a denunciation of this manager, with every justification, but it would not have been helpful to the team. I was baffled and stayed silent as the team discussed the telephone call. They identified with the deputy manager in his feeling of humiliation and hurt and they all recognized the controlling, racist element to the manager's rudeness. After a long, depressed conversation, one member of staff, a rather jovial man, a devout Muslim, said in a strong London accent: "It's that old colonialist attitude, innit?" They all agreed.

Conclusion

This wonderful 'free-floating discussion' taught me how these things come together. Both recent and established immigrants, and BAME NHS staff, generally tend to be left with difficult and poorly paid work. In psychiatry this has come to mean the care of psychiatric patients, particularly those who are the most unwell. The changes in the NHS have all led towards the illusory and deceitful goals of modernization, rationalization and economy, and the maddening, 'pseudo thought' systems of modern management theory, which, in the hands of senior NHS managers, have been a cover for rationalization and denial. In other areas of medicine, suffering elderly patients without services are turned into unwanted non-human objects, called 'bed-blockers'. In psychiatry the 'bed-blockers' are the patients that require long-term help, and in particular, those whose care needs land and buildings. I argue in this chapter that these patients are blamed and stigmatized as an obstacle to efficiency and progress and the staff that look after them become identified with this projective process. The effect on staff is then intensified by institutional racism and the social history of colonialism, so astutely picked up and interpreted by the staff member in the team.

This leaves a difficult task for the staff consultant, hovering between empathy and over-identification in the session. I over-identified with this team in their anger at the management and was anxious that I should not be associated by them, by being called 'boss' for example, with the middle-aged, white oppressors of the management and the colonial past, which was still so vividly present in the relations between young white managers and the older BAME staff. I learned something important and true in this group. It was said out loud in the staff group, and I am grateful to have been there to hear it. The staff group had worked towards it for many weeks, trying together to make sense of what was happening to them and their patients. They learned together to open themselves to a free-floating discussion and, as a result, found out how they had got from there to here.

References

Barton, R. (1959). *Institutional Neurosis*. Bristol: John Wright.

Bion, W.R. (1961). *Experiences in Groups*. London: Methuen.

Ezriel, H. (1950). A Psychoanalytic Approach to Group Treatment. In: S. Scheidlinger (Ed.) (1980) *Psychoanalytic Group Dynamics*. New York: International Universities Press.

Foulkes, E. (Ed.) (1990). *Selected Papers of S.H. Foulkes: Psychoanalysis and Group Analysis*. London: Karnac.

Foulkes, S.H. and Anthony, E.J. (1957). *Group Psychotherapy: The Psychoanalytic Approach*. Harmondsworth: Penguin.

Goffman, E. (1998). *Asylums*. London: Penguin.

Hartley, P. and Kennard, D. (2009). *Staff Support Groups in the Helping Professions*. London: Routledge.

Klein, M. (1998). *Love, Guilt and Reparation: And Other Works 1921–1945*. London: Vintage.

Lucas, R. (2009). *The Psychotic Wavelength*. London: Routledge.

Macpherson, Sir W. (1999). *The Stephen Lawrence Inquiry*. London: Home Office Cm 4262–1.

Menzies Lyth, I. (1988). *Containing Anxiety in Institutions*. London: Free Association Books.

Searles, H.F. (1986). *Collected Papers*. London: Karnac.

Skynner, R. and Schlapobersky, J. (1991). *Institutes and How to Survive Them: Mental Health Training and Consultation*. London: Routledge.

Thornton, C. (2017). Towards a Group Analytic Praxis for Working with Teams in Organisations. *Group Analysis*, *50* (4): 519–36.

Winnicott, D.W. (1965). *The Maturational Processes and the Facilitating Environment*. London: Karnac.

Chapter 4

Working between worlds of experience

Peter Wilson

Introduction

S.H. Foulkes' literary contemporary and fellow refugee from the Nazis, the Hungarian author, Robert Musil, concisely describes a group analytic model of mind . . .

> . . . the inhabitant of a country has at least nine characters: a professional, a national, a civic, a geographic, a sexual, a conscious, an unconscious, and possibly even a private character to boot. He unites them in himself but they dissolve him, so that he is really nothing more than a small basin hollowed out by these many streamlets that trickle into it and drain out of it again to join other such rills in filling some other basin. He unites them in himself, but they dissolve him. Which is why every inhabitant of the earth also has a tenth character that is nothing less than the passive fantasy of spaces yet unfilled.
>
> *The Man Without Qualities,* Robert Musil

. . . capturing perfectly the way in which universal, yet discrete, external forces converge towards the definition of each and every unique identity on the planet.

The greatness of S.H. Foulkes lay in his optimistic vision that conversation, or 'communication' could, in a group setting and with careful translation, ultimately transcend the differences between people whose identities have been forged from a confluence of diverse historical, geographical, cultural and familial backgrounds.

While clinical experience has demonstrated the truth of this apparently simple proposition, the notion that enormous differences in beliefs and behaviours, cultural assumptions, and even languages can be bridged, is severely tested when we seek to work with teams in institutions or organizations. This is because, as well as the challenge of working across disciplines, or professions, it is always the case that any team will evolve specific (sub-) cultural norms: beliefs, mannerisms and behaviour patterns that mutate over time in response to the demands of the context: the socio-political world, the organization, and the particular demands of the client or patient group.

A substantial part of Group Analytic theory is dedicated to understanding personal and organizational development in the context of social change. The Group Analytic understanding of sociocultural development is heavily influenced by the work of the sociologist Norbert Elias who, in *The Civilizing Process* (1994) undertakes a detailed exploration of changes in attitudes, manners and behaviours (etiquette) in post-medieval Europe. In doing so, Elias, echoing Musil, demonstrates how the psychic structures of individuals are shaped by configurations of power in the social world. This understanding, which influenced Foulkes' description of the individual as a nodal point in a communicational network, later led to Foulkes' assertion that "the individual" is, like the group, "an artificial, though plausible abstraction" (Foulkes, 1948).

The description of the individual as an 'abstraction' helpfully points us to an understanding that any definition of the individual and the group will be filtered not only through our sensual and perceptual apparatus but also through circumstantial factors related, as Elias demonstrates, to different contexts, including time, place, geography, and, most importantly, politics – or power. The suggestion here is that the truth, or reality, of any situation will be experienced differently, depending on the particular schemata, or set of assumptions that the individual or group has inherited. Taken to its logical conclusion and expanded globally, this relativistic theory takes us into a world such as that described by Yuval Noah Harari, whose book, *Sapiens* (2014), defines global 'culture' as being comprised of an "immense diversity" of "imagined realities" and "resulting behaviour patterns" (p.41). The obvious question provoked by such a scenario is how do we transcend or reach across these differing imagined realities and find a shared language?

The relevance of this to Reflective Practice is that, when entering any new situation, we are always going to be confronted by 'realities' and behaviour patterns that may challenge our own personal and professional understandings, beliefs, and ways of working or, as Harari might say, our "imagined realities". We could say that the work of a reflective group is to recognize and understand conflicting shared sub-group realities and how these serve to determine the culture of the particular group, which will, in recursive fashion, (re)inform our personal experiences.

In this chapter I will consider how the phenomenological, non-doctrinal approach of group analysis is highly appropriate to this task. To do so I will describe a Reflective Practice group undertaken several years ago in the unpromising situation of an Acute Forensic ward; an extreme situation where we might observe most vividly the contrast between different belief systems or realities.

First, I will offer a description of what we mean by Reflective Practice groups. Then, using H.G. Wells' short story, "The Country of the Blind", as an overarching analogue of the experience of entering into a team, to offer Reflective Practice, I will describe what happens when different, even opposing 'realities' come face to face and how analogy becomes an important tool used to try and bridge the alternative perspectives that are being described. I will explore how the apparent reality of one group, the nurses, may be unconsciously informed by the more dominant and congruent reality of the patient group, which is why these wards are so often prey to perverse dynamics and the destructive acting out of patient and staff alike.

Work on a forensic ward could be formally understood to be that of doctors and nurses trying to instil a discourse of respect, care, concern and responsibility into the disturbed world of dangerously psychotic and even psychopathic patients, with the hope of creating a therapeutic milieu. Instead, I will argue, the dynamics on a ward, and beyond, emerge from the far more disturbed world of the patient group who infiltrate and reinforce their own beliefs or 'imagined realities', through what Norbert Elias called the "gossip stream". As in the story "The Country of the Blind", the apparent 'disability' of the patient group, in this case a perverse and disturbed way of experiencing the world (imagined reality), shapes a way of behaving that the staff team may feel compelled to enter into or abandon.

Choosing to portray a Reflective Practice group that takes place under conditions that test the limits of such a group's viability, illuminates the ever present, but largely hidden, dynamics that can undermine our intention to create the conditions for honest and open reflection. There is always a struggle when we seek to develop an understanding of the complex dynamic relationship between the individual, the group, the institution and the social world. Our relatedness to others is not always welcome, most particularly when the differences between the 'us' and the 'other' is predicated on madness, badness, or both. While the work of the conductor is aimed at helping the team relate towards a more closely shared reality, in these instances the question frequently becomes one of how much 'reality' can be borne.

Moreover, relatedness itself can be disturbed by the very presence of the group analyst who enters a team from the 'outside'. An analyst comes laden with their own ideological baggage, a set of values that inform the whole purpose of the meeting. This can lead to a situation where the group conductor can easily find themselves in the position of the one-eyed man in the country of the blind, a position that is less advantageous than it first might seem.

I will argue that it is the phenomenological underpinning of group analytic theory that provides the conductor with the flexibility necessary to reach across and bridge different worlds of experience. The main tool applied to achieve this is the use of analogy, which serves to associate that which might otherwise appear unrelated.

Before entering, blindly or otherwise, into the world of Reflective Practice groups it might first be helpful to define how they are generally understood to operate by group analysts.

What is reflective practice?

In simple terms, Reflective Practice can be defined as an exploration of *what* happens in the workplace and *why*. What happens can include the consideration of issues as diverse as who makes the tea and buys the biscuits, to who takes responsibility for secluding a patient or devising a shift rota. We can think about what patients, residents, or staff actually do, their activities and interactions on a daily basis, what is offered by the team and how it is used. On another level, we can think about the relationship between the team and higher management. How does this impact upon the work and why? Other pertinent questions might be asked about how different members of the team relate to each other. How are power relations dealt with? How do difficult social issues, such as race and gender, interfere with the teams' capacity to communicate?

A successful Reflective Practice group is able over time to address and, more importantly, readdress these issues in a creative and fulfilling way. The group can enable individual team members to understand the powerful feelings they each have towards colleagues as a mirrored reflection of the dynamic interplay of the client group. Alternatively, a hospital team might understand disputes and acting out among the patient group as reflecting unspoken feelings about, for example, unwanted institutional changes imposed by management. Using the free associations of the group we can trace pathological dynamics such as splitting, projective identification and devaluation as they emerge in the dynamic matrix. The group offers, quite simply, a space for the practice of reflection. Unfortunately, however, as we are reminded, for example, by the story of Snow White, the mirror might reflect a truth we are unwilling to hear. For this reason, it is the conductor's task to create a space where uncomfortable truths can be heard. The first task towards this is to provide a sense of containment.

Containment

Containment is an analogical concept borrowed from psychoanalysis, referring to the process whereby the carer, usually the mother, bears the toxic anxieties of the infant until the infant is ready to take them back, detoxified by the very experience of the carer being able to bear them. The first step towards creating a containing experience is the development of secure boundaries. Creating the boundaries entails clarifying a regular time and place in which the group will occur, determining who will attend, discussing the remit of the group, and agreeing upon issues such as confidentiality. This is the 'dynamic administration' of the group, upon which the success of the group depends, not only because it helps to create a containing space but also because attacks on the boundaries offer invaluable material in the here and now that will aid understanding of workplace issues. 'Attacks' includes events such as the room being double booked, team members not attending, or the group being interrupted by acting out on behalf of users or uninvited authority figures in the organization.

Common themes in reflective practice groups

While Reflective Practice takes place in a wide variety of settings, which therefore produces an equally wide variety of experiences, there is, wherever people gather in the workplace, a commonality of themes.

Issues of power and control are a constant presence. Equally, the division of labour necessary to offer a professional service inevitably evokes feelings around value. Who is most valued by whom? Moreover, the basic experience of having responsibility for or being responsible to another adult can easily lead to the re-presentation of early family dynamics. Sibling rivalries can be reignited, unresolved dependency issues brought into play. These eruptions of familial issues, usually described in terms of who is most popular with the patients, or who is the manager's favourite, are particularly difficult to resolve in early sessions, where the team might be guarded about sharing personal experiences. If the aggression inherent in such feelings remains unacknowledged it can readily be located in the patient or user group who the team subsequently find 'surprisingly' difficult to contain.

Another common, though related, theme that must be carefully heeded, as later clinical descriptions will illustrate, is that of the external threat, which might take the shape of higher management, absent colleagues, or destructive patients. For example, working with a relatively sophisticated team in a crisis unit, the group quickly recognized that the unusually intense anger displayed towards an external Crisis Assessment Team who had recently secured two beds in the unit was actually displaced anxiety about a change of management in the team itself where a well-liked team member who was acting up had been deposed by a new manager.

Initially, however, references to an external threat will invariably refer to the group conductor. It is the conductor's role to identify these projections and bring them back into the room. This occurs most usefully when the conductor is able to establish that the group can safely express their ambivalence, or aggression towards him as they progress towards expressing ambivalent feelings towards each other. The modelling role of displaying how anger and aggression can be understood rather than reacted or retaliated to is an important task that falls to the conductor.

Other themes, or feelings that tend to recur, most often in the counter-transference are helplessness, inadequacy, hopelessness, humiliation, exclusion and shame. Again, it is the conductor's responsibility to be available to experience and then facilitate the expression of these feelings, which, while they remain covert, impede the task of honest communication and clear understanding that the work demands. If the timing is right, simply naming these feelings can help the team to feel understood and supported.

Yet it is sometimes the case that regardless of the conductors' efforts, the acknowledged willingness of the team, and the apparent concurrence of aims, these groups can feel an arduous slog for all concerned. From the group's point of view, it is often difficult to believe that the group is truly a safe place to communicate one's struggle with the work. The managers who commission the group are sometimes loath to acknowledge an anxiety about the flattened hierarchy and this readily transmits to other hierarchical relationships within the team who feel constrained from speaking directly by their professional position. Even experienced conductors can become disheartened when the hard work involved in preparing the team for the return of some of the projections is undermined by institutional defences against communication, such as sudden departure of staff, changes in shift systems, or even withdrawal or threat of withdrawal of funding for the post.

It is not difficult to find a reason why staff teams find this work so demanding. Working with disturbed and damaged people who have experienced emotional trauma *necessarily* evokes such disturbance in the carer. It is difficult, if not impossible, to be around seriously disturbed people for any period of time without experiencing disturbing thoughts and feelings. These feelings themselves can provoke feelings of shame and humiliation, which feel unutterable. This provokes the danger that staff teams enact this experience among themselves. Such an enactment might be expressed through creating scapegoats, forming sub-groups, or having a high turnover of staff or management. Arriving late for Reflective Practice meetings and simply not speaking are means of acting-in during the sessions. These methods avert the immediacy of distress but eventually, if not inevitably, a price is paid, not infrequently in the form of physical or mental health problems experienced by the staff. Often it is the users who pay this price as they experience inconsistent care, negligence and abandonment. This undermines the whole purpose of the organization and further devalues those involved in it.

If the conductor can bear the feelings of helplessness until the group is strong enough to take them back, this reintroduces an experience of value back into the work. The working Reflective Practice group eventually becomes a container for the necessary disturbance of the team. 'Necessary' because we begin with the understanding that in a psychotherapeutic relationship it is important, even essential, that the patient affects the carer. It is how the carer deals with the feelings that are evoked by the patient that will in the end determine the effectiveness of the therapeutic relationship.

The following clinical example, via a detour to the 'Country of the Blind', will help us to consider some of the reasons why communication in these groups can pose such a challenge, despite the fact that they generally take place in environments where care is the currency and honest and open communication is considered essential to the work.

"The Country of the Blind"

This short story, written by H.G. Wells in the early 20th century, describes how a lone traveller, Nunez, falls through a fissure in the ice and finds himself in a valley inhabited by a legendary people who have lived there cut off from the rest of civilization for hundreds of years. Many generations earlier, a mutation had rendered the whole community blind and recognizing this situation brought Nunez to recall a refrain that would soon haunt him with its irony, "In the country of the blind, the one-eyed man is king" (Wells, 1911, p.129).

The analogy I wish to draw from this story is that the first problem the conductor has on meeting with a staff team is that he/she is perceived as one who is able to see what otherwise cannot be seen. This 'seeing' is expressed initially in the group conductor's clarity about the need for clear boundaries: the establishment of a place, a time, a specified duration, the importance of confidentiality. These are indeed essential requirements for the proper functioning of a group, yet they carry with them an ideological baggage: the belief that experience can be shared, that authority is benign and can be shared, that communication, relationship and understanding are both desired and desirable. This might be true in many a context, however, workplaces develop their own culture over many years and often become as self contained and resistant to outside influence as "The Country of the Blind".

This is illustrated early in Wells' short story when our protagonist is borne towards the village elders where he hopes to assert his superiority. Instead he is thrust into a room of "pitchy darkness" where he trips and falls. His struggle to right himself is quickly taken as proof that he is "but newly-formed".

However, once he has gathered himself, Nunez tries to describe,

> ... the great world out of which he had fallen, and the sky and mountains and such-like marvels, to these elders who sat in darkness in the Country of the Blind. And they would believe and understand nothing whatever that he told them, a thing quite outside his expectation. They would not even understand many of his words.
>
> "The Country of the Blind", H.G. Wells (p.132)

This is not an unfamiliar predicament for the Reflective Practice conductor, particularly when thrust into environments where ordinary norms have been eroded.

The acute forensic ward

Bearing in mind our analogy with "The Country of the Blind", the work now to be described takes place in a small psychotherapy department in a large forensic hospital that is trying to institute reflective practice on the wards. The wards are designated as 'admission', 'acute', or 'rehab', according to the function they serve. The psychotherapy department has secured funds from the nursing budget to pay for annual contracts for several group analysts to provide Reflective Practice groups.

The Reflective Practice group takes place behind a series of locked doors, at the end of a labyrinth of corridors. We are deep inside a forensic hospital, a world split off from civil society and rarely considered unless something awful has happened to remind the social world of the threat contained. Unspecified problems on an acute forensic ward have led a nurse manager towards the idea that a Reflective Practice group would be a useful way to address them.

Having met with the manager, I duly attend a preparatory meeting, where I elicit the nursing team's thoughts about such a group. The team agree that the group would be helpful and welcome, yet despite my probing I am unable to elicit any but the most general reasons why. This could be seen as an idealization of the group potential that will later be denigrated. I suggest that it would be helpful if everyone who works on the ward, including the consultants, could attend. I am told this would be unworkable and is anyhow unwanted. They inform me that the admissions ward in a forensic setting is an extremely disturbed place to be. The nurses merely need help with the experience of being on the frontline.

At this meeting I acknowledge the difficulty of the team's task before laying down my suggestions as to what will make the group a safe place to develop our understanding of the work: a regular time, a suitable space, and an agreement that all available staff should attend. I also suggest that confidentiality can be an issue but that it can be overcome if we agree to consider topics that arise in the group as the property of the group. This way, if discussions continue *outside* the group, they can be brought back for further consideration *by* the group. Everybody agrees that this is fine, but contest that it will be difficult to maintain confidentiality when people who are absent from the group due to shift rotas will be curious as to what has happened.

Over the following weeks I am introduced to the team in stages, as they arrive in a variety of combinations. The manager is male, the clinical team leader female, and their approach appears to combine traditional male and female roles wherein the manager holds the responsibility for maintaining discipline while his deputy attends to the emotional and, not infrequently, physical cuts and bruises suffered by the team. The gender distinction is obliquely reflected in the structure of communications from the team, where most groups begin with a female staff member raising an issue and end with a male offering an authoritative response that usually contains what sounds like an empty threat along the lines of "you'd better get your finger out or there are going to be big changes around here".

In an early group, an experienced member of the team comments on how this group is so talkative compared to his previous experiences of such groups. But this optimistic beginning soon trails off until only a few months in, the groups consist of uncomfortable silences, broken only by recriminatory complaints directed at the authority structures of the institution: a higher management that introduced unhelpful policies, a consultant who refuses to listen to their concerns about a patient, a staff nurse (not, of course, present), who delegates while reading the newspaper. Attempts to focus on the group sometimes lead to discussions about dictatorial shift leaders or feckless colleagues, none of whom, miraculously, as the composition of the group changes on a weekly basis, is ever present. Mostly it leads to further silence. Occasionally someone demands that we introduce some structure. Everyone agrees that there is no point in trying to communicate difficulties. There is only one law in this institution I am told repeatedly: "Shit flows downwards".

Persisting in attempts to work in the here and now, I wonder aloud whether they perceive me as trying to pull them out of the shit or whether I am pouring more of it on them. Is the silence a way of making me helpless? Might it be the only way they can let me know how they feel? This particular intervention leads to a discussion about a patient, Dave, who is currently on a dirty protest. Staff members share their disgust at being forced to struggle with him in his room where they invariably end up rolling around in his excrement. One staff member talks about scrubbing himself under a shower and feeling unable to rid himself of the gut-wrenching stench. While this is a genuine illustration of the difficult work they endure, I am also left with the strong feeling that I am being told that the metaphorical excrement I describe is derisory when compared to the reality of working in such appalling conditions.

Disgruntlement with the group grows over subsequent weeks. Contempt is barely hidden as senior nurses laugh about the struggle they have in convincing the team to attend. The team tell me there is nothing to talk about. They say my time would be better spent on formal supervision. I say that if I can't help the team with each other why would they trust my interventions with the patients. Nonetheless, in between sustained silences they talk about the new problem Dave is causing. He is complaining bitterly about smoking on the ward and has even taken to standing outside his co-patients' bedrooms to ensure that no surreptitious smoking is going on. They fear that he will be badly beaten if it continues, but they can't convince the consultants to move him off the ward. I suggest that the silence represents the doors that are closed to me. There might be a feeling that I am trying to smoke something out. The group, I suggest, want rid of me as a way to avoid exposing what is actually happening on the ward. The team are baffled that I could make such a link. How helpful is this sort of comment when they are asking for assistance with a patient? In other words, they refuse to accept that that the answer might have something to do with them.

Perhaps, in retrospect, their bafflement was my fault. I was using a way of relating that I hadn't earned in the group. They didn't speak my language or understand things my way. There is a moment in the Wells' story when Nunez, irritated by the countrymen's refusal to acknowledge the value of his difference, asks:

Has no-one told you, 'In the Country of the Blind the One-Eyed Man is King?'
'What is blind?' asked the blind man, carelessly over his shoulder.
(Wells, p.134)

Nevertheless, my interpretation proves to have been more prescient than expected. The next week it transpires that a nurse has been suspended after forming an inappropriate relationship with a patient. The team say they cannot talk about it because the nurse is under suspension and anything they say might be prejudicial to her cause. The clinical team leader describes her guilt and anger but it appears not be shared by her mostly silent colleagues. I express surprise at the lack of response and suggest that there is an absence of trust between not just me and the team but within the team itself. Someone says they would talk to me if it were one to one. Others agree. I suggest that there is a wish for secret intercourse but this leads us into guilty feelings, which then must be hidden. The team appears unusually thoughtful in the ensuing silence.

At this stage I am growing increasingly hopeless. Presently, the patient who had held a dirty protest and subsequently complained about smoking develops a new symptom. He charges headlong at the wall from one side of the room to the other. Some members of the team feel they ought to restrain him, others that he should be left to it. Banging one's head against a brick wall, I suggest, is something we all know about. The group grimly agree.

Approaching the summer break, our signature patient, Dave, changes tack once more. He has become, to all intents and purposes, paralysed. Team members have seen him move when he thinks nobody is looking but there is genuine concern at his ability to remain static in such a contorted position. And in such a position the group drifts towards a four-week summer break.

I discover on my return that a freelance 'nursing support team' has been drafted in to meet with them during my absence. The group, I am informed, would like to share consecutive meetings between us. I refuse what I see as a further, institutionally supported, avoidance of the possibility of working through the difficulties. It becomes a bit of a battle. I am hurt and disappointed, furious with the team, the management who requested the extra support and the higher management who sanctioned it. The team members who have attended the other group compare the rival groups' lively vitality to my silent group. It's like the difference between GMTV news and BBC news someone suggests. The support group is great because it's really gossipy, while my group is all starchy and boring. One nurse imitates a BBC newsreader. I say that the group obviously find me starchy and boring. The group disagree. Nobody talks in my group they say because I *imposed* a rule that they couldn't talk to each other about the group during the week. I'm then informed at the end of the meeting that there is a staff away day the next week to decide whether my group should continue at all.

The gossip stream

It may be useful here to take a look at how group analytic theory might help us to understand the situation as it stands. The adjective 'gossipy' immediately caught my attention, as it reminded me of Farhad Dalal's description of the work of Elias and Scotson (Dalal, 1998, pp.87–126), who showed how gossip is used to sustain ideological belief systems. The means by which they do this is by dividing the world into binary opposites: good versus bad, smelly versus clean, etc. According to Foulkes (1948), we are "permeated to the core" by the social world. This means in effect that the psyche is structured, changes, and develops in accordance with the social structures of the world in which it exists. Our assumptions about the world and our place in it, including our thoughts and feelings about ourselves and others, are in turn determined by the prevailing ideology. Gossip is the oil in the ideological machine.

According to this theory then, gossip serves to maintain power structures in the favour of the powerful. While gossip is ubiquitous in human communications, the more powerful grouping, whose gossip streams run more deeply and therefore more persuasively, is usually the most established. The more established, powerful group are therefore more cohesive, have more effective channels of gossip communication and therefore have the power to define the values or ideology of the community.

Anyone familiar with the workings of a hospital cannot but be aware of the held professional hierarchy of the medical model. Consultants are perceived to be all powerful and inferiority is devolved downwards through ward managers, team leaders, numerical grades of Nurses and Health Care Assistants, to the barely acknowledged domestics. The nurses iterated this in one of my very first groups, "shit flows downwards". They were telling me that they were victims, awash in a feculent system, a system where power or authority is always used abusively.

This brought home the feelings I held about the group. The group felt like an imposition, something I was doing to the nurses against their will. My position was not caring but its opposite, aggressive, controlling, negligent, and each week as I left them to their task, abandoning. Not only this, but I had ostensibly proscribed the one release they felt they had from the oppressive pressure of the work, gossip. Gossip that permits the thoughtless attribution of negative or unwanted qualities towards patients, managers and absent colleagues alike. I was part of the negligent yet oppressive authority that dumps on those beneath it.

This, of course, takes us into the forensic experience, where the notion of a benign authority is barely thinkable, where power is invariably experienced as oppressive, negligent, or abusive. Janine Chasseguet-Smirgel in her book, *Creativity and Perversion* (1985), describes perversion as a regression to the anal sadistic stage, where all difference is disintegrated in the digestive tract. We might think of working in a special hospital as working in the bowels of society, where everything had to be turned into an undifferentiated mass of shit. The preoccupation with faecal matter may have been born of a culture where every difference, and more importantly the power differential that difference presents, is a threat.

From this point of view we could say that this shit didn't flow downwards, but in truly perverse fashion, upwards. For the forensic patient, power and authority is *always* abusive and therefore must be subverted or undermined. In the terms of this dynamic, my suggestion that it would be beneficial to avoid speaking about the group between groups was understood as a punitive demand. Instead of offering care, I was experienced as asserting control, restraining where I purported to be offering liberation. This, of course, reflects the patients' experience of nurses who present themselves as carers but are experienced as custodians.

Thinking of this inversion made me consider the different groupings that constitute a psychiatric hospital. It is most natural to ascribe all the power to the Consultants or Trust management and, in truth, they are the most reviled group in the eyes of the nurses. However, considering the work of Elias and Scotson (in Dalal, 1998) we will find that the group that meets most frequently, congregates most intimately and gossips most freely, is the patient group. After this the nursing team is the most cohesive group. They are also the group most closely associated with the dominant group, the patients. As we go upwards in the hierarchy, the groups become less and less cohesive. Consultants might meet regularly to consider management decisions but not to think together, share ideas or philosophical approaches. The group charged with that responsibility of instituting Reflective Practice, the psychotherapy department, barely exists as a whole but is instead fragmented, the work it offers, piecemeal.

We could then argue that the dominant ideology within the hospital belongs to the patients, whose gossip channels are deepest and strongest. The various professional groupings at the hospital cannot create an alternative powerful ideology based on a coherent model of care, because they do not share a common experience, rather they are caught up in their own battles for resources or prestige. What we are then left with is a community where a perverse ideology holds sway. Where authority is feared and reviled because with it comes the power to abuse.

The need to maintain this status quo arises because to get in touch with the awful feelings of shame, humiliation, depression and vulnerability has proven impossible to the patients who instead have developed mental ill health and criminality. Those left to cope with the unbearable feelings are the victims of their crimes (Wilson, 2005). The staff team joined in this gossip, identifying with the patients' view of a world where everything had to be soiled, or spoiled, in order to avoid the painful and frightening feelings evoked by depending on an unreliable other.

The wards where forensic patients live, often for long periods of time, in fact, "without limit of time" (Gordon et al., 2005) are unpredictable and violent places. Caring in such an unpredictable environment does not come easily, particularly when such caring is denigrated as weak, soft, or ineffectual. It is unsurprising in such an environment that negligence or casual carelessness becomes institutionalized. Consultants walk in on Community Meetings and demand to hold their ward rounds. Nurses miss meetings with patients to write up their notes. Managers move from ward to ward in the hope of finding somewhere they can make a difference. Patients assault their carers. Carers abandon their patients by moving on swiftly or staying safely in the office where the fear of attack is diminished. In order to avoid feelings of vulnerability and shame, patients have acted out criminally, the criminal act a manic defence against depression. Nurses too are drawn into this dynamic, so their only real contact with the patients where they feel they are doing something is when they are restraining someone, even if this entails rolling about in the shit.

In Wells' short story the protagonist constantly uses verbs related to sight: he sees, he perceives, he has an eye for, and so on. The villagers however experience the world through touch, hearing and smell. They do not, indeed, cannot, find a way to understand the different worlds they each subjectively inhabit. In my interventions I was concentrating on the way *to be* when the team were looking for the answer of what *to do*. I was in effect saying to them, "Don't just do something, sit there!"

Analogy in action

> . . . we emphasise the study of traumatogenic processes and the transgenerational co-construction of social facts.
>
> (Hopper and Weinberg, in Tubert-Oklander, 2014)

The group, perhaps surprisingly, did continue to sit there for several more months, until, in fact, my own contract came to an end. It survived the predations of my commercial rivals (ITV) and the resistance of its members, and at times we all left the room newly illuminated. An example of this arose several months in when the group, having arrived ten minutes late, found it had configured itself into a circle divided into black and white staff members. The two empty spaces in the room were on either side of me, black staff members on one side, white on the other. Dave's latest antic was discussed. He had called a team member into the room and demanded to be turned over in his bed. The nurse had refused. No sooner had he left than the alarm rang from Dave's room. The nurse returned to be confronted by Dave standing at the side of the bed pressing the alarm. "You are a piece of shit," Dave shouted. The nurse described a powerful urge to slap Dave around the face.

We looked at how the nurse felt he had only two options: to accede to Dave's request or not to. Someone laughed and said, "Black and white," gesturing at the room. "It would be simple if everything were black and white," I said, "yet Dave made you become the angry, violent one and suddenly it's not so black and white. That might feel frightening."

This led to a discussion on splitting and we acknowledged a further division, the nurses sitting separate from the group analyst. This is because we want to listen to you I was told. I noted how their lateness, which informs me they don't like feeling dependent on me, seemed to contrast with how they understood their positioning in the room as intended to let me know that they might want me to feed them. Perhaps, I suggested, I was a piece of shit, but still they wanted me to look after them.

The group began to talk about the experience of difference. White members of the team complain that black members talk in their own African language. Some black members point out that they are not African. African members say they do not understand the local dialect of some of their African colleagues and understand what it feels like to be excluded by language. We think about how in some ways we are different, in some ways, the same. In some ways we are like the patients. We can feel the wish to be violent. We are frightened of depending on each other for fear of not being understood. This is what we share black, white, patient and carer.

Closing thoughts

> . . . he heeded these things no longer, but lay quite still there, smiling as if he were content now merely to have escaped from the valley of the Blind, in which he had thought to be King.
>
> (Wells, p.146)

Group analytic theory has been criticized for its lack of rigour, or coherence. However, it is my view that the strength of group analysis lies in its non-doctrinal phenomenological approach, in which, while there is a recognition that we can use a range of analogies to approximate the reality of a situation, or the truth, our closest approximation can only be arrived at through dialogue. Group analytic theory is strongly informed by psychoanalysis but also by occasionally conflicting theories based in the social sciences, systems theory, or attachment theory. Foulkes' acknowledgment that groups and individuals are "plausible abstractions" (1948) permits us to understand all competing theoretical models as plausible abstractions and to use each one as required, along with other models derived from literature or philosophy, in the form of analogies that might offer "novel forms of approaching a truth that we intuit to be there, while knowing that we do not know it now and shall never have a complete knowledge of it." (Tubert-Oklander, 2014). In this sense we attempt to see the world holistically, or from the perspectives of the one-eyed, the bifocal and the blind!

"The Country of the Blind" ends ambiguously. Our protagonist lies on the side of a mountain surrounded by visual splendour, unwilling to forsake his sight to join the countrymen below who experience the world so differently. We do not know if he will choose to die or will finally relent and have his sight removed. This, like the clinical examples provided above, is an expression of our universal everyday dilemmas, starkly illuminated when observed at the extremes. What will we forsake of ourselves to join the group? How do we remain a unique individual with our own particular or 'special' way of experiencing the world while still belonging to a family, a group, a team, or an institution? At a broader level, the question is posed as to whether it is even possible to understand the world through the experience of another, when the cultural or even sensual context from whence our understanding has emerged is so different?

My aim upon joining the staff team was to meet in a collaborative attempt to think about the work. I would make suggestions as to how this might best be achieved. What I was not reckoning on was that the perception of my position of representing authority transformed my suggestions into demands. The language of collaboration was not shared or understood and nor was the notion of benign authority or helpful experience. I have an ideology, based on the assumed value of dialogue, that I am intending to impart. In extreme conditions, such as those that prevail in a forensic hospital setting, this ideological position becomes a part of the problem. In the binary world view, I have the choice of being an 'outsider' who shits upon them or I succumb to the shitty world they believe they inhabit. I am powerful or powerless. However, as Carl Jung said, and we do well to remember, the opposite of power is not powerlessness, but relationship.

How did the group survive despite all the difficulties described? In this group, rather than the epiphany of a mutative metaphor (Cox 1997), it was the slow accretion of shared experience that helped develop small important changes. The desire for relationship was always there and could be seen as present in the initial welcome I received from the staff team. It could also be understood to have been expressed, albeit destructively, in the nurse having a sexual relationship with the patient. Ultimately, however, it was the capacity to draw analogies between occurrences in the group and those that they described in their clinical and inter-professional encounters that helped us find a language of shared experience, to create between us a different 'imagined reality'.

Foulkes (1948) famously suggested that the group constitutes the norm from which individually we deviate. This suggests the group maintains an eternally elastic norm that expands recursively as it incorporates individual deviations. The danger of this is perhaps that we might find ourselves working with a perverse 'norm', as would be the case in a culture that was driven by shared fantasies, or 'imagined realities', where authority is always abusive and care is always com-promised. Morris Nitsun's (1996) concept of the anti-group suggests that there may be some destructive or dangerous feelings that cannot be incorporated, that must remain, like Nunez, outside the boundaries of a functioning group. Cer-tainly, work on a forensic ward or in a prison test the capacity of groups to accom-modate highly destructive dynamics.

However, within Foulkes' dictum is an understanding that the whole precedes the parts. The optimism in Foulkes (1971, p.212) is in the belief that human groups are *always* in some way related, an understanding that 'imagined reali-ties' can be bridged through finding a new, shared language of experience. It is the work of the Reflective Practice conductor to provide the analogies that will become part of the shared experience and the language that will be found to describe our relatedness.

Working with Reflective Practice groups, particularly those in dangerous or frightening settings, the group analyst must be prepared to spend time, like Nunez, alone on the mountain, in the liminal space between one experience of the world and another, maintaining Foulkes' optimism that eventually a language will be found where different perceptions and understandings can be used to recreate a picture of the work that is as close to a shared reality as we can reach. In this case, a language that allows us to share the human experience of being simultaneously creative and destructive without locating these impulses in a single individual or sub-group.

The phenomenological approach of group analysis has been often criticized for its lack of theoretical coherence and rigour. However, it is in the realm of Reflective Practice groups in the clinical or organizational setting that the appar-ent weaknesses of group analysis as a theoretical model become its strengths. The reality of life as a social animal is messy and incoherent. Foulkes' implicit recog-nition that the group is an analogy of the individual and the individual an analogy of the group provides the foundation, or font, for the creativity of the analogical approach that is at the heart of the group analytic endeavour. Group analysis with its capacity to incorporate a whole range of theoretical and creative approaches to thinking and being helps bridge the socio-political, psychological and cultural differences between persons and groups that inevitably arise when we are born, live, work and play in different worlds of experience.

References

Chasseguet-Smirgel, J. (1985). *Creativity and Perversion*. London: Free Association Books.

Cox, M. (1997). *Mutative Metaphors in Psychotherapy: The Aeolian Mode*. London: Jessica Kingsley.

Dalal, F. (1998). *Taking the Group Seriously – Towards a Post-Foulkesian Group Analytic Theory*. London: Jessica Kingsley.

Elias, N. (1994). *The Civilizing Process*. Bodmin: Blackwell.

Foulkes, S.H. ([1948]1991). *Introduction to Group Analytic Psychotherapy*. London: Karnac.

Gordon, J., Harding, S., Miller, C. and Xenitidis, K. (2005) X-treme group analysis: on the countertransference edge in inpatient work with forensic patients, *The Journal of Group Analytic Psychotherapy*, *38* (3): 409–26.

Harari, Y.N. (2014). *Sapiens: A Brief History of Humankind*. London: Random House.

Musil, R. (1997). *The Man Without Qualities*. Picador.

Nitsun, M. (1996). *The Anti-Group, Destructive Forces in the Group and their Creative Potential*. London: Routledge.

Tubert-Oklander, J.T. (2014). *The One and the Many: Relational Psychoanalysis and Group Analysis*. London: Karnac.

Wells, H.G. ([1911]2007). *The Country of the Blind and Other Stories*. Harmondsworth: Penguin Classics.

Wilson, P. (2005). Breaking down the Walls: Group Analysis in a Prison. *The Journal of Group Analytic Psychotherapy*, *38* (3): 358–70.

Chapter 5

What Makes a Staff Support Group (Un)safe

David Kennard

Staff support groups that are set up to enable staff to share and gain support for the emotional difficulties they encounter in their work can be experienced as a two-edged sword. The invitation to share your most difficult, emotionally challenging situations with your colleagues may be a pit you would rather walk around. Why is this?

All group situations carry social risks for the individual, e.g., of rejection, criticism, conflict, etc. As social animals we are good at oiling the wheels of social interaction that helps to protect us from such risks – what we call chit-chat, banter, common courtesy, making conversation, etc. In group analytic therapy, members are required to set aside these social conventions so that they can face and examine these risks in the interest of personal learning or to help overcome problems in living.

In groups that are known as 'sensitivity' or 'experiential' groups, the expectations are similar to those of group therapy, where members meet in an agenda-less, unstructured group in order to learn about themselves and about group dynamics. This contrasts with groups that are aimed at improving clinical understanding, competence and knowledge which have a structure in terms of presentations and theoretical input. These include supervision groups and reflective practice groups.

Staff support groups occupy a position somewhere in between. Like therapy/experiential/sensitivity groups, they are usually agenda-less, maintaining the flexibility to allow spontaneous topics to arise, depending on the issues that are uppermost in members' minds. But unlike these groups, they do not presuppose a commitment to learning about oneself and the aims are quite broad (potential benefits are listed below). It is worth mentioning that the terms 'staff support group' and 'reflective practice group' are sometimes used interchangeably, but I think it is helpful to maintain a distinction.

Reflective practice groups, originating in the work of Donald Schön (1984), are usually structured, with a presentation of a problematic situation or experience, followed by discussion and relevant theoretical input, leading to learning points/an action plan. This format has also been used in the development of Schwartz Rounds[1] to support staff in general hospitals.

Staff support groups, agenda-less and with the flexibility to pick up on issues that arise spontaneously, can be a source of anxiety for participants. They cannot come 'prepared' as they could to a more structured group and have to deal with the social risks inherent in an unstructured group situation. This presents the facilitator with a delicate task. The group must feel safe enough for staff members to come to, stay in, and speak in, which means that the social conventions we use to oil the wheels of group situations need to be allowed. Yet the group must also work with experiences, feelings and issues that can be a source of distress, shame, anger, or frustration: otherwise what's the point of meeting? Squaring this circle, keeping the group safe, while at the same time getting into emotionally painful areas, is what makes facilitating a staff support group one of the most challenging jobs a group analyst, or any group facilitator, can take on.

Benefits of staff support groups

Staff support groups have several potential benefits, both for the individual and the organization they work in. These have been summarized by Hartley and Kennard (2009) drawing on their own and other writers' experience:

> To provide staff with a protected time and space within the work setting but away from their immediate work tasks and responsibilities.
> To promote the value and the practice of open communication.
> To enable staff to express, discuss manage difficult or painful emotional responses – such as guilt or anxiety – to people and situations in their work
> "To enable staff to use the full range of their emotional responses in the service of the task – not to have to protect themselves by shutting down emotionally" (Farquharson, 2003).
> "To create an environment where the vulnerable parts of ourselves, which have been shielded by our defences, can be responded to and understood" (Rifkind, 1995, p.211).
> "To improve staff well-being in ways that are associated with better patient care and smoother unit functioning" (Lederberg, 1998, p.276).
> To enable the team to discuss obstacles to team working that may arise from issues between individuals, within the team as a whole, or between the team and the wider organization.

Risks associated with staff support groups

To achieve these benefits there are a number of risks that members of a staff support group must negotiate and overcome or manage. This chapter sets out to examine these risks.

Breaches of confidentiality

While the ground rules for the group will usually include the need for discussion in the group to be kept confidential, some staff may not trust their colleagues to respect this. This may be because of a general level of mistrust within the organization or between certain individuals or subgroups. In a group where attendance is intermittent, depending who is on the shift, I have often heard a participant say that their willingness to use the group depends on who else is there. Staff may even deliberately busy themselves to avoid attending if they know certain other staff will be going. Personal antipathies that have a long history may be beyond the reach of the group, unless a live situation occurs that provides an opening, as in the example described below. In this respect at least, staff support groups provide a freer space for newcomers who bring no relationship baggage to the group, though, of course, they have other anxieties about fitting in and not making mistakes.

When there is a floating membership, it is probably advisable to remind the group about the need for confidentiality, not necessarily at the start of each session but if there has been a discussion of a particularly sensitive nature. However, in my experience breaches of confidentiality are rare.

There may be occasions when a managed breach or broadening of confidentiality is appropriate. Members of the group may want an issue they have discussed to be brought to the attention of a manager. If the facilitator also feels this is appropriate, he or she can help the group decide how to do this and what information will be shared with the manager. The facilitator should avoid doing this for the group, as this could reinforce feelings of dependency or helplessness and also miss a useful learning opportunity.

Fear of being harmed or of harming someone else

In her classic paper, Stock (1962), highlighted the interpersonal concerns during the early sessions of therapy groups, which included anticipation of criticism or ridicule and concerns about hurting other members. In staff groups, where members attend irregularly, it is wise to treat all sessions as early ones and although the stakes are different from a therapy group, the interpersonal concerns can be similar, and in some ways more pressing, as other members are colleagues you have to work with outside the group. Moreover, in settings devoted to the care of vulnerable persons, staff are likely to be sensitized to the impact of expressing criticism.

> John mentioned his irritation at certain staff who avoided unpleasant jobs, like sorting the laundry. He felt he daren't challenge them, they were too clever for him. Joanna said her dad always said to rise above it. We thought about what you could say. Susan, a manager, said she didn't speak if she felt angry but when she was calm she might say 'this is one of the things the job involves'. I suggested, rather than challenging the other person directly, telling them the effect they had on you. We spoke about how people sometimes protect themselves by spending all their time with one resident. Susan joked there'd be bonuses for anyone who could tackle the difficult staff.

The need to maintain positive relations often takes priority over giving honest feedback. This can apply when one member dominates the group with a complaint or criticism about some aspect of the organization the group has no control over and other members either agree or stay silent: a classic 'fight/flight' group that staff sometimes refer to as a 'moaning session'. The silent members tend to be reluctant to challenge or disagree with the complainer because they fear they would either face criticism themselves or risk having to go back into the work situation with increased tension in their working relationships. Dealing with monopolizers is familiar territory for group therapists, but in the context of a staff support group may be best responded to with interventions aimed at giving everyone a chance to speak or raise a topic rather than interpreting the individual's behaviour or the group dynamics – though this may depend on the psychological sophistication of the group.

The fear of causing harm can also come from altruistic motives. In one session, staff discussed their reluctance to tell a popular colleague who had recently been promoted to the role of team leader, not present in the group, about a complaint a resident had made about a staff member because they didn't want to burden her with an extra problem.

The task of the facilitator is to steer a course between recognizing and acknowledging anxieties over potential harm while offering ways forward, e.g., alternatives to confrontation (as in the above example) or using opportunities in the group to demonstrate that feedback can be managed constructively.

> In one group meeting, two staff, who had disagreed strongly over how a particular care plan should be implemented on their shift, aired their differences in the group. I commented on both having strong opinions and could see both sides – sticking to the agreed plan but also being flexible. What did others think? Only one responded, taking the position of doing what you think is best at the time. At the end I asked the two if they thought they could deal with differences more amicably if they found themselves working on the same shift again. One said she would try. As everyone left the two stayed behind to talk – it sounded as if a resolution was happening.

Being seen as 'not up to the job'

This is one of the risks felt most acutely by some people, depending on the individual's self-confidence, level of experience and also on the culture of the setting. This may be particularly the case for new staff members who are trying hard to prove their worth and fearful of getting things wrong, whereas more experienced staff may be comfortable with lacking some specific knowledge or skill or making occasional errors – as long as they are not serious. Hearing this can be especially helpful for newcomers.

> In a staff support group in a children's hospice, a new member of staff expressed concern that she hadn't known what to say to a colleague who had asked her

how to carry out a certain procedure with a child. She'd felt bad not knowing. An older staff member recalled breaking into helpless laughter on one occasion when she repeatedly failed to complete a particular procedure, or another time having to admit she had never seen a piece of equipment before.

The inclusion of senior staff (clinicians or managers) in a support group raises particular issues that need to be recognized. If they are willing to share their own anxieties and difficult experiences, this can make it feel less risky for others to do so. On the other hand, the senior member may feel that to 'moan about things they find difficult' would risk undermining team morale. Where there are issues in a team around management actions or decisions, the staff may feel it would be risky to raise these for fear of a negative reaction and an adverse effect on future job references. Including senior staff in a support group increases both the potential benefits and risks – the benefit of greater mutual understanding between occupants of different roles and levels in the hierarchy and the risk of negative value judgements leading to defensive closing up or smoothing over.

The culture of the setting also plays an important part. In settings that value action over talking and have a 'macho' culture, and where physical containment may be the priority as in some secure units, 'just talking' may be denigrated as irrelevant, and participation in a support group may be viewed as a sign of weakness (Milton and Davison (1997) give a good example of this). It is also not uncommon for the staff culture to be split, with some staff valuing the opportunity provided by a staff support group and others avoiding it, with the risk that the facilitator is drawn into the split and loses perspective on the setting as whole.

Exposing splits in the staff team

As quoted above, a risk factor for participants in a staff support group with a fluctuating membership is who else is present in the group. Large staff teams inevitably develop subgroups of staff who work closely together or who feel comfortable with each other, perhaps sharing details of their personal lives. Personal antipathies between individuals can also develop, which tend to remain undiscussed and unresolved, and are managed where possible by avoidance or minimum interaction. The extent to which participants feel safe to disclose personal feelings in a staff group will therefore be closely related to who they find themselves in the room with. Staff may even decide to absent themselves from a support group meeting, on the pretext of having jobs to do, if they know that a certain colleague will be attending.

The history of such splits can be long ones. In a long-running staff support group where the question of whether managers should be invited to attend was being considered, it emerged that when the group had started, managers had attended regularly but that following a contentious disciplinary issue, they had stopped attending and that was how it had stayed.

Where the split involves particular individuals, this can be a difficult issue to address, partly because the relevant parties will often succeed in avoiding being in the group at the same time, and partly because the issue may have personal resonances for the individuals concerned that go beyond the scope of the group. The strategy chosen by the protagonists of letting sleeping dogs lie may be the only realistic option, unless the split can be caught early.

In the example given above illustrating a strong difference of opinion between two staff working on the same shift in regard to how a care plan should be implemented, the conflict between the two had begun earlier on the shift: A had been preparing food for lunch, not expecting to have to do it all. B had asked if she wanted a hand. A said she was fine so B went to do something else. A ended up preparing the whole meal and feeling too angry inside to say anything. It was later on the same shift that the disagreement about the care plan had occurred.

On this occasion the issue surfaced in the group and was sufficiently fresh to have something done about it. If it had been left, it is possible that these two staff members would have developed a lasting antipathy, or at least a coolness, towards each other.

Being analysed

This risk is part fantasy – part reality. As a young clinical psychologist, I got used to being asked, after I told someone at a party what I did for a living, if I was analysing them. (It doesn't seem to happen now I'm retired, either the parties I go to are with others in the psych. world, or people aren't interested in what I'm thinking.) While it is an important rule, and usually an explicit one, that staff support groups are not therapy groups and an individual's unconscious wishes and fears are off limits, it is, of course, still true that the facilitator will be thinking about the dynamics, conscious and unconscious, at work in the group. Hartley and Kennard (2009) suggest that "it is often the most anxious and sceptical group members that ask whether they are being analysed. We find it helpful to say that we are thinking about what is happening in the group and will usually share our thoughts".

When the facilitator is known to be a group analyst or group therapist, the suspicion of being analysed may be quite persistent and may be fuelled by the facilitator's style. Some months after taking over the role of facilitator of an established staff support group from a non-analytic facilitator, I carried out a feedback exercise using an anonymous questionnaire that included space for comments. Under the heading of comments on the facilitator, it was clear that for several staff there was great discomfort at my style. Here is a brief selection:

> "David appears unwelcoming and cold – never smiles or looks at you, looks in mid-distance when speaking – he mumbles and is difficult to understand and tends to stop conversation in mid-flow – appears to need 'meatier' topics."
>
> "David reads in more serious issues – laughter is important to –. He goes off onto subjects nothing to do with issues brought up."
>
> "David often says something that stops discussion."

"David looks for an issue even if there isn't one."

"David tries to steer group – thinks we need to talk about 'doom and gloom', not affirmation of positive events."

"Awkward silences due to people feeling if they say anything it is 'scrutinized' by David as it is not 'deep enough'."

"Sometime staff support involves laugher and 'silliness' as a way of dealing with issues, which is just as important as intense times – a facilitator needs to enable the whole group to feel as able as possible to engage as they want to, and should never be directive, critical outwardly, or intense."

This feedback made for uncomfortable reading and clearly pointed to mismatch of expectations. What it did enable me to do, after swallowing my narcissistic pride, was to bring these comments back to the group and work on developing a more collaborative style. A year later, I carried out the same exercise. The feedback had improved:

"I think he helps the group move forward in the discussions, more so than if we were alone."

"He lets conversation flow, listens. Could possibly pick up and challenge a little more."

"I feel the group leads the majority of the session."

"Overall a good facilitator, but at times I feel it may be difficult to facilitate due to the amount of people in the session and the difference of opinion and the topics covered."

"I find David's observations helpful on the whole, sometimes asking/putting an awkward point into the arena, which discomforts people, but I quite like questioning the status quo. However, I do know some people find his interventions cut across the discussion or are too problem focused when they feel there are none."

There are various points to be drawn from this comparison, including the value of carrying out a feedback exercise like this and the point made in the final comment that different staff want different and sometimes incompatible things from a staff support group. One can notice in the transition from the first to second set of comments a greater acceptance of the facilitator's approach at the cost of what might be called analytic edge. "Could possibly pick up and challenge a little more". How the facilitator of a staff support group who is also a group analyst manages the staff group's attitude to the risk of being analysed is one of the core challenges of the role.

Breaching the personal/professional boundary

Work in the caring professions carries the ever present risk of overstepping the boundary from a professional to a personal relationship This is one of the reasons for the importance of clinical supervision and staff support. Wojciechowska (2009) cites several examples of staff support groups sensitively exploring these issues arising in everyday practice. The risk in the staff support group is slightly different. It is that the content of the discussion will overstep the boundary. Given that one of the aims of staff support groups is to enable staff to use the full range of their emotional responses in the service of the task, it is easy to see how discussion of a staff member's emotional response to a work situation might spread into their personal life. Where the individual and the group are comfortable with this, it may be an acceptable temporary breach – e.g., touching on domestic stress, an experience of bereavement or miscarriage – but the facilitator should manage this carefully, fostering the mutual support available in the group, while not allowing intrusion into an individual's personal life further than they are comfortable with. A gentle steer towards individual counselling or therapy may be required. Wojciechowska (2009) suggests that if a staff member has a highly personal and embarrassing issue, it can be helpful for them to see the staff support group facilitator individually.

Getting upset or leaving the group feeling worse

As indicated above on the risk of being analysed, staff want to leave a group session feeling better not worse. Lederberg (1998) has pointed out that, "in staff support groups the members work together all day and extreme emotion is not containable". On the other hand, Bolton and Roberts (1994) point out that "support is needed to enable staff to face rather than evade difficult issues".

Hartley and Kennard (2009) have noted that "it is not uncommon that if someone becomes visibly upset and tearful in a group, it somehow percolates through the whole team, and attendance at the following session plummets". They give the following example:

> A normally cheerful and robust member of a group for the staff of a large community mental health team broke down in tears when describing the shock for one of her patients whose young son had been involved in a near fatal accident on a school river trip. It turned out that her own brother had drowned when she was 16 and the pain of that time had come flooding back, taking her and the rest of the group by surprise. Outwardly the group was very supportive, but quickly changed the subject.
>
> The facilitator sensed that the impact on the group had gone underground and that the other members were anxious not to say anything that might upset her further. About ten minutes before the end, he gently suggested that this is what had happened. This provided an opportunity for the person concerned to say that she felt alright now and that it had helped her to be able to cry in the group. Nevertheless, only four people came to the next session and it was two or three weeks before attendance was back to full strength.

In this case, as often happens, the individual who was able to express her feelings felt better afterwards, but the onlookers were left with unexpressed feelings to process outside the group.

In the staff group I facilitated in a children's hospice, there was an initial mismatch of expectations concerning the way a group session should be concluded. As a group analyst I was used to leaving unresolved issues in the air or closing with a brief comment reflecting the question or problem the group was facing at that point. What the staff team wanted was a supportive rounding off or a humorous story to send them out of the room ready for whatever they had to face. What this also meant was that the last word would more often be theirs rather than mine. Here are two examples:

> At the end of an animated session that had highlighted the need to share information in a fast developing situation because 'anything could happen at any time', I said the group members were like a spider's web, with very thin but strong connections. One of the experienced staff team present made the perfect rounding off: "We're a cracking team".
>
> A session centred on the death of a three-day-old baby and how her parents and siblings had been dealing with this in ways that the staff working with the family had found very moving. A new staff member who had not been directly involved said he sometimes found himself getting tearful for no reason. Others said that this was natural and gave their own examples. At the end of the session, an experienced staff member told the group the following anecdote: She had been discussing alternative ideas for a baby's funeral with the granddad and she had remarked on his "thinking outside the box". She had apologized and said she had wished the ground would have swallowed her up.

No group facilitator could have come up with an ending to a painful session as sensitive, apposite and reassuring as that.

Managing the risks

In the above descriptions, I have suggested ways in which the facilitator might respond to a particular risk. There are also some general points that can help to reduce the risks and free the group to function as effectively as possible.

Setting up the group

A mismatch of expectations can be avoided, or at least reduced, if the aims of the group are discussed, before the group starts, with the staff who will be participating in it. If the invitation to facilitate the group has come from a manager, the facilitator should arrange to meet with the team so that they feel it is their group and not something that has been imposed or arranged behind their backs.

Key questions to discuss with the team include where the idea for the group has come from, previous experience of such groups, the aims of the group, when it will take place, who will attend, and the ground rules, e.g., about confidentiality, whether attendance is voluntary, the role of the facilitator, etc. Following this, it may be a good idea to have a written contract or letter to staff setting out all the relevant information.

Dynamic administration

This covers everything the facilitator does outside the group sessions to 'keep the show on the road' and ensure the meetings take place as planned. At its most basic level it is to ensure the group meets at the agreed time and place. This can be more problematic for a staff group than a therapy group. A session may be cancelled because of a staffing crisis or lack of cover to replace the staff attending the group, or moved because the usual room is not available. The possibility of these occurrences should have been raised in the preliminary meetings – the reliability of arrangements for staff 'cover' is particularly important in residential settings – but unforeseen problems can still arise. It is helpful if the facilitator maintains a close liaison with the manager(s) responsible for staff and room allocation so that problems with these can be quickly addressed. It is not uncommon for management decisions to appear arbitrary and it is important for the facilitator to identify lines of authority so that decisions affecting the integrity and stability of the group can be responded to appropriately.

Boundary maintenance

Within the group itself, there may also be challenges to its integrity and stability, especially during early sessions when group norms are being established. Members may arrive late, leave early, or come and go during a session and need to learn that such behaviour is disruptive to the working of the group, while allowing that occasional emergencies may be unavoidable. Erratic attendance may be unavoidable in a team working a shift system but it is helpful to group trust and cohesion if the norm develops of commitment to attend as regularly as possible. The facilitator's role is to promote and protect the group's capacity to address the aims agreed with the team. Members whose behaviour undermines this capacity may need to be challenged, but this should be done on the basis of the effect on the group rather than the individual's possible motives.

Promoting a culture of mutual support and empathy

Beyond protecting the group as a going concern through dynamic administration and boundary maintenance, this is the facilitator's main task that addresses the risks staff face when they join a staff support group. Hartley and Kennard (2009) suggest the following intervention strategies to help with this task:

Asking questions

Open questions can help to get the group started or encourage interaction.

Encouraging empathy

If a member takes the risk of talking about a difficult experience, it is important that they get an empathic response. If this is not forthcoming, the facilitator can show interest and empathy and elicit responses from other members, e.g., asking if others have had similar experiences.

Clarification

Specifics are always helpful, especially as an antidote to generalized expressions of dissatisfaction or frustration. Asking for details of what actually happened to generate a feeling of dissatisfaction, done in a spirit of genuine curiosity rather than criticism, can facilitate a more constructive discussion and also conveys the personal interest of the facilitator in the issues the staff are contending with.

Modelling

As in any group, the behaviour of the facilitator/conductor provides a model of interaction for the members. If the facilitator shows empathy, curiosity and an effort to understand before giving an opinion, this will be noticed as a good example of how to be in a group.

Self-disclosure

The use of self-disclosure is always a potential tool for the facilitator, but one to be used with care. It can facilitate greater openness in the group if the facilitator shares something of their own feelings or experience, or it could have the opposite effect.

Confrontation

Care should also be taken over challenging or confronting the group and should probably only be done to express something the group tacitly knows anyway, e.g., "This seems to be a group that avoids conflict at any cost".

Avoiding interpretations

The members of a staff support group have not signed up for personal awareness or learning about their unconscious fears, wishes, or motives and any intervention aimed at this would be an unwarranted intrusion. It would reinforce any lurking stereotypes about the facilitator as a detached omniscient onlooker and damage their credibility as a useful external resource. This does not mean that interpretations do not enter the facilitator's mind. Awareness of transference or projections in the group may be helpful in shaping interventions, e.g., asking for specific examples to counter the tendency towards 'them and us' splitting.

The one kind of interpretation that might be made is where it concerns group parallel process. For example, it is not uncommon for staff in the caring professions to feel inadequate in the face of their clients' level of need and at the same time to feel angry at the lack of support they feel they get from their own managers. Recognizing the parallel process here can help staff to separate out the two issues of unmet need so they can think more clearly about each of them. Humphreys (2009, pp. 163–70) describes such a situation in more depth.

A group analytic approach to staff support groups

Much of the above will be familiar to group analysts, in particular, dynamic administration and boundary maintenance. There are also other ways in which the group analytic model works well in staff support groups.

Health = open communication

A basic premise of group analysis is that the healthy parts of an organism have free flowing communication between them. By extension, a healthy group or social system is one with open communication between its members and subgroups. I sometimes illustrate this with a circle that represents the current limits of what members are willing to share. At a simple but fundamental level the aim of the facilitator is to expand the circle:

What can't be talked about

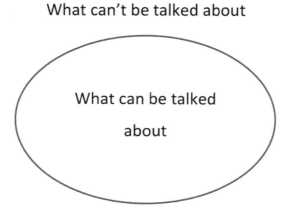

What can be talked

about

FIGURE 5.1

The advantage of this view is that it can apply equally to a therapeutic group or a staff support group. The group analyst can 'read across' from one to the other without having to change models, though there may be a need to recalibrate.

Split focus on the individual and the group

Models of group therapy can be divided into those that focus on individual members, those that focus on the group as a whole, and those that use a combined focus on individual members and on the group process. Group analysis is the third type, with its core image, taken from gestalt psychology, of figure and ground. Group members move back and forth between occupying the foreground and background, collectively forming the sounding board for the member's individual experience. This fluid approach is appropriate to working with staff support groups, where the facilitator has simultaneously to hold in mind the needs of the individual, their position in and relationship with the immediate group, and the relationship of the group to the wider organization.

Role of facilitator

I use the term facilitator rather than conductor to de-emphasize the therapeutic connotations of the role in this context. In a staff support group, the facilitator is not a therapist and it is important that members do not feel they are being 'treated' or analysed. However, certain core aspects of the group analytic conductor's role fit well with the requirements of a staff support group. One is the attitude towards authority and leadership. Group analysts refrain from active leadership, but do not reject the need of the group to confer on them the attributes of a leader at times. More importantly, in group analysis the conductor is not a blank screen or omniscient observer but is fully present as a real person – albeit one who knows that they are in receipt of transferences and projections. To quote Foulkes,

> The therapist's own personality is of fundamental importance. It must be in line with his[2] position and attitude so that he can be completely honest with the group and mutual trust can develop. He need not be perfect or in any way share the unconscious fantasy of the group of an omniscient leader . . . he need only be what he is, but naturally should be adequate and competent.
>
> (Foulkes, 1964, pp. 285–86)

Conclusion: limits to risk management

Three attributes of staff support groups make them inherently risky for those attending:

First, in residential settings, sporadic attendance due to shift working means that the group cannot develop stability of membership and cohesion over time, so that most sessions are like the early sessions of a therapy group when members are still testing the water.

Second, unlike a stranger group, where the risks are mainly restricted to what happens within the group, what comes up in a staff support group, even if it remains confidential, will influence members' working relationships for better or worse for the rest of the week.

Third, the simple truism: at work one's colleagues are likely to be both the main source of support and the main source of stress. Clinical emergencies and therapeutic failures, difficult and painful as they are, are part of the job staff are trained for and supervised in. Colleagues are another story. Put simply, good working relationships mean work heaven, bad working relationships mean work hell. You tamper with the status quo at your peril.

Three reasons, then, to be cautious in a staff support group.

And yet, people do attend staff support groups and benefit from them. Evaluating the evidence, Hartley and Kennard (2009) concluded that there was clear evidence that well set up and well run staff support groups are experienced as beneficial. They found that the most successful groups were those set up as a joint undertaking by a staff team that recognizes it has problems, its leader, and the facilitator. However, they noted that, "even when these ideal conditions do not occur, staff groups with an external facilitator are likely to be experienced as helpful by around half of those taking part".

The potential benefits of staff support groups, as outlined at the start of this chapter, are considerable and worth pursuing. The risks can also be considerable. The aim of this chapter is to enable the risks to be recognized, managed as far as possible, and accepted when unavoidable.

Notes

1   https://www.kingsfund.org.uk/projects/schwartz-center-rounds
2   Foulkes wrote at a time when the masculine pronoun was used to represent both sexes.

References

Bolton, W. and Roberts, V.Z. (1994). Asking for help: staff support and sensitivity groups re-viewed. In: A. Obholzer and V.Z. Roberts (Eds), *The Unconscious at Work*. London: Routledge.

Farquharson, G. (2003) Personal communication.

Foulkes, S.H. (1964). *Therapeutic Group Analysis*. London: George Allen and Unwin.

Hartley, P. and Kennard, D. (2009). *Staff Support Groups in the Helping Professions*. London: Routledge.

Humphreys, N. (2009). Working with disturbed states of mind. In: P. Hartley and D. Kennard (Eds) *Staff Support Groups in the Helping Professions*. London: Routledge.

Lederberg, M.S. (1998). Staff support groups for high-stress medical environments. *International Journal of Group Psychotherapy*, 48(2): 275–304.

Milton, J. and Davison, S. (1997). Observations of staff support groups with time limited external facilitation in a psychiatric institution. *Psychoanalytic Psychotherapy, 11*: 135–45.

Rifkind, G. (1995). Containing the container: the staff consultation group. *Group Analysis, 28* (2): 209–22.

Schön, D. (1984). *The Reflective Practitioner: How Professionals Think in Action.* New York: Basic Books.

Stock, D. (1962). Interpersonal concerns during the early sessions of therapy groups. *International Journal of Group Psychotherapy, 12*: 14–26.

Wojciechowska, E. (2009). Managing personal and professional boundaries. In: P. Hartley and D. Kennard (Eds), *Staff Support Groups in the Helping Professions.* London: Routledge.

Chapter 6

Consulting to doctors in general practice

"Don't talk to me about work"

Cynthia Rogers

The health service in crisis

Some years ago, the then Chair of the Royal College of General Practitioners, Dr Clare Gerada, was concerned for the future of the profession, as many of her peers were taking early retirement and numbers entering the profession were dwindling. The profession was being challenged and doctors were unhappy. She recognized that a Group Analytic approach could address this complex situation; using small and large group meetings to explore the pressures GPs were exposed to in the consulting room, in the surgery, fighting for local resources, and as respected professionals. She wanted to create a kinder profession and needed to identify the structures and assumptions that discouraged GPs from taking care of themselves and doing what they knew would be good for them and their patients. This chapter describes how this group analytic consultation was conceptualized and implemented. The success of the approach has led to established national funding, and it continues.

The challenge

The National Health Service (NHS) is experiencing continuous change, with a marked impact on the assumptions general practitioners can make about their professional lives. Their identity and professional culture is coming into question. What constitutes surviving as a caring doctor now is unclear. Thoughtful doctors are grappling with what their response to the changes can be and whether there is a narrative that will enable them to engage with and negotiate their way through the changes.

The current structures have evolved to fit life before the changes, and some assumptions may no longer be fit for purpose. Feelings of anger and upset arise when doctors face making changes they do not feel confident with or that challenge their ethical and moral perspective. It becomes difficult to think. While medical clinicians often think that they have answers, those also involved in management or leadership are likely to be frustrated that they have no answers, only more choices, often bad choices, where one has to settle for the least worst option.

Doctors who have strong clinical and operational skills are being asked to think strategically in a complex medical model with reduced financial resources. The answers are not clear and are demanded against a background assumption that the government does not always trust them. Doctors are expected to get decisions right, even when they lie outside their primary area of competence. There is inevitably a fear that this questioning of their expertise might become generalized and extended to clinical competence. At the same time, complaints are rising and complaints procedures experienced as persecutory.

The infantilization of the professional

Gerhard Wilke (Wilke and Freeman, 2001), a group analytic consultant who has researched the professional lives of GPs dealing with change, brings a helpful analytic conceptualization of their difficulties. Referencing Iliffe (Iliffe, 2008), he sees the industrialization of family medicine as a malign phenomenon that negates the individuality of the patients and the creativity of the doctor. He recognizes that the NHS is no longer a good enough environmental mother for the GP and has turned into a neglectful and persecuting parent. Clinicians can feel like naughty children and managers are seen as enforcers of utopian visions generated by out of touch politicians. He suggests that the constant change, disturbance and dislocation are disorientating and can reduce adult functioning.

Solving problems directly can be helpful but it may not influence the overarching narrative about role and identity that creates and sustains the problem. To paraphrase Einstein: "expecting to get a different result from behaving the same way defines madness".

Thinking about the natural responses to change

Professionals undergoing massive change can experience feelings of loss similar to bereavement. It is hard to believe the enormity of the task of operating within parameters that seem to have nothing to do with why they became doctors in the first place. The familiar grief responses of anger and helplessness are to be expected. Self-sacrifice is no longer an option and other intuitive responses, such as just doing a good job somehow, no longer bring the rewards they used to.

Fight–flight (Bion, 1961, pp.63–64) might be another natural response. One can flee the NHS, fight the changes, or stay with the uncomfortable feeling of really minding what is happening. It is easy to see the attraction of retiring, with the understandable feeling that it is not they who have left the profession but rather that it is the NHS that has left them. Others might be seen as identifying with the aggressor when they enthusiastically embrace the new opportunities. Particularly sad is young doctors giving up their life's ambition in despair.

Doctors no longer function in a world of individual relationships. In the main, the individual GP is functioning in a group practice that is linked to a network of independent practices, each nestled in, and accountable to, the wider NHS. One has to see the individual in the context of their complex competing relationships. The practice dynamic is the sum of the constraints enacted between individuals. What doctors allow themselves to do is influenced by conversations with colleagues. Doctors care about their reputation in the eyes of their colleagues, so tacit injunctions around what is considered 'professional behaviour' are powerful. Thinking in the midst of conflicting expectations is difficult (Wilke, 2005).

Personal relationships come under pressure when it is not possible to meet colleagues' reasonable requests. The challenge is to bring some creativity to the dialogue. John Ballatt (Ballatt and Campling, 2011) in writing about the need for intelligent kindness to reform the culture of healthcare, has talked about the value of kinship relationships and how important, but difficult, it is to stay with the feelings of our colleagues. What does it mean to see the individual in the context of their complex competing relationships?

The group analyst consulting to the profession

How can a group analytic approach help doctors change their narrative to create different ways of behaving and achieve successful outcomes? Approached for help, I want to know how they are formulating the problem. Do they want help fighting change or are they looking for ways to make the new situation work? Can they actually imagine making it work for them and their patients or are they overburdened with depressive anxiety? Why might they be finding it so difficult to create space to think about the problems? No one wants to take the comfort of existing defences away from practitioners but it is important that the defences work constructively. Can GPs be interested in the underlying dynamic that might be driving the difficulties or are they too attached to the rather more concrete ideas and formulations they have already arrived at? Group analytic reflective practice is not about finding the answers to the doctors' dilemmas. It is more about helping them to manage themselves in the face of these dilemmas and feel they will have the support of their colleagues in doing so. It is about identifying what needs thinking about and what the barriers are to thinking about it.

Group analysts consult to every level of the profession, providing input to leaders of the profession, national and local conferences, medical education, practices and individual GPs. Resistance will be encountered. A structure, a language, and a process is evolved that might best make a connection, hold any anxiety, avoid a clash of professional cultures, and nudge the participants towards authentic participation. This dynamic administration creates the environment in which a group analytic attitude can flourish.

Consulting to the individual GP

Individual GPs may be offered one-to-one consultation to understand the projections and constraints they are subject to, reflect on their role in maintaining them, and examine what aspects might be open to influence. For example, a GP, whose early family experience as the eldest girl with responsibility for caretaking within the family, might find herself resentfully taking the same position in the practice. Avoiding positions where she might have some authority but assuming responsibility and irritated by the senior partner who seems always to be in meetings elsewhere. The consultation would look at ways she can resist this pattern and whether, indeed, she wants to. There will be gratifications that she may be unwilling to forgo. The senior partner's sense of entitlement may be beyond her influence but she can cease to encourage it. Becoming involved in management and exercising authority, or delineating more accurately her areas of responsibility, will change the dynamic in the practice and potentially give her the opportunity to be a more equal partner. Ongoing support might be provided by joining a local reflective practice group that focuses not just on the doctor–patient relationship but on the whole experience of being a doctor. Personal therapy is a resource for many doctors, either individual therapy or in a stranger analytic group. Analytic groups open only to doctors provide an experience where the hurdle of assuming the identity of a patient is circumvented (Gerada, 2016). The common experience provides the ballast that a group can quickly coalesce around.

Consulting to the practice

A GP is asked to be a doctor, a manager, a leader and an agent of social change. In this multi-layered complex world, it will be harder to hide differences and disagreements between colleagues. Partners, sessional doctors and locum doctors each have a good argument for why they have drawn the short straw. The question is how to manage difference in a way that builds resilience. It is not always easy to hear another's views and assumptions without experiencing it as an attack on existing perceptions. Is it possible to hold different views without being seen as disloyal? Differences can seem so insurmountable that doctors feel it is better to avoid talking about them. Where a practice keeps saying that they must talk about the difficulties but fails to do so while day to day operational issues fill the agenda, one has to wonder what is happening.

Where they all have different needs as GPs, it may be difficult to talk about it, for fear there may not be an answer that satisfies all. Differences lead to disagreement, which can become personalized, resulting in emotional disinvestment by some partners, as they feel their efforts are unappreciated. It would not be difficult to predict the dynamics of a practice with one older disenchanted GP partner longing to retire alongside a bright eyed, keen, new GP partner and a third who just wants a quiet life and to be allowed to get on with the job. An authentic conversation allows them to stop each fighting for their own corner, start to understand where each is coming from and think about how they can manage to support one another in the very different things each wants. Having the conversations may raise the emotional temperature between people, but it deepens understanding and strengthens the partnership as the differences are acknowledged, not taken personally, and become used creatively. It is the consultant's role to elucidate the underlying dynamics and conflicts, reframe them as inevitable or understandable, accurately identify the feelings generated, and locate the disturbance where it can be addressed.

Consulting to local meetings and national events

GPs meet at a local level for continuing professional development. Workshops with titles like 'Resilience in Practice', provide an opportunity for reflective practice with an educational element. A psychoanalytic perspective on the GP's experience is described and then explored in intimate reflective small groups or sophisticated median groups that reflect wider concerns and experiences. GPs often know intuitively when they are being manipulated by patients but an understanding of unconscious psychological interplay, can give them the confidence to resist the pressure. Being together and discovering that others share their experience is in itself invaluable.

National events maximize the potential of median and large groups. They allow GPs to think together as colleagues, develop a dialogue that questions the orthodoxy and support one another in creating a profession that is fit for purpose. Larger groups can be threatening and if dialogue is to evolve, projective processes need to be mediated and digested. Setting the tone for dialogue rather than stimulating anxiety is essential. A careful introduction or short provocation can set the tone. The provocation, a stimulating short talk that asks questions rather than provide answers might provide new language for the discussion or a new psychosocial framework from analytic thinking, which will encourage serious attention to the real issues people struggle with.

A respected senior doctor might introduce the group, setting an example of honest communication, by talking personally about professional experiences. A larger group can grow from a small goldfish bowl. Volunteers in the centre of the group discuss a topic such as, 'what is the value of reflective practice?'. As the observers join in the discussion, it becomes a median or larger group. The median or large group is conducted to maximize intimacy and communication. Where there is a resort to splitting and projection this is attended to thoughtfully and incorporated into the dialogue. All views are considered and listened to. No one person is allowed to dominate. The convener will be confident to intervene in any destructive dynamic, for example, to contain the narcissistic individual or to deter scapegoats being made and massification, by naming and reframing it (Rogers, 2013). "David I think you should be aware that the group are exploiting your willingness to talk", can be a useful intervention if one voice is heard above all others.

Why use a group analytic approach?

A group analytic approach is particularly suited to GPs who work for themselves as independent practitioners but as part of a practice funded by the NHS. Group analytic consultants employ a tripartite paradigm that addresses the network of competing relationships and priorities in the workplace. They bring a psychoanalytic conceptualization, a systemic or complexity perspective, and an awareness of the psycho-social forces at play. A group analyst might be thinking analytically about a GP's insecurity and notice how this is amplified by the group dynamic that reinforces the power relationships.

Group analysis is not a rigid method of consulting, more a way of conceptualizing and relating. The individual is understood analytically in the context of their experience and relationships. The individual is also seen as constantly influencing and being influenced by others. The GP practice and wider profession is viewed as a collection of individuals all relating to one another and subject to identifiable interpersonal constraints. In this way, considerable complexity is embraced whilst not losing sight of each individual. Group analysts employ a quality of free-floating attention that allows them to shift their focus, drawing attention to whichever perspective provides the simplest, or most acceptable, way to engage with the particular difficulty. The method is to facilitate authentic free flowing conversation.

How does a group analyst work?

Participants engaged in authentic exchanges see their own anxieties and struggles mirrored in their colleagues and are able together to have new thoughts and conversations. The challenge is to encourage the participants to look in the mirror. Those who look, risk exposing themselves to feedback that is devoid of the familiar distortions built up over the years. The consultant actively creates the structure and intimacy that allows this to happen. The key elements are demonstrating real interest in what people say, thinking intelligently and analytically about contributions, and discouraging attacks on thinking and linking (Bion, 1984 pp. 105–106).

A hardworking, caring, exhausted GP will see aspects of herself mirrored back by others. Kind, simple feedback may enable her to sit and recognize her depression and exhaustion and that she cannot continue as she is. Talking with a colleague who is the mirror image of herself will be containing but also enlightening and sobering. Seeing him also try to do the impossible will stimulate her compassion, but also reveal quite how futile and delusional her own efforts are and encourage her to desist. Normally she might be contemptuous or dismissive of those not trying as hard as her but in this setting she has to take everyone seriously, including those with very different values from her. Encouraged by the consultant, she starts to take an interest in the person who, (in her mind) cavalierly, just gets the work done. How does he do it? Those held in contempt frequently have much to offer and talking can reconnect a weary GP with split-off, denied and more selfish aspects of herself that she needs to rediscover and develop.

As the group goes on, the consultant will notice how the GP interacts with the others. Perhaps her helpfulness in the reflective practice group starts to be experienced by others as some kind of rebuke or irritant. If this parallels her reports of relationships in the practice, it can be explored in the group, with people giving honest feedback of what it is like to be in a relationship with someone who is relentlessly helpful and exhausted.

On occasions, these interactions can become stuck in a form of malignant mirroring (Zinkin, 1983). A young GP who grew up with a rigid, controlling father might react rather badly to an old school GP who, rather than enter into reflective dialogue, insists on telling her what she should do on a practical level to solve any dilemma. In the world of projections and transference, she is back at home with her father and he with his headstrong daughter. As they get into entrenched positions, interesting fixed projections and assumptions emerge. If the group can insist that the protagonists think about the other members' more nuanced perceptions, the debilitating projections can gradually be acknowledged and withdrawn. The discussion then broadens out into how much each member of the group lives their life in the shadow of projections, and how this manifests in difficult relationships at work. Stepping out of malignant projections is a fruitful avenue to explore (Ogden, 1979).

Where the contract is to work at a superficial level, talking about a minor issue provides a focus for quite complex exchanges. What does it mean if the overworked GP invites the patient to take their coat off and sit down? Does a coat hook on the back of the door suggest the appointment will last only 10 minutes or longer? Once they are happily ensconced and the minutes are over, how does the GP encourage them to leave without being rude or stimulating a time-consuming complaint? Have GPs really come to terms with the change in culture from revered doctor to entitled, informed patient or are they intimidated by the consequences?

Working with roles, constraining and enabling

GPs can struggle with the concept of role identity. Formal identified roles provide the containing structure of the practice. The unconscious roles that GPs fall into meet the less conscious needs of the practice. GPs enjoy the role of doctor in the consulting room. Management and political (albeit non-partisan) roles sit less comfortably. In a reflective space, the ambivalence about embracing these formal roles can be explored. A discussion about exerting authority might evolve but what is interesting is precisely what it might mean to each individual to take on the responsibilities. Previous experiences would be explored alongside the challenge to self-identity. Acknowledging the contribution of the different roles each member of the practice plays, facilitates good relationships in a practice. The practice that has been encouraged to distinguish between the person and the role will be well placed to handle conflict. In highly charged conversations, role clarity ensures it is a professional conversation, rather than unpleasantly personal. "It is my job to talk to you about . . ." GPs readily, and perhaps unwisely, accept roles they are unconsciously assigned, provided such a role complies with their own phantasy of themselves or meets a need.

A group analytic reflective space will usefully explore how these operate. These come alive in a reflective practice space. A practice manager needing to cover a session intuitively understands how to flatter the young doctor looking for approval, or shame the locum with a persecutory super ego into giving her what she needs. It is in their interest to learn to resist this. Similarly, a doctor sensitized to sibling rivalry can be relied upon to give voice to feelings of unfairness. If others know she will do this, they will leave it to her, knowing the issue will be attended to and that she, not they, will be seen as the difficult sessional doctor. Splitting involves separating the good and the bad objects. Good objects need to be split off and located where they will be kept safe in this dangerous environment. Pity the poor doctor who the practice needs to embody perfection. Particular attention is needed when a group scapegoating dynamic comes into operation. The consultant told of anxious nurses, incompetent receptionists, or rude sessional doctors will naturally wonder whether this is a scapegoating dynamic that allows the partners to operate in denial of their own concerns: "At least I don't lose my temper as often as her". Where the source of the splitting can be identified, it mediates the toxic feelings and the projection can be withdrawn.

GPs who can be interested in the unconscious communication can limit projective processes, provide more containment, and reduce the distress in the practice. The doctor who has some insight into his or her valency to engage in projective processes will find engaging in projective processes easier to resist (Rogers, 1987). In a reflective practice group with mutual trust and open discussion, doctors can start to talk about themselves and develop some insight into what they need from their colleagues, how that makes them vulnerable to influence, and which feelings they may pick up on. "Whenever the therapist feels a great urge to make an individual interpretation, she should pause and ask herself why the rest of the group are not thinking or saying what she is itching to say" (Garland, 2010, p.35).

Problems and difficulties

Many doctors go into this caring profession because of unresolved personal conflicts. Devon (2018, p.85) in an overview, draws attention to medical students motivated by unresolved conflicts from childhood (Leif, 1971): a medical career as a defence against the impotence experienced in the face of an early experience of death (Feifel and Hanson et al., 1967); and care-giving as an attempt to resolve early emotional neglect (Tillett, 2003). In a consultation I would expect to see 'helping profession syndrome', in which the professional compulsively gives to others what he would like to have for himself (Malan, 1979) and what Johnson (1991) characterizes as 'fragile grandiosity' leading to emotional detachment and denial of personal vulnerability.

Depressive anxiety

A GP, defeated in trying to do the job well, will experience depressive anxiety. This is the treacherous internal voice that says it cannot be done, producing the feeling of anxiety and sadness at one's own limitations. Often it is amplified by colleagues. If it is noticed and given a label of depressive anxiety, it becomes less toxic and can be resisted. Where the situation they find themselves in is less than optimal, reflective practice can enable GPs to carry on thinking and resist depressive anxiety. It is frightening to think that one might be working in a situation that does not provide the support needed to do the job or that the demands might actually be overwhelming.

GPs who keep trying harder, and failing, become stressed. Seeing the situation for what it is, however depressing, will allow the GP to know that it is not their failure but that the situation and expectations are quite unrealistic and cannot be met simply by goodwill. This might be particularly difficult for a GP who has gone into the profession in an unconscious attempt to repair an early experience of bereavement or illness by being there for others. Put in a position where they feel they are letting their patient down, it would not be surprising if feelings of guilt escalated to depression.

Persecutory anxiety

Any consultation to the NHS has to confront the real persecutory elements and the persecutory anxiety that pervade the service. A reflective practice group can explore how the participants habitually engage with persecutory events, perhaps masochistically identifying with the aggressor, sadistically retaliating, and diverting the aggression through scapegoating, or resolutely denying their limitations and trying to meet the needs of the practice, like the Dutch boy with his finger in the dyke.

Persecutory anxiety is often associated with the friction and misunderstanding that arises in a bureaucratic environment when colleagues are under pressure (Menzies Lyth, 1960). GPs who confidently undertake difficult conversations with their patients often still prefer to avoid confrontation with their colleagues. Group analysts demonstrate conflict resolution skills in conducting the group and model how to engage with rage, disagreement and difference. More practically, an exercise using a pro forma that guides the GP through how to have a difficult conversation, can be useful. (Rosen, 2014, pp. 63–64).

Thinking about anxiety

Much unnecessary anxiety and frustration is due to a failure to distinguish between problems and difficulties, particularly those involving colleagues. A problem does have a solution that is within the influence of the person who is experiencing the problem. A difficulty is something that has to be accommodated or managed, because any solution is beyond the remit of those experiencing the difficulty. Trying to 'solve' difficulties that do not have a solution or accommodate problems that could be solved with a little more courage, is to be discouraged. Every GP has their Achilles heel in personal relationships with colleagues and patients.

A reflective space provides an opportunity to think about this in a non-judgmental setting and perhaps gain some insight.

There may be a tendency by the GP to any one of the following traits:

Needing approval and appreciation.
Getting involved in sibling rivalry.
Responding awkwardly to authority figures.
Exhibiting masochistic tendencies.
Suffering from a persecutory super ego.
Having a propensity to hold a grudge.
Feeling excluded.
Needing to be at the centre.
Being quick to see other's faults.
Being uncomfortable being in the wrong.
Holding and voicing the anxiety for others.
Reacting awkwardly to being mothered.

How might a group analytic reflective practice group help?

A reflective practice group contains and mediates both depressive and persecutory anxiety and facilitates thoughtful discussion of the anxieties that GPs are subject to. GPs need to carry on thinking in the eye of the storm to do a good enough job. A reflective practice space enables them to:

Be aware of their own sensitivities and see how others exploit these.
Discourage the idea that people behave logically and move to an understanding of how the real world works.
Be prepared to behave counter-intuitively and ruthlessly engage with insisting that others meet their needs.

Conducting a reflective practice group

A group analyst conducting a reflective practice group looks for the underlying dynamic that will solve a number of possibly unrelated problems. The GP's language will be used in a supportive, uncritical atmosphere, where the tricky question can be asked thoughtfully. The group analytic model thinks analytically and systemically about both, the individuals in the room and the group as a whole and the influence of the power dynamics in their wider environment. The patients, the practices, and the NHS are all part of the picture. The skill is in knowing which level to attend to at any given moment, to promote the most helpful conversation.

In a complex reflective practice group, it is wise to anticipate a variety of reactions to any attempt to offer substantial support. While the GPs may want to engage, it would be naïve to assume they will not simultaneously actively resist attending to the very issues they need to grapple with. Importantly, the group is the perfect setting for GPs to try out new behaviours, rejecting the ideal of the resourceful, inexhaustible doctor. Behaving counter-intuitively, they can put themselves first, ask for help, not be masochistic, set limits, and expect their needs to be met.

Can GPs rediscover their resilience?

GPs tend to think in terms of resilience (Howe et al., 2010, p.92). Medical training was designed to build in the resilience necessary to do the job in a particular way with a whole set of assumptions that doctors more or less bought into. Doctors looked after the patients and the NHS looked after the doctors. Doctors were given the support they needed and that was where the resilience came from. However, with the industrialization of the NHS, the space for that support has been squeezed out. It is hard for doctors to accept that this contract no longer exists and nothing is replacing it.

It is easy to think of resilience in a slightly brittle way, as some kind of inbuilt quality that an individual either possesses or doesn't. I am not sure that is helpful or accurate. Psychological resilience is defined as an individual's ability to properly adapt to stress and adversity. How each individual manages the stress and how the practice responds as a group of colleagues will determine the level of resilience. Christopher Rance (Rance, 1998) suggests that managing oneself in the presence of others, in the context of a collaborative task, constitutes good management.

The literature on building psychological resilience suggests that care and support for each other is vital, including acknowledging disagreements (McCann and Beddoe et al., 2013). When things change as significantly as they have, the fundamental assumptions of the profession are disrupted. The challenge is to retain what is good and vital. At a practice level, the multiplicity of individual responses and the need to survive emotionally and financially increases the pressures on how doctors work together in their practices. Inherent in being resilient is how these tensions are brought into conversations and which conversations can be had.

For many doctors, some ways of working have to be given up and doing so feels like a betrayal of everything one has worked for. In these circumstances, it is particularly difficult for professional colleagues to have honest conversations. When groups are under stress and in constant transition it is easy for them to split and enact a conflict. To look to blame members who are struggling and to operate more as individuals rather than as a group. The aim of a group analytic consultation is to introduce a group analytic way of thinking that promotes reflective conversations. It shifts the focus from any blame of individuals and looks to the interactions between people in the context of their environment, by bringing in an outside perspective. Keeping this fluid allows the issues that really matter to be talked about. The challenge is to build resilience individually but also ensure that the group acts supportively and increases its resilience.

Through this process authentic quality relationships are developed that acknowledge difference, anticipate needs, and manage the balance of being an individual – an individual in a role and a member of a practice. Realistic limitations can be acknowledged and opportunities explored.

"It is not the strongest of the species that survive, nor the most intelligent, but the one most responsive to change."

Quote attributed to Charles Darwin

References

Ballatt, J. and Campling, P. (2011). *Intelligent Kindness: Reforming the Culture of Healthcare*. London: RCPsych Publications.

Bion, W.R. (1961). *Experiences in Groups, and Other Papers*. London: Tavistock Publications.

Bion, W.R. (1984). *Second Thoughts: Selected Papers on Psychoanalysis*. London: Maresfield Reprints.

Devon, A. (2018). CBT versus the unconscious: Ignore countertransference at your peril. In: Valerio, P. (Ed.) *Introduction to Countertransference in Therapeutic Practice: A Myriad of Mirrors* (p.85). London: Routledge.

Feifel, H., Hanson, S., Jones, R., et al. (1967). Physicians consider death. *Proceedings of 75th Annual Convention of the American Psychological Association*. Washington, DC: American Psychological Association.

Garland, C. (2010). The Groups Manual. In: C. Garland, *The Groups Book: Psychoanalytic Group Therapy: Principles and Practice*. London: Karnac.

Gerada, C. (2016). Healing doctors through groups: creating time to reflect together. *British Journal of General Practice, 66* (651): 776–78.

Howe, A., Smajdor, A. and Stöckl, A. (2012). Towards an understanding of resilience and its relevance to medical training. *Medical Education, 46*: 349–56.

Iliffe, S. (2008). *From General Practice to Primary Care: The Industrialization of Family Medicine*. Oxford: Oxford University Press.

Johnson, W. (1991). Predisposition to emotional distress and psychiatric illness amongst doctors: the role of conscious and experiential factors. *British Journal of Medical Psychology, 64* (4): 317–29.

Leif, H. (1971). Personality characteristics of medical students. In R. Coombs and C. Vincent (Eds). *Psychosocial Aspects of Medical Training*. Springfield, IL: C.C. Thomas.

Malan, D. (1979). *Individual Psychotherapy and the Science of Psychodynamics*. London: Butterworth.

McCann, C.M., Beddow, E., McCormick, K., et al. (2013). Resilience in the health professions: a review of recent literature. *International Journal of Wellbeing, 3* (1): 60–81.

Menzies Lyth, I.E. (1960). A case-study in the functioning of social systems as a defence against anxiety: A report on a study of the nursing service of a general hospital. *Human Relations, 13* (2): 95–121.

Ogden, T.H. (1979). On projective identification. *The International Journal of Psychoanalysis, 60*: 357.

Rance, C.K. (1998). Organizations in the mind: the interaction of organizational and intrapsychic perspectives. In: S. Hardy, J. Carson and B. Thomas (Eds), *Occupational Stress – Personal and Professional Approaches* (pp.351–64). Cheltenham: Stanley Thorne.

Rogers, C. (1987). On putting it into words: the balance between projective identification and dialogue in the group. *Group Analysis, 20* (2): 99–107.

Rogers, C. (2013). Engaging with the median group. *Group Analysis, 46* (2): 183–95.

Rosen, D. (2014). *Vital Conversations: Improving Communication between Doctors and Patients*. New York: Columbia University Press.

Tillett, R. (2003). The patient within – psychopathology in the helping professions. *Advances in Psychiatric Treatment, 9*: 272–79.

Wilke, G. (2005). Beyond Balint: A group-analytic support model for traumatized doctors. *Group Analysis, 38* (2): 265–80.

Wilke, G. and Freeman, S. (2001). *How to be a Good Enough GP: Surviving and Thriving in the New Primary Care Organisations*. Abingdon: Radcliffe Medical Press.

Zinkin, L. (1983). Malignant mirroring. *Group Analysis, 16* (2): 113–26.

Chapter 7

Reflective practice groups – a hall of mirrors

Sue Einhorn

Introduction: Narcissus, Echo, and reflective practice

The loneliness of Narcissus, who drowns in his own reflection, and the loneliness of Echo, who has no self but merges in a bleak desire to be Narcissus and, so, loved by him, reminds us that relationship is reciprocal. As group analysts we may be stifled by a world seen only through our own eyes, or a world through the eyes of a person who I hope will know me better than I know myself, and so allow me to exist. Both positions are safer than the unknown in a dangerous world, where not knowing leaves people open to challenge or even accusations and blame when things go wrong. Working with people is not an exact science and so things do go wrong and many clinicians are preoccupied with covering their backs while working in highly stressful settings. However, training is fundamentally about helping to build enough confidence and trust in a clinician so that they feel able to work with integrity, which includes not knowing and being curious to learn.

This chapter is about the nature of reflective practice with examples from the use of reflective practice groups on our training at the Institute of Group Analysis.

The reflective practice framework

Some years ago, the Institute of Group Analysis (IGA) decided to introduce reflective practice groups for those enrolled in the second year of the diploma course in group analysis. The introductory year introduced students, from both organizational and clinical settings, to the basic ideas of group analysis. However, after this first year, people who wanted more but who did not wish to train as group psychotherapists could not take things further at the IGA, except through short courses and workshops. Training to become a therapist is not for everyone.

The second year of the course now offers a diploma in group analysis and a group practitioner status to all who complete it. The format of the course includes a seminar on group analytic theory followed by reflective practice groups of up to six, plus the 'conductor'. Each student is expected to bring a group that they are conducting. These are not supervision groups and are carefully structured so that the content of the seminars can be linked into the discussion of the groups being presented. In the ninety minutes of the reflective practice group (RPG), two students take thirty minutes each to make a presentation and discuss it with the RPG. The final twenty minutes is an allocated reflective space for us to think about how we have worked together that day.

Most of the students who progressed onto the RPG from the foundation year were hungry for more group experience. However difficult their foundation experiential group had been, those who continued often talked about the loneliness of their work situation and how important it was for them to be a group member. It often raised a wish for more personal work but also reminded them of the tantalizing nature of groups. The desire to share and be heard, while struggling with the fear of feeling shamed or humiliated as they revealed themselves, sometimes clashed with their wish to hear about other group members. The echo here was that these were the very dilemmas being faced by the members of the groups they were facilitating.

The emotional mind

The greatest challenge for many of us in working as counsellors, therapists, or group workers is learning how to think with the heart and feel with the mind. A capacity to reflect on what we are doing or hearing or seeing depends on translating our emotional responses into words. The opposite is also true, so that our ideas can be translated into useful connections with what is being emotionally experienced in the group. This is the challenge, the development of what I call 'an emotional mind'!

As clinicians or group conductors, what those we teach or those who come for help need from us is our minds. Whatever our intuition or capacity to recognize feelings in others and in ourselves, we need to be able to *feel with our minds*. Most theories could really be regarded as pegs on which we recover our minds and help us to think with our emotions. I look on many of our theories and techniques as pencil sharpening. To be able to feel with my mind or think emotionally in the service of my group members, I need ideas and words to translate what they are saying or feeling or projecting, so that my mind can engage as a separation between us. I need my mind to remain intact as a therapist or group conductor if I am to be of service to my groups.

To do this, our theories and techniques offer us particular ways of understanding the 'reflective space', but they should never impede the value of simply staying with not knowing. Our emotional minds may struggle hard to remain with such confusion, sometimes even with panic, but I believe that is the real value of a reflective space in groups. This is a shared, sometimes unknown, space where we wait for understanding to emerge, often through metaphors or dreams, but eventually, over time, in words.

Reflective practice

In this context, the reflective practice group is an opportunity for dialogue between different points of view. The space and time to want to understand each other is that reflective space. It is this time and space that our RPG members want, as there is usually very little time and opportunity to articulate their practice dilemmas with others who are simply interested in them as clinicians. All public sector agencies seem to be in crisis themselves, often mirroring the crises of both clinicians and those who come for help, which then influences how clinicians can talk about their work. It is the freedom to be away from the pressures of their agencies that enables the RPG members to talk openly about themselves in their work.

In a reflective practice environment, each clinician needs to understand that what they see is reflected through the lens of their own understanding, training, and life experience. In acknowledging that framework, the risk of drowning in their own reflection recedes, because there is the wish to extend their world through dialogue with others. There is a respect for what others have to say, but to be open to allude to their life experience as part of that understanding does mean creating an atmosphere of trust, collegial trust.

A reflective space such as this is not easy or straightforward. These are not therapy groups and yet they do require members to be able to acknowledge how their life experiences have influenced them to become such thoughtful clinicians. Perhaps it makes more sense to say that it is '*the use of self in the service of one's work*'. That is why I use the term, 'allude', because the experience is not explored, as in a therapy group, or connected to transference implications. It is personal information that a clinician feels confident to share, so that they can show what has influenced them but they also want colleagues to know about them, so that they can feel understood. It is the importance of a real connection between colleagues who understand and are comfortable with the notion that professional roles are carried out by real people!

Vignette 1

A woman reports that in her group one of the group members has become the focus of hostility. She feels helpless because group members are taking up positions that entrench their point of view. They cannot hear what the other is saying and keep declaring that this particular group member is not listening to them, as they continue to silence her. How can a reflective practice group bring some quiet into the noise of all this?

The RPG members then explore the feelings brought up in them, and one member talks about her experience of being silenced and feeling that what she has to say in our group will not be heard because we don't want to hear what she has to say! The woman who had brought the issue begins to feel very anxious, as though her issue would be hijacked by the RPG member. A parallel process.

As you can hear from this, the RPG members were working very hard to link their life experiences with her group problem, and, after much discussion about who should be heard, there was a realization that entrenched views are evidence of anxiety – the anxiety of not being understood. The need to feel understood resonated with all. It became clear that these entrenched views also needed to be heard before people could be open to new ideas.

The woman who brought this issue felt very helped because the RPG simply told her to be patient and wait for the group itself to feel heard, while also making it clear that they agreed that scapegoating is not on! In other words, the complexity of the problem was heard and understood in the RPG, and their respect for her capacities as a clinician gave her the confidence to feel helped.

Self supervision

Taking these ideas into account, I would like to suggest that in valuing time for the 'emotional mind', the capacity for self supervision develops more gently. The RPG can be internalized so that a lone practitioner can hear different aspects or levels of thought by relating back to the sorts of discussion that deepened understanding when in the RPG itself. Internalizing is a way of making other ideas and experiences one's own. It is a crucial capacity for practitioners, when opening themselves to challenging ideas. When we are listened to and feel heard, we can then hear ourselves more clearly and may also wish to articulate ourselves differently. Listening carefully to others within the context of the person we are getting to know can broaden our own understanding and even change how we think at times.

What is a reflective practice group?

We are seven people sitting in a circle in a building that is comfortable with groups. In our first meeting we discover first names and who has links from previous encounters but, importantly, we learn of the groups that each member is bringing to us:

- A community psychiatric nurse is bringing her Mentalization Based Therapy (MBT) group for day patients in a psychiatric hospital. It is a carefully structured group that she co-conducts.
- A young psychiatrist works in a closed forensic unit for 'lifers', where he plans to set up a second therapeutic group for men who have little chance of ever leaving the institution.
- A therapist working with substance abuse in a private hospital uses a variety of approaches, including rules about members' entitlement to be in her group if they lapse.
- A counsellor who is re-thinking his work is about to set up a young adults group in a local authority Child and Adolescent Mental Health Service (CAMHS).

A male youth worker who is thinking about further training is setting up a group in a drop-in centre for depressed mothers.

A senior manager in a hospital service wants to set up a group to support nurses on an eating disorder ward.

As we begin, it is clear that each person is steeped in the culture of their own practice and, although one or two may have regular supervision, most of the group rarely get to talk about their work beyond a monitoring activity. They are nervous and excited but, as with any new group, bring their beginning anxieties with them. In the final 20 minutes I ask how they have found this beginning and, after a nervous silence, members begin to talk about their confusions. In fact, they are really puzzled about how to use this last bit, this time set aside to process how we are working together and, as I know what it's all about, could I guide them? We seem to have to finish before this can be properly articulated and so the first cliffhanger happens.

The cliffhanger

My experience was that almost every session ended on a cliffhanger, as we moved from the task of understanding each other's group issues to attending to the process of the RPG. Gradually, reporting the progress of their groups moved into a link with the previous week's unfinished business.

Vignette 2

A woman began her presentation by saying that she was aware that she had spoken too much in the past few weeks but really felt she needed to be heard. She then began to get her notes out to present her group but one of the men said that he felt that he was the same and had been thinking about it when challenged for talking so much last week. Another group member commented that perhaps it was because they were both only children. They were delighted and interested and wanted to take it further. We agreed to return to this later in the session, as we now needed to hear about her clinical work. She said that being thought about in this way really helped her to be more open about the struggles she was having in her clinical work. However, we couldn't return to it that week.

We are trying to fit so much into these 90 minutes!

The entire Diploma Group attends the seminars, about 18 or 20 students, and they often come into the RPG filled with the dynamics of their larger group. We need some time to debrief, or at least to let me know if there is an important emotional issue before we start the presentations. The RPG is a space for all these influences to have a voice but how to balance the task with the process is always tricky. Fortunately, as the year progresses, it stops being primarily my task and is taken on by the RPG itself. However, I am there to demonstrate a group analytic perspective.

A lone voice

For most of the RPG members, their relief in being heard was palpable. Some had supervision at work and were not quite so isolated, but for many, the groups they were conducting may have been managed but the emotional impact and reflective thought needed was not even recognized as a need. It could even be said that the students themselves didn't know what they were missing until they brought their work to the RPG.

Vignette 3

A consultant clinical psychologist had been running a group for inpatients of a locked ward for ten years. As the senior staff member, he offered supervision to others but had little for himself. His commitment to these very damaged patients meant that the group meant a great deal to him as well as to them. Early in the RPG he was very taken with Foulkes' dictum that the conductor is a group member but a special group member (Foulkes, 1986).

In this particular RPG, others understood the demands of working with this client group and were impressed by his group. However, as we gained his trust and colleagues questioned why he was allowing other professionals to interrupt his group sessions, he gradually opened up to the notion of being 'a special group member'. To quote, he "has used this year to separate himself and become the special member he is". He is now able to present the group so that we can see him in it and the different members of the group as personalities in their own right. He is now a group conductor doing a professional piece of work, that means he can instruct others not to enter while the group is in progress. His compassion for his group members had led him to merge with their distress and feelings of being forgotten so that he did not value sufficiently what he had created for his patients on this locked ward.

He described himself as now "swimming in the same waters but with a different skin". In all the years of conducting this very difficult group, he had never been listened to so seriously and had not even known how much he had needed his experiences reflected back to him. His experience of being a 'lone voice' resonated deeply with others. This connection between the group members developed a growing trust. Foulkes' basic law of group dynamics (see below) describes how a well-functioning group enables enough trust, so that the individual can flourish within a nourishing group culture. This was how the member's lone voice helped in creating a matrix of trust in the RPG.

A group analytic perspective

In describing my understanding of a group analytic perspective (GAP), it is important to begin simply and acknowledge a commitment to groups and to the importance of respect for the individual in the group. The 'facilitator's' or 'conductor's' key function is to keep the group safe enough for members to engage in the difficult work of opening their work to the scrutiny of their colleagues.

A group analytic perspective understands that, from the very beginning, we are born relationship-seeking. We are born into a group and social context that creates who we are in interaction with what we bring into the world of ourselves. Who we are and who we become is constantly mirrored and reflected back to us and from us in an interaction between ourselves and the influences around us. However, as we grow older, we also need to develop some judgement about which relationships help us to grow and which inhibit us. Sometimes, of course, it is the same people or groups that do both!

A group analytic perspective is based on Foulkes' 'Basic Law of Group Dynamics', which states that, "collectively they (*the group members*) constitute the very norm, from which, individually, they deviate" (Foulkes, 1948).

This basic law then defines a well-functioning group as one in which there is a collective culture that values each member of the group being different and developing on their own journey, provided their work does not threaten the safety of the group. Paradoxically, it is the safety found in the group that enables members to develop the relationships that makes a group reflective.

Initially, it falls to the group conductor to work with group members in building a safe group. I think a safe group is where there is space to reflect on oneself and think about the other members. I have written about this before (Einhorn, 2010). It is a place where the difficult, often unsafe – because painful and shaming, relationships of the past are re-lived through the present relationships in the group, but this time they can be thought about and their meaning understood. For the group conductor, safety resides in the regularity of the group and sufficient confidence in her authority to help group members feel safe enough to manage conflict or attend to 'unspoken' themes. It is not the conductor's responsibility alone.

When I suggest that my task is to offer a group analytic perspective, then as the group conductor I am responsible for looking after the group boundaries until this becomes a task shared by the group. It is a democratic perspective, as the group analyst is regarded as a group member, but a 'special' group member whose task is to protect the group culture so that it remains safe if these rather unsafe feelings are to be part of the work of the group.

What, then, is a 'group analytic understanding' of a group?

Foulkes (1986) included in his theory four levels of communication that acknowledge the complexity of our lives. He did not leave the 'real world' at the consulting room door and so demands of us a capacity to remember the social context, while focusing on the group members' needs, both internal (psychological and emotional) and external. I do not see a separation between a person's psychological struggles, their family's social and emotional history, and the social dilemmas within which we all live. All these influences are present in every person and every group. As people work together in a group, they form a network of relationships, unique to their group, but interlaced by all these different levels. We call this the group 'matrix'.

The matrix of the RPGs is complex, because the theory seminars raise issues that will influence all the clinical presentations. The dynamics of the training community will also resonate in the RPG, sometimes loudly and sometimes quietly, but they are there. Who wants to continue training, who is getting the best essay marks, who are the 'difficult' students, etc? Palpably there are the social crises of the welfare state as well as the increasing desperation of those who come for help. How to choose what needs attention in the RPG is part of the group dynamic but is a constant open question.

In the RPGs, the Current Level is meeting at the IGA, which itself offers a context where groups are valued. The community of members brings the social context of each individual's background – class, gender, ethnicity, age etc. plus their agency work contexts.

Then there is the Transference Level of communication, where the group can represent the family, or past relationships with parents, siblings, or teachers. Members bring these relationships from the past into their expectations of how people will treat them or what they might need from people in the present. This is not always very conscious but it can help to understand when current feelings are triggered by past experiences, especially when the other person seems bewildered by a response!

Foulkes also included the psychoanalytic perspective, using bodily and mental images, where group members can experience themselves or others as what we call 'part objects'. For example, the group itself may take on a maternal function, such as a womb or breast. What is useful is how the body can express, for example, an anxiety that does not seem warranted in the moment. This is where the 'emotional mind' may well have to translate what has been triggered in the body.

Foulkes also included what he called the 'Primordial Level', which he thought of as a collective unconscious common to all human beings.

Perhaps the most useful concept for our RPGs is that of the 'social unconscious'. For group analysts, quoting Foulkes, "the social permeates to the core" (Foulkes [1948]1983). Because it permeates to the core, it is also part of our unconscious mental activity. The unconscious knows no time or place or separation between the social or the individual, and so, we are deeply influenced by ideas that we take for granted. We do not notice how some social norms become so deeply embedded that we do not even question them. We become aware of this when norms change e.g. the current discussion about whether biology and gender are fixed.

We need an awareness of the social unconscious to make us ready to understand things such as our resistance to difference, and that such resistances may well permeate us to the core.

Conclusion

A group analytic approach is taken in the RPGs and demonstrates that all groups, whether time-limited, drop-in, or open-ended, consist of members who need help to begin; courage to explore themselves; and the time and space to end. These RPGs are permeated with evaluations about the members' progress in understanding theory, participating in the groups, and also having essays marked.

However, all groups have to deal with an ongoing evaluation of how effectively they are working, as well as the importance of group members developing more judgement about who is helpful for them in their lives. We lived a parallel process as members' groups also resonated with these themes. The competitiveness of members in the groups and on the course was very much part of the matrix, and both helped some to challenge themselves while inhibiting others. It is a theme worthy of its own chapter.

This chapter began with Narcissus and Echo but has explored what turns a reflection into a thought. A reflection itself, mirrored back through water is distorted by what is being sought. Narcissus sought his beauty but, I have attempted to show, that the courage to see oneself through others' eyes, as an adult, can open the interaction to a different form of reflection. A reflective practice group offers a space where members can see themselves as clinicians through others' eyes. However, this only works well if each member is also prepared to say what they have understood and seen of the other. It takes courage to be seen and perhaps even more courage to express what you see in others. It would be easy to simply echo what has been heard. However, a key skill is learning how to express these views kindly and helpfully as part of offering challenges and understanding, so that colleagues experience the importance and interest of their clinical work for themselves and for each other.

References

Einhorn, S. (2010). Sleeping Beauty's kiss: The birth of the IGA training in St Petersburg, Russia. *Group Analysis, 43* (3), 268–81.

Foulkes, S.H. (1986). The conductor in action as a group analyst. In: *Group Analytic Psychotherapy – Method and Principles* (pp.107–108) London: Karnac.

Foulkes, S.H. (1948). A basic law of group dynamics. In: *Introduction to Group-analytic Psychotherapy*. In: *Foundations of group analysis for the 21st century.* (Ed.) J. Maratos (2015). NILGA/Karnac.

Foulkes, S.H. ([1948]1983) *Introduction to Group-Analytic Psychotherapy: studies in the social integration of individuals and groups.* London: Karnac.

Chapter 8

Getting comfortable with the uncomfortable

Reflective practice in anxious times

Ian Simpson

Facilitating reflective practice with staff teams in social care is always a challenging task. It has never been easy. The group dynamics are complex, particularly when there is a dissonance between the essential requirements for the clinical work and the underlying organizational priorities. Similarly, it can be difficult translating group analytic principles suitable for psychodynamic psychotherapy groups into organizational working settings (Bramley, 1990; Hesse, 2001).

In this chapter I would like to raise some basic questions about the implications of working with staff teams in these settings, for the participants, for the organizational structures in which they work, and for the facilitators doing the work. As facilitators we are often confronted by realities that we find hard to think about or process. Similarly, the implications for the facilitator are particularly challenging in terms of the ethical and political questions that can emerge. This is all the more relevant when social and healthcare systems are under tremendous additional pressure from austerity measures and management systems that foster unsafe and unhealthy working conditions that leave staff deeply insecure and struggling to survive and thrive.

Reflective practice is increasingly being acknowledged and valued as a significant means of improving the working lives of team members, individually and collectively. The Department of Health booklet, 'See, Think and Act' (2010) acknowledges the importance of the contextual setting and relational dynamics in workplaces, by highlighting the importance of relational security:

> Relational security is the knowledge and understanding staff have of a patient and of the environment; and the translation of that information into appropriate response and care.

It is good that this has been recognized as a major focus, as it ostensibly acknowledges the close connection between quality of care and the setting and organizational culture in which it takes place. Group analytic theory, focusing as it does upon contextual containment, inter-subjectivity and relational dynamics, is well placed to contribute to our understanding of the complexity of these processes.

The group analytic perspective

Group analytic theory emphasizes the importance of the cultural context and setting as we live our lives, and it highlights the essential interconnectedness and relational dynamics in human interaction as paramount in any comprehensive understanding of individual and social developments. It also illuminates how self-destructive reciprocal relational structures and ideas can lead to limiting internal and external horizons that distort how we see ourselves in relation to others and constrict and constrain our ability to adapt and change. Group analytic and other relational approaches also challenge the current widespread cultural notions that human life can only be understood in terms of empirical scientific enquiry or by neoliberal economic theory, which advocates individual advantage over social needs. Group analytic theory can influence and expand our understanding of how we function together individually and socially outside, as well as within, the boundaries of the clinical setting.

From a group analytic perspective, the reflective practice setting is a dynamic phenomenon that functions within its sociocultural context. In this sense, the reflective practice group is not only a dynamic entity in its own right. It is also a representation of the wider organization in which it operates, and it mirrors this in its interactions and reflections, constellating the explicit and implicit dynamics from within the community of which it is a part. It offers a space in which the interpersonal, systemic and institutional factors that help or hinder the establishment and maintenance of effective therapeutic relationships between staff and those they work with can be explored and worked through. Accordingly, the solutions to work-related difficulties must be appropriately located and sought in that contextual setting.

A fundamental group analytic principle holds that individual group and social contexts are interdependent. The aim is to consider the relationship between the individual, the team they work in, and their work setting as intrinsically and actively linked together through dialogue in meaningful interaction. This acknowledges and recognizes that the group members are the best people to sort out issues and difficulties that may arise. The power is located with them and should not be invested in facilitators, as if they held the solutions.

The role of the staff group consultant is to facilitate communication and dialogue in the group. If there are underlying tensions and strains within the team, these need to be brought to the surface and therefore enable the group to make sense of them. Staff tensions, rivalries and conflicts can inhibit the potential for developing good practice. When these are addressed in a collaborative, supportive environment, the members have the potential to develop the quality of their work through better understanding of interpersonal and institutional dynamics and how these can impact on everyone involved. Communication and active participation between members is encouraged and enhanced within a holding/containing, facilitative environment. A group analytic facilitator is aware that relational dynamics are context sensitive and that open and direct dialogue and communication in the interplay between group members and within the group context is what influences positive therapeutic outcomes and the potential for positive change.

Group analytic facilitation should concentrate on the group and its members doing the work. The group does the work for itself and the facilitator takes a less intrusive role, concentrating on holding and analysing manifest and latent processes, rather than interpreting or directing. However, interpretations and interventions identifying underlying processes are made when appropriate or considered helpful. The correct technique is to minimize excessive or inappropriate dependency upon the facilitator and accustom the group and its members to seek their own solutions to problems.

Settings

The contexts or settings in which we live and work are of primary importance for our sense of meaning, safety, security and continuity. Establishing a relatively safe enough and good enough setting is essential in social and health care work. Experience suggests if you get the context right then you optimize the treatment outcome and therapeutic potential (Simpson, 1995). A supportive setting must be created that is safe enough for us to begin to trust and take risks as the treatment or therapeutic process and attachment to clinicians and services goes through the different phases of illness to wellness. Also, we must have these conditions in place if we are to manage the inevitable distress when things do not go well. The setting has to feel physically as well as emotionally safe. When we are anxious and concerned about our physical or mental health, we are vulnerable and frightened. At these times, we need to feel held and contained (looked after) to enable us to stay with the difficult process we are going through. Good human relationships based on consistency and continuity, underpinned and informed by what John Ballatt and Penelope Campling have called 'Intelligent Kindness' (2012) is what is required at these times, not fragmented, transitory contact with different people or services. Compassion, continuity and relational safety and security are also important, when we consider the needs of the staff working in social care. The psychological and emotional distress generated by the work must be recognized and acknowledged as a priority.

We cannot ask staff to hold and contain the anxieties and distress of those in their care if they themselves do not feel held and contained, encouraged and supported by the organizations in which they work. If the basic underpinnings of the structure, the foundation upon which it stands or falls – the staff – are not seen as primary, if their welfare is not given priority, then this raises questions about the quality of the work undertaken and highlights the all too apparent dangers evident in the high levels of staff sickness, absence and distress that currently plague many teams in social and health care. The nature of the wider organizational culture is of the greatest importance in establishing the quality of care provided both for those in care and those providing that care.

The culture of care

There is a considerable body of evidence supporting the view of human beings and their well-being and effectiveness as being developmentally socially formed and located (Ormay, 2012; Gantt and Badenoch, 2013; Brown and Zinkin, 1994; Pines, 2002; Stern, 2000; Trevarthen, 2017; Trevarthen and Aitken, 2001; Kerr, 2009; Dalal, 1998, 2016). This social and relational view of human beings emphasizes our essential interconnectedness. This is an open-ended, emergent phenomenon that requires a safe-enough containing context to thrive, integrating and promoting healthy biological and social processes. The necessary conditions for the establishment of any social or healthcare system should be based upon this understanding of human relationships. The model should allow for flexibility and creativity when considering working relationships and organizational dynamics, recognizing that the safe containment and holding of clinical staff and those they care for is a group/social phenomenon, embedded in our interrelatedness and connectedness. This is important, because staff teams are also intrinsically linked and connected into their wider cultural, political and economic organizational structures, influencing professional practice and expectations. Working models should be informed by a set of principles acknowledging this contextual understanding, with reflective spaces for staff put in place that facilitate dialogue and the working through of issues and difficulties.

Regrettably, this way of thinking is largely disregarded by the proponents of the neo-liberal/managed care model (New Public Management) currently being imposed upon our social and healthcare systems. The cultural paradigm lying behind this view is rooted in the belief that unfettered free enterprise, elevating self-interest over social needs and well-being will optimally organize every facet of society, including economic and social life. This is an economic ideology that has utilized empirical scientific principles that conclude that the nature of reality can be understood by behavioural and materialistic theories discoverable by evidence based research, like randomized control trials. Of course, evidence based approaches are not bad *per se*, it is rather how the 'evidence' is construed and how alternative approaches or models are dismissively excluded that is problematic. The neoliberal model is underpinned by a series of dogmas that fuel the fantasy of discovering a perfect, all-encompassing understanding of how we function together, over-objectifying and reducing rather than valuing what is human (Simpson, 2016; Dalal, 2017a).

The context of care

Someone presenting with a mental health problem should not be seen as only bringing a separate individual problem. Their problem represents only one aspect of an intricate and complex social/group phenomenon. Individual disturbances should be located in all the aspects of a person's life and in their network of interpersonal relationships. We cannot conceptualize or consider individuals as if they were in isolation from the formative, social and cultural context in which they live and work. In the attempt to maintain relational security and organizational containment, the business/performance model, in my view, actively deconstructs these principles and is, in fact, self-destructive and traumatizing for both staff and those they work with, and therefore it is an unethical and unacceptable basis for social care. This is the underlying contradiction that permeates our current social and healthcare systems and creates such a problematic division between the needs of staff and those they care for, and the structure in which they are compelled to work.

As a basis for social care systems, these principles foster a cultural context where health and well-being becomes commodified and the human relational elements that are intrinsic to care become devalued. We get a health care ethos, which, at its worst, turns patients into demanding and potentially litigious consumers, and clinicians into alienated production-line workers.

This model, as it attempts to reduce anxiety and risk, actually achieves the opposite and creates conditions that perversely cause trauma, resentment and a reactive defensiveness that inhibit the very thing it purports to deliver (Hoggett, 2010; Long, 2009). Tasks are organized with other aims in mind and this can create a climate that distances clinicians from each other and from personal contact with those in their care. An oppressive bureaucracy is created that reframes need in the context of what is available or expedient, rather than looking at what is responsive and empathic. The concentration upon prohibitive and time-consuming processes, which reduce face-to-face clinical time and increase paranoid anxieties around blame and censure, closes down the possibility of creative, professional solutions between managers, clinicians, and those in their care. As clinical staff struggle with the day-to-day anxieties of managing and containing patient distress and disturbance, they also end up resentful and disaffected, feeling uncontained or unsupported by the wider organizational structure. Those being cared for also become the victims of this approach as treatment models are devalued because they are considered uneconomic or wasteful. Models of short-term work are valued above longer-term ones, irrespective of the consequences for those with complex and difficult presentations.

Layard's (2006) vision of improving access to psychological treatments is commendable. However, in practice, this has been expropriated by those advocating one particular clinical model. The predominance of cognitive behavioural therapy as the panacea for mental distress sustains the convenient fantasy that society's ills can be contained within one limited model that views them as simple technical problems or medical illnesses, as if they were individual problems divorced or separate from the social, culture, and context within which they occur (Rizq, 2014, Ryle and Kerr, 2002, Simpson, 2016).

Discursive and imagined functional spaces

Society is based on shared meanings and practices, which constitute culture. It is linked by relationships that are set by people in order to live and work together. It is formed by shared, enfolding and unfolding meaningful interaction. This takes place in the lived context of daily relationships and in the search for personally and socially significant meaning with others. Our families, friendship networks, and our working relationships constitute our evolving sense of self and selves. This process always happens within the context of the small, medium and large groups in which we live and work. It makes sense to think about ourselves in dynamic, group terms, and for us to explore interpersonal relations in that forum.

Within a wider, commonly identified, national culture, there are many diffuse and differentiated cultures, forming, re-forming, enfolding and unfolding over time. These represent a variety of belief systems all interlinked and interrelated. Similarly, an organization does not exist as an entity, outside of ourselves. It is a dynamic, creative and evolving project that emerges in the relationship between the people who form it and are formed by it in lived experience as we continually create discursive worlds and imagined spaces to establish order in our understanding and perception of social and individual meaning (Weegman, 2014, pp.57–80, 139–44). These organizing principles help create social cohesion, giving us a sense of living within safe enough containing contextual structures. However, the consequences of this can be good or bad, ordered or disordered, depending upon the particular individual and social perspectives in any given cultural or historical situation. These constantly changing spaces are adaptive to setting, cultural conditions, and to external and internal events. They are not false or illusory, but are essential as significant and meaningful good enough working hypotheses, enabling us to function individually and socially.

Social and healthcare settings

When this is translated into social and healthcare work settings, it is important to distinguish between settings that are ordered and effectively functional and those that become disordered, dysfunctional, and intrinsically perverse. Although an organization ostensibly has a common objective, the discursive world of those who manage can be very different from that of those who undertake the clinical work. When anxiety permeates an overburdened, overstretched service, the disparity between managerial and clinical anxiety can become polarized. The discord generated can result in staff feeling devalued, as if their clinical concerns are of secondary importance, while managers justify their position by highlighting the need for efficiencies and effectiveness through cost improvement plans or top–down control measures. In these circumstances, management proposals can feel censorious, undermining, or punitive, including to many managers who work in these contexts. This invariably creates a disordered discursive world that is essentially dysfunctional, distressing, and perverse, in the sense that the culture can create conditions diametrically opposed to that which it is supposed to accomplish (Rizq, 2014). Rizq (2016) has also highlighted how when anxiety is unbearable, the powerful compulsion to expel or eject the disavowed, toxic aspects within us by abjection can manifest itself in social care organizational dynamics. This creates circumstances where contextual settings can become iatrogenic and cause further difficulty and distress. Such a situation is extremely uncomfortable to manage, both for workers and for managers. In essence, it requires us to either resort to defensive, self-protective denial, world-weary cynicism and passivity or we confront the awful reality and manage and bear the discomfort and distress as best we can.

Ethical and political issues

Political and ethical questions are inevitably raised when we facilitate groups with teams obliged to operate in these patently unsafe conditions. This raises the wider boundary issue of whether we should or should not act if we clearly see this happening. Should we do more than facilitate? Should we abandon our professionally neutral stance and address this at another level in the organization? Should we actively encourage the staff to do something about it themselves or can we trust the reflective process to find solutions? These are not questions that I personally find easy to address. They raise important issues about the role of the reflective practice facilitator, particularly around boundaries and their areas of remit. Difficult ethical and political issues arise around whether or not to try to influence the wider organizational structure if we consider that unsafe or harmful practice is taking place. Also, what is the best way to do this if we decide to follow that course? Should we even be considering such a course? This can be a risky business where confidentiality and professional boundaries have to be respected.

I know from experience that if I go outside the boundaries and approach managers further up the hierarchy, that this only works if they are supportive of the process and appreciative of the merits of reflective practice and are prepared to handle any issues that I identify with sensitivity and common sense. In other circumstances I know that to attempt such a move would be counterproductive, resulting in either a defensive reaction or overcontrolling punitive responses directed towards staff in the team I am working with. Back channels can be useful, but they should be treated with caution. These boundary issues are with us anyway, even when conditions of practice are more favourable and accommodating. However, when working conditions are destabilized and impoverished by austerity measures, what should we do? Do we leave things as they are and allow staff to maintain the pretence that they are doing something professionally fulfilling, enabling them to keep turning a blind eye to the awful reality of their working lives, or should we encourage them to take action against the debilitating structure in which they are forced to participate? There is an ethical and political dimension here that we cannot ignore. As facilitators, knowing this, should we become advocates rather than facilitators and say what we really think? And if so, where and how should we say it? Or should we trust that the reflective process itself will enable staff to find a way through?

Organizational anxiety

The genesis of organizational anxiety, like individual anxiety, is based upon the fear of things going out of control, of fragmentation and collapse. Similarly, organizational change is, by its very nature, anxiety provoking. Repetitive organizational change provokes massive anxieties each time it is implemented. Anyone who works in the NHS knows this is often management's response to solving service problems. Quite some time ago Isabel Menzies Lyth showed the inherent fallacy of this but little attention has subsequently been paid to these insights and they have largely been disregarded (Menzies Lyth, 1960). As mistakes and problems occur in services and changes and new developments arise to correct them, this generates occupational and personal anxiety. As Hopper and colleagues (2012) show, this will invariably manifest itself as traumatic, particularly if the underlying structures are failing or struggling because of limited resources or with confused, misguided, or inappropriate attempts to stabilize things.

In social care services, the basic issue is the tension between capacity and demand, especially in times of reduced resources. It is also about managing or not managing unrealistic expectations, including the management of risk in services and the impossible roles they are expected to fulfil in dysfunctional work settings. In these situations, the emotional and psychological effects of the work upon clinical staff are often unacknowledged and denied. When capacity is reduced, demand increases, as waiting lists get longer and services become stretched. This can lead to day-to-day professional and ethical dilemmas about how to exercise a realistic and proper duty of care. This will normally manifest itself within internal team dynamics in reflective practice settings emerging in the form of rivalry, envy and resentment between those practising different clinical treatment modalities or job functions, when certain treatment modalities may be prioritized over others.

Similarly, when resources are reduced, collective frustration and rage can emerge. If resources are being cut, the inevitable level of anxiety this generates throughout an organization increases and can create a volatile situation. A defensive, blame culture may also mean staff get persecuted for limitations, failings and mistakes. In these circumstances, people feel pressurized, resentful and embittered, and incidents and the possibility of abusive or divisive responses increase. The inability to enable and maintain appropriate commitment, compassion and humanity by overstretched and disillusioned staff can create potentially dangerous situations.

When financial cuts are implemented in the name of efficiency or effectiveness and staff teams are expected to maintain the same work levels with reduced resources, this is experienced as an imposition from above with little apparent concern for or understanding of what is actually required to address the pressures of managing the clinical work. Anxiety increases if we are asked or required to do something we are unable to do because the conditions and the context of the working environment conspire to thwart us in the task. While individual clinicians struggle with the effects and consequences of change, managers have to implement policies and priorities determined and directed from above. They, too, are located in their own particular world of meaning and significance and they are often put in an intolerable situation. They are concerned about their personal and professional need to be approved and valued by peers and their own management. This draws attention to the likelihood of a basic and structural misunderstanding about how to contain and manage anxiety, depending upon the position from which it is viewed. The overarching organizational aim may be to create and maintain a viable, efficient and effective service. However, in a context of austerity, management priorities are more than likely to diverge from those of clinicians on the frontline.

The reflective space

The value of establishing a reflective practice space is well documented and the benefits are manifold (Simpson, 2010; Carson and Dennison, 2008; Thorndycraft and McCabe, 2008; Hesse, 2001; Bramley, 1990; Rifkind, 1995; Hartley and Kennard, 2009). It offers a space for staff to share their experiences together as members of a team and it can help team members recognize and acknowledge the underlying forces and processes that may be at work. The work is by the team, for the team. It should provide a facilitated space for creative dialogue to support and challenge individual and group thoughts and feelings about the working environment, the wider organizational context, and the nature of work undertaken by the team. This can mitigate isolation, defensiveness and a sense of helplessness. Similarly, a shared understanding of the commonality of pain and trauma can alleviate distress and lead to positive action, combating the sense of powerlessness often engendered by the nature of the work undertaken. Arguably, in times of depleted resources and the overwhelming pressures and anxieties that accompany this, a space to reflect and think about what this means is even more essential for staff welfare. This principle applies not just to frontline clinical teams but should be put in place throughout organizations up to the highest levels of management.

Most staff teams operate within a hierarchical structure with clear differences in status, responsibilities and priorities. Managers and staff are both 'victims and supporters' of the organization in which they work. They can be both powerful and powerless at times. For team members, the tension of being sandwiched between the clinical work with very damaged and disturbed patients and the demands from management can often lead to resistance or inappropriate defensive responses as attempts to reconcile these demands are made (Scanlon and Adlam, 2012, Hinshelwood, 1994). Similarly, managers may be pressurized by those above them who, for whatever reason, do not understand or appreciate the practical difficulties involved in implementing new policies and protocols with clinical staff, and they may be required to do things they are not comfortable with. None of us are immune from the distress and anxiety generated when things go wrong, and managers, just like clinicians, need support and containment as well.

Managers themselves will often report they feel traumatized by organizational dynamics (Hopper, 2012). In reflective practice the differences of responsibility and status implicit within a hierarchical structure should be acknowledged and worked with.

An essential aspect for generating a healthier dialogue is enabled when managers and clinical staff are prepared to share the reflective practice space. Unfortunately, in my experience, this is all too rare and is often resisted, primarily by managers or senior staff who may wish to preserve an understandable but misguided professional distance. This is a sensitive area where issues of authority and status can be keenly felt, and it is not always easy for managers to place themselves in situations where they or those above them may be challenged or criticized. They may also be fearful of showing their own vulnerability or of expressing views in opposition to those being imposed from above. Similarly, team members may be reluctant to share a reflective space with managers fearful about what may emerge in terms of their own safety. This is all too prevalent in the current climate of disciplinary action, referral to registering bodies, other punishments and sanctions and fear of loss of employment.

Nevertheless, a willingness to share a space for reflection can provide the opportunity for the different tasks and priorities to be expressed, mediated and negotiated. A group analytic understanding of the relationship between similarity and difference is helpful here. Managers and clinicians may have different perspectives but they share a commonality of anxiety and distress when working conditions are difficult. This may take different forms as it manifests itself and is experienced from particular positions, but if the commonality can be expressed, shared and understood, the potential for resonance, as opposed to dissonance, can develop between the participants. Each group can, hopefully, begin to understand and empathize with the other as their commonality of experience is shared and their differences are recognized and acknowledged.

Managerial and clinical expectations

Managers and team leaders will often see the reflective practice sessions as spaces to help staff improve performance, morale and generally create a happier, more productive and efficient team. While we may be in agreement about those aims, a problem emerges when the working reality is compromised, or it is one in which it is extremely difficult to carry out the required clinical tasks, practically or professionally. Requests may come from managers whose underlying motivation is often a reflection of their difficulties managing their team and will therefore look for external help to compensate for management deficiencies. An outside facilitator is not there to compensate for inadequate or poor line management. Managers in these circumstances may also hope that the reflective practice facilitator can help staff maintain the illusion that conditions are viable when they patently are not, or that they can somehow miraculously reinvigorate and motivate demoralized and disillusioned teams in the hope that the team will make the best of things – in effect, turning a blind eye to what is essentially a difficult and desperate situation in terms of clinical integrity or viable working conditions.

The divergence of perspective between clinical and management aims and objectives is also reflected in the different ways reflective practice can be viewed. Managers, for instance, can see reflective practice from a very different standpoint than that of clinicians or outside facilitators. I remember one rather extreme example of this difference in priorities and positions when some years ago, I was meeting with the head of an NHS trust and the trust head of HR, trying to get reflective practice groups established throughout the trust teams. At one point I emphasized the importance of reflective practice in empowering staff. The HR head looked askance at me and retorted, "Oh no! It's taken twenty years for us to get rid of the unions and now you want to empower staff!" In another more recent instance, one of my supervisees told me that the managers of the team she was facilitating issued the following pronouncement in the form of a reflective practice group contract that they were required to sign:

> I understand that issues I have with my workload, working environment or my relationship with other team members and managers are not appropriate to bring to the RP Group.

Constraints like this highlight what Chris Argyris (1980) calls the 'undiscussable', when organizations in times of difficulty are unable to face risky or threatening issues, particularly when those issues question underlying organizational assumptions and policies. In this way, the organization colludes in maintaining and reinforcing the problems. At times like these, the facilitator is left in an extremely tricky situation. We could go outside the boundaries of the group and try to convince the managers that reflective practice is limited and inhibited in these circumstances, hoping they will see sense and change their position. If we do so, we will not always be thanked for exposing what is, in effect, a wider organizational dysfunction, and we are in danger of becoming a 'subversive' rather than a 'saviour'. In cases like these, the wider organizational issue has to be tackled, but an external reflective practice facilitator may not have the power to influence management in that way. Alternatively, if we accept the mandate outlined above, the most we can realistically offer is case discussion or case supervision groups. Even then, teams will invariably end up talking about all the things they have been told not to, but that puts the facilitator in a secretive, collusive relationship with them, if they allow this to take place. Again we are faced with problematic ethical and boundary issues.

Reflective practice in anxious times

When conditions are particularly severe, reflective practice groups are extremely uncomfortable and hard to bear for all concerned, including the staff group facilitator. In these conditions, staff groups can be very resistant and reluctant to participate. Anyone who has tried to organize and facilitate reflective spaces in most current social care settings will know how hard it is to maintain regular attendance and will be well versed in the many and various excuses used to avoid attending. It is commonplace in reflective practice work to have to cope with a 'virtual' group.[1] This again presents another example of having to hold and contain the discomfort and anxiety of dealing with what can feel like a less than satisfactory set of circumstances.

There is also an understandable self-preserving desire to avoid obviously painful or recriminating experiences. We are all capable of living in denial, maintaining the deception that our work environment is OK, when it is not. The discomfort and distress that emerges from the cognitive dissonance created, when our beliefs and intentions do not match the practical realities, is very hard to bear. The practicalities and pressure to pay the rent or mortgage or look after our families can hold us in untenable situations. Also, we all need to feel that the work we do is personally meaningful and significant, and hold on to a sense of professional integrity, even under extreme conditions, and we all need to get through the day reasonably intact, difficult as that may be at times. I am constantly struck by the patience, resilience and forbearance exhibited by staff who continue to try to give their best while suffering under the most extreme conditions.

As facilitators, irrespective of our chosen theoretical model, we need to accept that, individually and collectively, team members will be struggling with the tension generated in uncomfortable spaces, and we must position ourselves accordingly. For instance, if a team is feeling helpless and powerless, this can encourage a rescue fantasy with a powerful and unrealistic projection on to the facilitator. At times like these, we must resist any urge towards 'therapist omnipotence', imagining that we can intervene and effect radical change.

Recognizing that we cannot or should not expect to exert unilateral power and control over any complex dynamic group culture, we can, however, act through the power and control we actually do have in our special role as facilitator. Facilitation is the key word here. Although the term necessarily implies some form of leadership, we should offer leadership that enhances rather than shuts down interactive group dialogue. The challenge is to gauge when or how we should or should not intervene, acknowledging that our most important function is to hold the space and the boundaries of the space. Using our understanding of group dynamics in these settings, we can affect and enhance the nature of interpersonal communication by choosing when to intervene. We should be sensitive and understanding when defensive measures are adopted and, at times, suspend our desire to offer interpretation or to 'open things up' or 'shut them down'. Although we may empathize and acknowledge how difficult it is, we should resist the temptation to 'do the work' for the team. If we can hold the group within the area 'between' the powerful desire to act or interpret and the pervasive sense of helplessness that we may feel, then possibilities for the expression of latent material are opened up.

The notion of 'suspension' or not saying what we are thinking or feeling as a means of seeing or sensing something without explicitly stating it involves trust in the reflective process and the therapeutic potential implicit in the context created by the reflective space (Bohm, 1996). We need to trust that the 'safe enough' continuity and boundaries of the context will enable material that is not immediately openly expressed or understood, hopefully, to manifest itself at some point. We need to have faith that the implicit will become explicit. I have often been surprised and intrigued when I feel that I need to make an intervention or interpretation in a group when, if I remain silent, the issue will emerge in the group spontaneously. We need to trust in the group process, as uncomfortable and frustrating as this may be at times, and we need to hold the space as best we can, knowing that the discomfort generated in us is appropriate and normal in the circumstances.

In bearing the 'uncomfortability' inherent in many of the settings in which we work, particularly if we are faced with the distressing reality in the disordered, discursive worlds described above, we need to consider the implications of the emergent nature of these situations. If we accept that these are open-ended processes, we are obliged to accept that this open-endedness necessarily creates uncertainty and apprehensiveness and faces us with the unknown and all the fears that this brings forth. We are relationally interconnected with the staff group members in the lived experience of our interaction with them. We may be in a special position, but we are still in it with them. We may struggle with the urge to come up with a rescuing solution or make it easier, and we will often feel we have failed them. Before we can enable those we work with to become comfortable with the uncomfortable, we must manage our own 'uncomfortability'. There is no easy, definitive way to do this, but I would argue that it becomes easier if we accept that it is not easy or determinable. The uncomfortable can be borne and managed better if we embrace the notion of 'radical uncertainty' (Dalal, 2017b, Tubert-Oklander 2017, Doron, 2017). This involves an acceptance that we are participating in an emergent, creative process that we must engage with, not knowing what will come but trusting that it can be endured and managed. As Farhad Dalal puts it:

> It is in this place of deep uncertainty, that I require commitment. And what I am committing to is my sense of things in the moment, my thoughts, emotions and experiences as they arise in me, committing to the gestures and responses that are being called out of me. I am trying to be true in the moment, in relation to the person or persons I am sitting with, and with whatever is taking place between us in that moment.
>
> (Dalal, 2017b)

This encourages me when I am overtaken by doubts and fears. I must hold my position with the group, trusting that my own feelings of distress and pain can be borne and survived with theirs. If I use my experience and understanding of the contextual setting – uncomfortable as that may be – I can hold the group process together with the team in a creative tension acknowledging the difficulty but not succumbing to it. To quote Dalal again:

The situation is one of paradoxical tension, a tension that cannot be, and ought not to be resolved. I try to immerse myself in the moment and trust that I will be able to manage to stay true in the turbulence that is bound to follow.

(Dalal, 2017b)

Importantly, if we are able to bear the 'uncomfortability' together in this way, it does not necessarily imply that we are left only struggling to manage pain and distress. On the contrary, it can open up (enfold/unfold) a potential space for creative positive action when things are not defensively shut down, and new possibilities are opened up, and teams can empower themselves. If difficulties can be borne, something positive can be born. Although we may feel it is alright to recognize and acknowledge the awfulness of the work setting, this does not mean that the team are powerless or helpless. They can find ways to creatively support each other, take positive action, and survive and thrive even in the hardest of times.

Note

1 The notion of a 'virtual' group can be helpful when working with a team where some members are regularly absent from sessions. For myriad reasons, it is extremely rare to get a whole team at sessions. Practical issues, like shift patterns, irregularity of consultant or manager visits, can sabotage the ideal of full team membership reflective practice groups, and it is not always possible to maintain continuity of membership or inclusion of all relevant staff members in all meetings. Members are on 'more important' work, the medical consultant does not attend, the administration or reception staff do not think it is appropriate, the night shift can't be there, and so on. In reality, we are often only working with the 'virtual' group. But this does not mean that effective or important work cannot be done. On the contrary, in the 'virtual' context, the team can be 'held and contained' and 'held in mind' without everyone being present at any given time, as the regularity and continuity of the reflective space is maintained (Simpson, 2010).

References

Argyris, C. (1980). Making the undiscussable and its undiscussability discussable. *Public Administration Review, 40*: 205–13.

Ballatt, J. and Campling, P. (2012). *Intelligent Kindness: Reforming the Culture of Healthcare.* London: RCPsych Publications.

Bohm, D. (1996). *On Dialogue* (pp.83–95). London: Routledge.

Bramley, W. (1990) Staff sensitivity groups: a conductor's field of experiences. *Group Analysis, 23* (3): 301–16.

Brown, D. and Zinkin, L. (1994). *The Psyche and the Social World: Developments in Group Analytic Theory.* London: Routledge.

Carson, J. and Dennison, P. (2008). The role of groupwork in tackling organisational burnout: two contrasting perspectives. *Groupwork, 18* (2): 18–25.

Dalal, F. (1998). *Taking the Group Seriously: Towards a Post-Foulkesian Group Analytic Theory.* London: Jessica Kingsley.

Dalal, F. (2016). The individual and the group: The twin tyrannies of internalism and individualism. *Transactional Analysis Journal, 46* (2): 88–100.

Dalal, F. (2017a). Group analysis in the time of austerity: neo-liberalism, managerialism and evidence-based research. *Group Analysis, 50* (1): 35–56.

Dalal, F. (2017b). The analytic and the relational: inquiring into practice. *Group Analysis, 50* (2): 171–89.

Doron, Y. (2017). Radical uncertainty in action: a response to Dalal's 'The Analytic and the Relational'. *Group Analysis, 50* (2): 255–63.

Department of Health Booklet (2010). *See Think Act: Your Guide to Relational Security.* Produced by COI for Department of Health.

Gantt, S.P. and Badenoch, B. (Eds) (2013) *The Interpersonal Neurobiology of Group Psychotherapy and Group Process.* London: Karnac.

Hartley, P. and Kennard, D. (Eds) (2009). *Staff Support Groups in the Helping Professions: Principles, Practice and Pitfalls.* London: Routledge.

Hesse, N. (2001). The function and value of staff groups on a psychiatric ward. *Psychoanalytic Psychotherapy, 15:* 121–30.

Hinshelwood, R.D. (1994). The relevance of psychotherapy. *Psychoanalytic Psychotherapy, 8* (3).

Hoggett, P. (2010). Government and the perverse social defence. *British Journal of Psychotherapy, 26:* 202–12.

Holmes. J. (2002). Acute wards: problems and solutions – creating a psychotherapeutic culture in acute psychiatric wards. *Psychiatric Bulletin, 26:* 383–85.

Hopper, E. (Ed.), (2012). *Trauma and Organisations.* London: Karnac Books.

Kerr, I. (2009). Addressing the Socially-Constituted Self Through a Common Language for Mental Health and Social Service: A Cognitive–Analytic Perspective. In: J. Forbes and C. Watson (Eds), *Confluences of Identity, Knowledge and Practice: Building Interprofessional Social Capital.* ESCR Seminar Proceedings (4), Research Paper, 20: Aberdeen: University of Aberdeen: 21–38.

Layard, R. (2006). The Depression Report: A New Deal for Depression and Anxiety Disorders. London: LSE.

Long, S. (2009). Greed. *Psychodynamic Practice, 15:* 245–59.

Menzies Lyth, I. (1960). A case-study in the functioning of social systems as a defence against anxiety: A report on a study of the nursing service of a general hospital. *Human Relations, 13* (2): 95–121.

Ormay, A.P. (2012). *The Social Nature of Persons: One Person Is No Person.* London: Karnac.

Pines, M. (2002). The coherency of group analysis. *Group Analysis, 35* (1): 13–26.

Rifkind, G. (1995). Containing the containers: the staff consultation group. *Group Analysis, 28:* 209–22.

Rizq, R. (2014). Perverting the course of therapy: the fetishisation of governance in public sector mental health services. *Psychoanalytic Psychotherapy, 28* (3): 249–67.

Rizq, R. (2016). States of abjection in managed care. In: J. Lees (Ed.), *The Future of Psychological Therapy* (pp.69–83). London: Routledge.

Ryle, A. and Kerr, I.B. (2002) *Introducing Cognitive Analytic Therapy: Principles and Practice.* Wiley.

Scanlon, C. and Adlam, J. (2012). On the (dis)stressing effects of working in (dis)stressed homelessness organisations. *Journal of Housing Care, Care and Support (special edition on Psychologically Informed Environments), 15* (2): 74–82.

Simpson, I. (1995). Group therapy within the NHS: We all know about 'Good Enough' but is it 'Safe Enough'? *Group Analysis, 28:* 223–35.

Simpson, I. (2010) Containing the uncontainable: A role for staff support groups. In: J. Radcliffe, K. Hajek, J. Carson and O. Manor (Eds), *Psychological Groupwork with Acute Psychiatric Inpatients*. London: Whiting & Birch.

Simpson. I. (2016). Containing Anxiety in Social Care Systems and Neo-Liberal Management Dogma: In: J. Lees (Ed.) *The Future of Psychological Therapy* (pp.51–68). London: Routledge.

Stern, D. (2000). *The Interpersonal World of the Infant: A view from Psychoanalysis and Developmental Psychology* (2nd edn). New York: Basic Books.

Thorndycraft, B. and McCabe, J. (2008). The challenge of working with staff groups in the caring professions: The importance of the 'Team Development and Reflective Practice Group'. *British Journal of Psychotherapy, 24* (2): 167–83.

Trevarthen, C. and Aitken, K.J. (2001). Infant intersubjectivity: research, theory and clinical applications. *Journal of Child Psychology and Psychiatry, 42*: 3–48.

Trevarthen, C. (2017). The affectionate, intersubjective intelligence of the infant and its innate motives for relational mental health. *International Journal of Cognitive Analytic Therapy and Relational Mental Health, 1*: 11–52.

Tubert-Oklander. J. (2017). Between imagination and rigour: A response to Farhad Dalal article 'The Analytic and the Relational: Inquiry into Practice'. *Group Analysis, 50* (2): 238–54.

Weegman. M. (2014*). The World Within the Group: Developing Theory for Group Analysis*. London: Karnac.

Chapter 9

Resistance to reflective practice – an anti-group perspective

Morris Nitsun

Introduction

Reflective practice in organizations usually starts with the best of intentions. There may be enthusiasm in the team and hopes in the consultant for a fruitful collaboration. However, the initiative, not unusually, runs into difficulty and the outcome is often less than satisfactory. The work group falters and fragments, attendance at meetings is sporadic and dwindles over time, and both the team and the facilitator end up frustrated and demoralized. This chapter argues that resistance to reflective practice is a powerful dynamic that needs to be recognized and addressed in its own right. The resistance emanates on the one hand from the threat of organizational rupture, and on the other, the threat of participation in an open group with colleagues. Resistance to the challenge of regularly attending a group, dealing with interpersonal tensions in the group, and the invitation to openness and sharing complex and difficult feelings, against a background of organizational dysfunction, undermine the potential for reflective practice. Using his concept of the 'anti-group', the author explores the group-related aspects of resistance to reflective practice and how this may be understood and worked with creatively.

A vein of pessimism has crept into the literature on reflective practice in organizations. A special edition of the Newsletter of The Group-Analytic Society (Group Analytic Contexts, 2017: 75), focuses on the theme of reflective practice, written mainly from the perspective of group facilitators and consultants. While generally agreeing on the relevance and importance of reflective practice in health services and other organizations, several writers convey a sense of despair about the work. The oppressive atmosphere of organizations in the contemporary ethos appears to undermine the aim of promoting awareness and understanding in a reflective, containing space. Organizations are often described as traumatized by relentless restructuring, the bleeding of resources, and at the same time the pressure to provide more and more services (Nitsun, 2015a). Also highlighted are the conditions of great uncertainty under which staff work, with threatened closure of services and staff redundancy a common preoccupation. Some writers even question the ethical basis of offering support in such an embattled environment (e.g., Simpson, 2017).

I agree with these concerns and have myself in a previous managerial capacity witnessed the destructive impact of political manoeuvring and economic stress on organizations, sometimes wondering how staff and services survive at all in these circumstances (Nitsun, 2015a). While unequivocally recognizing these stresses, I consider that the process of reflective practice is obscured by the anxiety about everything happening outside the group, both in the wider organization and the environment at large, probably because the tensions and stresses are so great. But this may be at the expense of looking at what happens in the actual group process. Resistance to reflective practice, which appears to be widespread in organizational environments, is seldom explored in any depth. Why is it so difficult for intelligent, mostly well-intentioned people to come together in a spirit of shared understanding of the difficulties they all experience in one form or another? Why is attendance at the reflective practice group often so grudging and inconsistent? Why, when the process is meant to help and support staff do they seem so sceptical, even averse? Very few papers address the specifically *group* aspects of the process. What is it about reflective practice groups, or some of them at least, that makes them so difficult? Why do they quite often fail?

Reflective practice groups vary in composition. They could be uni- or multi-professional: of different levels of seniority; clinically or managerially focused, or both. They vary in structure and duration from one-off meetings to long-term commitments. Their aims also diverge – from seeking solutions to immediate problems to deeper exploration of roles and interpersonal tensions. These differences naturally influence the dynamics of the groups and how they function. But what they share in common is the challenge of a staff team coming together in a group, with the particular anxieties and sensitivities people feel in the group setting, against a background of organizational stress.

This chapter sets out to examine:

1) Resistance to reflective practice and why our best efforts may be derailed.
2) The group aspects of reflective practice, since much if not most endeavours are undertaken in a group format.

I particularly highlight the anti-group dynamics that seem to me a crucial part of the difficulty. Drawing on my publications on this topic (Nitsun, 1996, 2015), as well as my ideas about the organizational mirror (Nitsun, 1988a, b), I attempt to understand these difficulties and offer suggestions as to how they may be met in the interest of more reliable and satisfactory intervention. My main theses are:

There are inherent resistances to reflective practice that are akin to psychological resistance more generally, but take specific forms in groups.
Stress in the organizational environment creates a background of anxious insecurity that penetrates the group.

The resistance emanates further from anxiety about exposure, both professionally and personally, in the group.

The anxiety may be compounded, not necessarily alleviated, by being in a group.

The reflective practice group, established as a supportive venture, can become an anti-group – a group that is mistrusted, avoided, potentially undermining and undermined. By recognizing these difficulties, we may as consultants and facilitators be in a better position to manage them constructively. Alternatively, we may consider different ways of approaching the task, ways that are less likely to generate anxiety in unproductive ways.

Two sources of anxiety

Two main sources of anxiety are outlined here:

1) Rupture in the organizational environment leading to chaos and confusion in staff teams.
2) Anxiety aroused by participation in a group with other colleagues.

These anxieties in turn interact with anxiety about the primary task.

1. Organizational rupture

There is a growing body of literature on the destructive impact of organizational change. These observations apply to all organizations, but my particular focus is on healthcare organizations, especially the National Health Service (NHS), which I know best, having worked clinically and managerially in the organization for almost five decades. The NHS is the largest and most influential healthcare organization in the UK. It is subject to continual reorganization, to the powerful influence of political and economic trends, to enormous tensions of demand versus resource, as well as generating a host of social and interpersonal dynamics through the working relationships of staff. It epitomizes many of the problematic processes within organizations at large.

I have myself written about the adverse effects of NHS organizational restructuring, emphasizing the repeated nature of reorganization in a way that is relentless and ruthless, with seemingly no reflective stance at the heart of the process (Nitsun, 2015a). I give examples of the "change management" process, a euphemistic term describing the almost total lack of people management in a process that can become agonizingly protracted, with decisions constantly delayed and staff left feeling directionless and unsupported. Typically, jobs are deleted or downgraded and post holders are required to compete with colleagues in an atmosphere fraught with anxiety about survival and fears of annihilation. In one NHS Trust that I am familiar with, the thin layer of staff who survived the process felt they did so by the skin of their teeth. At the same time, the Trust witnessed an exodus of some of its most talented clinicians. Remaining staff were left with shrunken services, struggling to meet more demanding performance targets than ever. The sharp vein of insecurity, paradoxically, united personnel at all levels. Ironically, in a splintered community the one unifying factor is the shared dread and moral disorganization. This is one version of the anti-group – a disunited group bound together through fear and rage.

Both Rogers (2009) and Grace (2016) have written about the specifically devastating impact of mergers and acquisitions. Grace emphasizes endings and loss as a crucial dynamic in the unfolding of mergers and acquisitions, but describes how difficult this is to deal with when the purpose of the change is ruthless merger, increased competitiveness and hyper-cathected efficiency. Instead of the mourning required to deal with loss, these events trigger overwhelming anxiety and regressive group responses, reflecting persecutory fears of abandonment and disintegration. Both Grace (2016) and Oliver (2016), in a commentary on Grace's paper, agree that these processes create the conditions for anti-group developments where goodwill and collaboration break down and yield to a dog-eat-dog environment. Grace, though, referring to my own elaboration of the function of the anti-group, points out the creative potential of the anti-group and the possibility that, in the throes of organizational stress, ways to understanding and constructive action may emerge, facilitating a "regenerative" rather than a "murderous" outcome (Grace, 2016).

2. Anxiety about the primary task

A further source of organizational anxiety relates to the performance of the primary task, which in health services concerns the delivery of safe and effective treatment for the full range of physical and mental conditions. Whereas the anxiety arising from organizational change is usually sporadic, rising and falling in line with the vicissitudes of political and/or managerial impingement, anxiety arising from the primary task of healthcare remains a constant. The challenge of dealing day-to-day with illness ranging from mild to severe and life threatening is fraught with anxiety. Few if any other jobs carry the same weight of responsibility, not in some abstract way but in the immediacy of human beings in states of considerable distress, as well as their families and friends. Further, it is not only the individual patient's recovery that is at stake but whole groups of patients, clustered together in clinics and hospitals, whose care requires robust organizational and management systems in difficult and under-resourced conditions, with painful questions about prioritization and clinical risk. Staff at all levels, from the nursing assistant to the specialist consultant, are caught in spirals of anxiety about the treatment they deliver and constantly face the prospect of failure and criticism. The whistle-blowing culture that has grown in the NHS adds fuel to these anxieties: fears of being found out, of being discovered, wrongly accused, or punished for imagined or real failures or misdemeanours.

It is now well-known that anxiety at this level and of this intensity generates organizational defences – Menzies Lyth's (1959) idea of social defences – that do make it possible to carry on the work without undue strain. But there are consequences. The humanity underlying care is compromised if not eroded, there is a retreat into bureaucracy, and the relationships between staff are organized in defensive rather than facilitative modes. Of course, there is good practice in the midst of this anxiety, but all too often defensive modes are adopted in order to survive. A number of writers (eg., Hirschorn, 1988, Obholzer, 1994) have further developed this theme. While defences serve a purpose, underlying anxiety often haunts the individual practitioner. However strong the motivation to undertake this work in the first place, the stress cannot but evoke ambivalence in the practitioner. This ambivalence can erupt into resentment, even hate or rage at the unwieldy system that makes them responsible without adequate support or recognition – rage at patients and their families for their unrelenting demands, their lack of appreciation and gratitude and, not unusually, their hostility. This is the organizational equivalent of Winnicott's (1949) "hate in the counter-transference", regarded as inevitable and essential in therapeutic work. However, such feelings are difficult to bear, particularly without support or the opportunity to share the emotional load, and when vulnerable patients' survival is at stake.

In psychodynamic terms, there are ongoing processes of projection and identification between staff and patient. Various writers comment on the process whereby carers may project the vulnerable, if not ill, parts of themselves onto the patient (Nitsun, 2015b). There may be an inherent tendency in caring staff to split off the vulnerable parts of themselves and look after them vicariously in others, through a process of projective identification. While this process serves a purpose, it leaves such carers, paradoxically, more vulnerable, since the projection of dependency needs estranges these carers from their needs, from care and treatment for themselves, ultimately depriving them of vital support when really needed. The way this affects medical doctors has been described by Gerada (2016). Under the heading of "the medical self", she suggests that doctors are taught to ignore their own needs in the interests of commitment to the treatment of others. She describes the defensive avoidance of dependence and the concealment of vulnerability that has contributed to a crisis in medical services to disaffection and burnout of serious proportions in the profession.

The overlap of personal and organizational anxiety

These dilemmas of the human conscience, of agency and accomplishment, of anxious responsibility, have probably existed since the beginnings of organized healthcare. But if the ambivalence is difficult to tolerate in an organizational environment that is relatively stable and secure, how much more so in the face of the massive and disruptive organizational change that is a feature of our times? Given the degree of organizational stress in many work environments, the difficulty of tolerating one's own vulnerability as a staff member is sharply accentuated. Do you dare reveal your worries and concerns, your mistakes and misdirected efforts, in an environment in which you risk losing your employment? The tendency to hide, to cover up, to feign strength and invulnerability may be proportional to the sense of looming threat – which in the NHS is a fact of life.

Resistance to reflective practice

I have described in some detail the stresses that prevail in healthcare and what is at stake for services as well as individual practitioners, in order to highlight the resistance to reflective practice that is my main concern in this chapter. While these stresses highlight the growing need for understanding and support within services, they also reveal the defensive processes that have propped up services and individuals over generations of healthcare. Hence, the opportunity for reflective practice may be welcomed in some quarters but in others it poses a threat – of exposing all that is concealed under the banner of responsible health care. Can staff risk revealing the feelings of helplessness, the loss of self-esteem and self-agency that undermines their confidence and disabuses them of the hope that they can influence and change their services?

Reactions of this sort may account for the fact that reflective practice rather than being welcomed is viewed in some situations as irrelevant, an irritant, and, furthermore, potentially dangerous. Consistent time has to be set aside for regular reflective meetings. Some regard this as an intrusion, an interference with busy timetables, an additional commitment in an already fraught day or week. The initiative may be viewed suspiciously as prying into personal and interpersonal matters that are best left unknown. It is no surprise then that the best initiatives may run aground. What is meant to help and support is perceived as intrusive and potentially undermining. In a competitive environment, these fears are compounded by rivalry and envy in the team and the anxiety of losing face. Further, while reflective practice usually aims to look at the patient in all of us, so as to help staff to own their vulnerability, this challenges the necessary split that may exist for some between patient and staff. I have seen this especially in mental health services, where the idea that we all have the potential for psychological dysfunction, that many staff actually do have mental health problems and that there may exist in us all a mad or psychotic part, is seen as alien and unwelcome.

What seems to me new in the literature is the despair expressed by group analysts who for years may have supported the need for reflective practice in organizations: the element of despair that leads some writers to question whether there is any point at all in offering reflective practice groups that make facilitators want to abandon their own hopes of making a difference (e.g., Simpson, 2017). How much are these writers reflecting a powerful and widespread process of resistance, in addition to their despair about the current degree of organizational fallout? Further, how much does this position, wanting to withdraw from group work in organizations or actually withdrawing, reflect the resistance of practitioners unwilling perhaps to plumb the real depths of fear and despair that haunt the organization and how they resonate with this?

The anti-group

Most reflective practice initiatives take place in a group. While there are other forms of reflective practice, the method is mainly practised in groups. The rationale for this has been summed up by Thornton (2017). In essence, she suggests, groups offer a multi-perspective, democratic approach that adds value to the task by opening up the discourse to all those present and that draws on the strengths of the group. While I mostly accord with this view and have myself conducted similar groups, I have reservations about their uncritical application in the organizational setting. For one thing, these are not stranger groups. I highlight this because group analysis originated and developed as a method for groups of people who have not previously met each other and were required to have no contact outside the group. The reason was to keep the analytic frame clear, to focus all interactions in the group, and to strengthen confidentiality. This, however, is very different from groups of staff together attending a group. Staff group members usually know each other, sometimes over many years, have variable but sometimes considerable contact and, moreover, have to work together in the difficult circumstances described above. When the group is over, they have to return to the workplace. Inevitably, there is hesitation about how open to be in the group, how revealing, how confronting. Apart from the general tensions I described above, there are tensions about leadership, hierarchical differences, power and powerlessness that are part of the interpersonal work matrix. These tensions vary in intensity and duration but can create considerable animosity and conflict. Part of the resistance to group reflective practice is the fear of exposure of these tensions. Much as the method aims to approach such difficulties constructively, within a non-blaming stance, and while some teams use the opportunity constructively to do this, others are anxious about wading into troubled waters, and still others report an unhelpful escalation of hostilities following reflective practice. In such circumstances, the group comes to be seen as a risky, if not dangerous, space and the potential to constructively engage with fellow practitioners is outweighed by mistrust of the process.

I formulated the concept of the anti-group (Nitsun, 1996) in order to address difficulties of this sort in both therapeutic and organizational groups. Originally a reaction to what I perceived as the idealized and sometimes over-optimistic aspect of group analysis, I offered the anti-group as a critical principle that challenges the tendency to naively assume the value of groups and to ignore the problems groups can create rather than resolve (Smith and Berg, 1988). The concept emphasizes that groups have negative and not just positive potentials and outcomes and that this is rooted in attitudes of mistrust and fear of groups. Actual negative experience of groups, both in one's personal life and the workplace, reinforce these attitudes. Anti-group dynamics, varying in intensity, may be present in all groups, at least potentially, but groups dealing with sensitive personal and interpersonal issues potentially more so.

Although the concept of the anti-group aims to recognize difficult and potentially destructive processes, the intention is a constructive one: to strengthen group integrity and development. I have suggested throughout my writing that the anti-group has creative potential. Once the impulses and fantasies propelling group destructive behaviour are understood and addressed, including the impact of hostile environmental forces, the group has a greater chance of accessing its constructive and creative potential. But the group first has to be established and maintained, to be held in a state of sufficient safety and security for the transformation to take place and this requires patience, resilience and consistency on the part of the conductor.

Resistance and the anti-group

Before exploring more fully the anti-group and its manifestations in reflective practice groups, it is necessary to consider how resistance as a psychological defence may differ from the anti-group and how it may overlap. For the purposes of this chapter, I suggest there are two forms of resistance.

The first is resistance in a general sense, the sense we are familiar with from psychoanalytic writings, starting with Freud. It reflects the avoidance of psychological inquiry that may uncover unwanted, repressed, or denied aspects of the self. This form of resistance is often described as a feature of psychotherapy that inhibits psychotherapeutic progress, although the 'classical' notion of resistance as residing in an individual has to some extent been superseded by the view that resistance is a product of context, including the therapist or facilitator.

The second form of resistance that is relevant here is resistance to participation in a group. This has more to do with anxiety or discomfort about the group format, reflecting fears that are commonly generated by groups. Another way of looking at the difference is that the first form of resistance is aimed at the reflective process itself, irrespective of the setting in which it takes place, so that it might occur with just one other person. The second form is specifically linked to the group with anxieties about exposure and hostility in the group context and is tantamount to the anti-group.

Of course, the two aspects of resistance usually come together and reinforce each other, which is probably why group settings can be so difficult for many people: the combination of underlying resistance to the reflective process aggravated by resistance to participation in a group.

Anti-group manifestations

I have often pointed out that anti-group phenomena are varied. They occur differently in different groups but there are certain common characteristics that apply to most anti-groups, whether in group psychotherapy or organizational groups. The anti-group usually reflects a group under duress; a group in conflict with itself; a group that lacks trust in its own process; a group that is overcome by doubt and despair; a group that is prone to hostility and aggression that cannot be understood or managed; a group in impasse; a group that fragments.

Group behavioural manifestations include: poor and erratic group attendance; more than usual drop-outs; disruptive sub-grouping; difficulty in generating a group discourse; lack of cohesion and coherence; "attacks on linking" (Bion, 1967) that obstruct the thinking/reflective process; and the establishment of a negative counter-group in opposition to the reflective practice group.

Determinants of the anti-group

I have previously pointed out that isolating specific determinants of the anti-group has limited value, since they are all inter-linked and likely to operate in a circular rather than linear form. However, it is also useful to consider which factors contribute to anti-group formations, both in psychotherapy and reflective practice groups. The following is a summary of these factors, bearing in mind that the determinants may generate each other – and that both generate the group and are generated by it.

Survival anxiety

The fear of annihilation in the organizational milieu is paralleled in the group by anxieties about surviving the group and also whether the group will survive.

Narcissistic injury

Anxiety about being revealed and shamed mirrors earlier experiences of shame and creates resistance to group inquiry, sometimes with a fear of re-traumatization.

Failures of communication

Like psychotherapy groups, reflective practice groups depend to a large extent on verbal communication and offer scope for clarifying and deepening communication. But this cannot be taken for granted. As in all communication, understanding through words is often flawed and incomplete, creating misunderstanding and misattunement (Stern, 1985).

Projective identification

Where words fail, a more primitive form of non-verbal communication, often through disowning unwanted feelings, is projected onto others and creates states of confusion and fragmentation.

Destructive rivalry and envy

The workplace is often the site of intense feelings, rivalry and envy not uncommonly stirred up in the competitive atmosphere. Teams that harbour such feelings may have difficulty collaborating in the spirit of reflective practice, with a fear of rivalry and destructive envy erupting in the group.

Unresolvable conflict

In line with the above, there may already be significant conflict in teams joining a reflective practice group. While this may be aired constructively in the group, there also is the risk of further enactment and exacerbation of conflict.

Alienation of desire

I suggested in an earlier publication (Nitsun, 2006) that desire is an important though often hidden dynamic in groups. This is not necessarily sexual desire but the range of desires that propel people in their work and personal lives. Some groups facilitate the healthy expression of desire but in others anxiety can result in a deadening of desire. This is akin to the 'anti-libidinal group' and may impair the group as 'an object of desire' (Nitsun, 2006).

Defensive agglomeration

I use the term 'defensive agglomeration' to describe a process whereby disowned and denied difficulties are projected massively into and onto the group (Nitsun, 1996). The group then becomes the receptacle of all that is difficult and bad, rendering it a fragile or implosive container.

It will be clear from the above that the reflective practice group is vulnerable to a range of dynamics that may undermine the group. Looking at each of the determinants above and how they may enter an organizationally-based group, the following observations apply:

ANXIETY ABOUT SURVIVAL

Anxiety about survival is widespread in health care and is likely to be stirred up in the process of a new group forming, with corresponding anxiety about whether the group will survive.

NARCISSISTIC INJURY

Narcissistic injury, and the fears of re-injury arising from unwelcome exposure, is also common in the workplace and will have echoes, at least, in the reflective group.

FAILURES OF COMMUNICATION

Failures of communication and the operation of projective identification are similarly ubiquitous in work settings, creating a great deal of confusion and misattribution. It may be very difficult for members to convey adequately and safely the complexity of feelings aroused both in the work environment and the group itself. Misunderstanding is a common fear and feature of groups of this kind.

RIVALRY AND ENVY

Rivalry and envy are 'normal' components of work relationships in a competitive environment. Where excessive, however, they can damage relationships in both subtle and obvious ways. The reflective practice group may trigger existing rivalries and generate new ones.

CONFLICT

Conflict erupting in the group, which may be inevitable if the group is an open forum for difference, can of course be productive and transformative but sometimes deteriorates into intractable, self-righteous and divisive hostility.

DESIRE

Desire is also likely to be present in the group, whether sexually or in other forms of desire, but with particular tensions about its expression in the workplace. This, too, is likely to complicate the process, creating secrets or other forms of restraint. Inhibition and restraint are necessary at times but potentially create a repressed, alienated group.

Defensive agglomeration

I want particularly to highlight the phenomenon of defensive agglomeration, described above, through which a host of problems, sometimes unseen and unverbalized, infiltrate and contaminate the group. At its worst, this lays the ground for an intractable anti-group formation, the group regarded as of no use, a waste of time, even destructive. The most difficult, even hated, aspects of the team, the organization and the outside environment, are all projected onto the group. Of course, this is crucial information and an indirect message to the facilitator of the many problems the team is struggling with in the work setting. But it needs a vigilant group conductor to recognize the link. Facilitators may feel overwhelmed and undermined by the intensity of the group's behaviour and may not have the available insight to make sense of what is happening. My concept of the organizational mirror (Nitsun, 1998a, 1998b) aims to clarify some of these links, explaining the phenomenon commonly known as 'parallel process' as a process of dysfunctional communication from one level of the system to another. Through this 'faulty' mirroring, the group is made to absorb the unprocessed data. But in a similar way to the 'giving back' of the projection identification described by Bion (1967), there is the potential to 'return' the processed content of the projection onto the group and help group members to own what belongs to them as individuals and teams, so enabling the group to acquire a meaning and value of its own.

The role of the facilitator

The role of the facilitator in these settings is demanding. The idea that the group will welcome and appreciate the reflective practice venture, and that a high standard of cooperation may be assumed, is often misguided. Groups are usually not how we expect or want them to be, especially in the chaotic world of healthcare and organizational life more generally. The unpredictability of change combined with organizational pressures and uncertainties provides an unstable background to this work. In my experience, running groups with staff is more challenging and difficult than conducting psychotherapy groups, and anti-group phenomena are more pronounced and sometimes more intractable. Often, work routines, such as shift changes, handover periods, and unexpected staff movement are blamed for inconsistent attendance and the group not working. These are usually valid reasons, but used as ways of avoiding the reflection group, with resultant discontinuity and fragmentation.

The problem for the facilitator is a sense of inadequacy and helplessness in the face of such resistance. The feeling of incompetence may be difficult to bear. It is hard to countenance poor and grudging attendance, a group sometimes consisting of just one or two members surrounded by empty seats, without feeling demoralized. In any case – and this may be the point – the sense of demoralization and helplessness mirrors the widespread loss of morale experienced across the organization, so that the conductor feels entangled in a web of despair. Additionally, the group's anger and criticism may be directed at the conductor himself, with demands to justify the group's existence, to explain the process, to give more direct answers and advice, all of which may compound the conductor's sense of inadequacy. Anti-group is often anti-conductor (Nitsun, 1996). However, there are also instances of a split transference: the group is repudiated but the conductor appreciated or vice versa. All these dynamics are difficult for facilitators to contend with and the facilitator himself needs a supportive/supervisory setting in which these difficulties can be explored. Facilitators provide a containing function in very trying circumstances and their own needs for containment are an essential part of the process.

The conductor's staying power is crucial. The capacity to withstand confusion, hostility, aggression and despair is vital. Even where the group does not appear to be appreciated, where there is enormous projection and 'defensive agglomeration', an important job may be being done. Years ago, as a head of department in the NHS, I was a participant rather than facilitator in a staff group consultation process. All hell broke loose. There was a great deal of expressed disaffection and conflict, including attacks on the group and in particular on the facilitator. I remember being shocked, wondering what on earth was happening and what could be gained. Interestingly, in the aftermath of the process there was a distinct sense of change in the department – for the better. Some of our thorny issues as a group of people working together in difficult circumstances seemed to ease and relationships generally improved. What interested me, in particular, is that most of our well-rehearsed difficulties had not been addressed as such in the group. The group was so consumed by irritation with the process and the facilitator that our 'problems' were hardly aired. Clearly, what must have helped was the enactment in the group of strong emotion, frustration and hostility – and the facilitator's ability to withstand the onslaught. I highlight this experience to make the point, as I often do, that the anti-group, if given a voice, can pave the way for more constructive developments, but also that the facilitator's endurance and capacity for containment are essential requirements.

The creative potential of the anti-group

The above example of a group that benefited from the opportunity to express its anti-group strongly and openly illustrates the point that the experience may ultimately prove to be constructive. As I have noted in several of my publications, the resistant force of the anti-group conceals the more creative potential of the group and once this sees the light of day, in a supportive environment, the positive strengths of the group are freer to develop. I link this to Winnicott's theories about the value of anger and hate acknowledged (Winnicott, 1949). His concept of the "use of an object" highlights the developmental need to test out destructive impulses against a real object. If the object survives, there is a strengthened belief in the resilience of the good, in one's own survival, and in the value of ambivalence in which both loving and hating can be tolerated. Winnicott's writing refers to the mother–infant relationship, but a similar principle applies to other relationships, including group relationships, where ambivalence is often amplified.

Why some reflective groups are 'easier' than others

My purpose in this chapter has been to address the more difficult and resistant kinds of groups encountered in the reflective practice initiative and the way this reflects anxiety about survival. But the example above of a group I once attended myself as a participant illustrates the way in which a seemingly bad experience can have a positive effect. This leads onto another point about why some groups respond well and others react badly. The degree of psychological mindedness in the group is an important variable. Groups that comprise members who are familiar with the process of reflection, perhaps based on professional and training background, are rather obviously more likely to appreciate the reflective process.

Groups of staff that do not have this advantage are more likely to be challenged, if not threatened. Unfortunately, many staff in NHS mental health services have minimal exposure to psychological thinking and are likely to react with surprise, disbelief – and resistance – to the approach. Where there are so many other factors mitigating against the process, such as organizational pressure and insecurity, demanding and inflexible work schedules, anxiety about performance, and the susceptibility to criticism and shaming – all outlined above, failure to grasp the essence of the reflective practice method makes it all the more difficult for staff to identify with the group and to remain committed. Unfortunately, the most vulnerable staff, those working in the most difficult, demanding and deprived settings, often with acute psychosis or intractable long-term conditions, are the ones who most need the understanding of reflective practice but are the least able to access it. Having said this, there is a reverse argument: less psychologically sophisticated staff members may react in immediate and robust ways that are enlivening and useful, whereas more sophisticated members tend to mobilize intellectual defences. This highlights the differing needs of those attending reflective practice groups and what sort of modifications of technique may be appropriate.

Implications for technique

Given that reflective practice generally meets with greater or lesser resistance, I wish to highlight some technical issues that have a bearing on the process and that are open to consideration or revision:

1   The most important technical point concerns the facilitator's management of the reflective practice group. The group analytic concept of dynamic administration is key here, particularly boundary management. Fundamental requirements include the provision of a consistent time and space for group meetings and the protection of boundaries from intrusion. If this is necessary in all process groups, it is all the more important in running reflective practice groups. These groups, more than most, are prone to interruption, sabotage, time and space violations, whether through organizational carelessness or the more subtle impact of envy and resentment. As many have experienced, the setting up of a new group may attract suspicion and censure. Others feel excluded and resentful of the initiative. This is often true of reflective practice groups, and for this reason the effort at effective dynamic administration must be redoubled. Although most facilitators are aware of this in principle, I have known facilitators to let their boundary maintenance slip unwittingly or unconsciously, resulting in complications that are difficult to remedy.

2   The structure of the group is an important consideration. The group analytic method encourages free-floating discussion in an unstructured, undirected group (Schlapobersky, 2016). However, minimal structure and lack of direction create – and may exacerbate – ambiguity and anxiety. Conversely, clear structure and guidance help to create safety and trust. Although heightened

ambiguity may be seen as productive in triggering projections – transferring into the group key issues from outside the group – in my experience this is a risky way of running reflective practice groups, especially in the early stages, when anxiety is likely to be at its highest. This is particularly the case with participants who, as described above, are unfamiliar with reflective practice. I suggest that it is appropriate and useful to initiate a clear discussion about the aims of reflective practice with guidance as to what to expect and how to make the most of the experience. The reflective practice group is not a psychotherapy group, where there is continuous engagement and where the purpose is to explore personal problems, often with minimal structure and guidance. The reflective practice intervention lends itself to a different approach, explaining the frame and the purpose to participants, and possibly initiating exercises and modified group events to introduce the reflective practice process in a more structured and comprehensible way. Oliver (2016) makes a similar point about organizational groups, suggesting a more active, educational approach.

Taking further my suggestion of a more structured group with a greater degree of guidance than might be usual, there is an interesting question about how direct or indirect the reflective task might be. In other words, is it best to embark directly on reflective practice or to create a structured setting that invites reflection but does not make this the overriding aim? While arguing for transparency of aims and methods, I have been aware of how a spontaneous reflective process can begin unexpectedly in a situation in which this is not the primary aim. I have often given talks and run workshops on group process in organizations in which an open, reflective discussion about organizational and clinical problems emerges spontaneously and voluntarily. In setting the scene, I usually refer to the importance of context, in particular the organizational context, and the way this influences group dynamics through

The transmission of organizational preoccupations to groups.
The organizational attitude to group methods.

Additionally, I address group process issues as part of a range of potential group interventions. Without my necessarily intending this, participants in the training event often begin talking about organizational tensions and pressures in their own workplace, their relationship to work and how they are viewed as staff members, either individually or in groups. There is often greater openness, readiness to share and interest in exploring these issues from a reflective stance than I have encountered in groups set up specifically as reflective practice groups! These are surprising and useful events, often making for a creative day.

There is something paradoxical in the above. When a group is set up openly as a reflective practice group, there is often resistance to using the opportunity. When a group is set up for training purposes rather than as a reflective group, there may be a spontaneous and productive discussion about work-related issues. This arises voluntarily and differs from the 'imposition' of a reflective practice agenda.

Conclusion

The great challenge of reflective practice groups is that the very problems that require understanding, often urgently, are the same problems that create resistance to the group: for example, defensive survival strategies, denial and concealment of difficulties, and hidden shame about mistakes and inadequacies. This is akin to psychotherapy, where it is well recognized that the index problem, embedded as it is in a pattern of unsatisfactory relationships, will enter into the psychotherapeutic process and influence its positive development. The difference is that organizational groups do not generally seek help, they are contextualized in different ways, are part of embattled organizations, and do not generally relish or trust psychological inquiry. They are also not stranger groups as people usually know each other and work together, with all the implications this has for boundary infringements and enactments. It is therefore not surprising that they evince a high degree of resistance. I have suggested that resistance is compounded in the group setting and that the process is likely to trigger anti-group developments that may impede or undermine the intervention. The group conductor's capacity to survive the despair and aggression of the group is vital. But the possibility of creative growth is always there. The anti-group often holds the key to a constructive unfolding of relationships and hence the presence of anti-group developments may be seen in a positive light. However, it is a delicate balance and the possibility of group derailment is always there. In order to meet resistance and ease the process of reflection, I suggest that the free-discussion group analytic approach, generally with limited guidance or explanation, is not necessarily the intervention of choice. A more structured, explanatory approach combined with introductory exercises, as well as judicious use of analytic group work, may provide a container that offsets rather than exacerbates anxiety and resistance.

References

Bion, W.R. (1967) Attacks on linking. In: *Second Thoughts*. London: Heinemann.

Gerada, C. (2016). Healing doctors through groups: creating time to reflect together. *British Journal of General Practice, 66* (651): 776–78.

Grace, C. (2016). Endings and loss in mergers and acquisitions: an exploration of group-analytic theory. *Group Analysis, 49*: 134–48.

Group Analytic Contexts (2017). *Issue 75 (Special Edition on Reflective Practice in Organisations)*.

Hirschorn, L. (1988). *The Workplace Within: Psychodynamics of Organizational Life*. Cambridge, MA: MIT Press.

Menzies Lyth, I. (1959). The functioning of social systems as a defence against anxiety. In: I. Menzies Lyth (1988) *Containing Anxiety in Institutions: Selected Essays, Vol. 1*. London: Free Association Books.

Nitsun, M. (1996). *Destructive Forces in the Group and their Creative Potential*. London: Routledge.

Nitsun M. (1998a). The organizational mirror: a group-analytic approach to organizational consultancy, part 1 – theory. *Group Analysis, 31* (3): 245–67.

Nitsun M. (1998b). The organizational mirror: a group-analytic approach to organizational consultancy, part 2 – application. *Group Analysis, 31* (4): 505–18.

Nitsun, M. (2006). *The Group as an Object of Desire*. London: Routledge.

Nitsun, M. (2015). *Beyond the Anti-group: Survival and Transformation*. London: Routledge.

Nitsun, M. (2015a). An anti-group perspective of organizational change: the case of the National Health Service. In: *Beyond the Anti-group*. London: Routledge.

Nitsun, M. (2015b). Being a group therapist: a journey through life. In: *Beyond the Anti-group*. London: Routledge.

Obholzer, A. (1994). Managing social anxieties in public sector organizations. In: A. Obholzer and Z.V. Roberts (Eds), *The Unconscious at Work*. London: Routledge.

Oliver, C. (2016). Response to: 'Endings and loss in mergers and acquisitions' by Corina Grace. *Group Analysis, 49*: 175–82.

Rogers, A. (2009). Organizational reconfiguration in in health care: a life and death struggle. *Organizational and Social Dynamics, 9* (2): 225–48.

Schlapobersky, J. (2016). *From the Couch to the Circle: Group-Analytic Psychotherapy in Practice*. London: Routledge.

Simpson, I. (2017). A reflection on reflective practice. In: *Group Analytic Contexts (2017) 75, (Special Edition on Reflective Practice)*. Available at: https://www.yumpu.com/en/embed/view/5ZKB6kOpqotlhRrX

Smith, K.K. and Berg, D.N. (1988). *Paradoxes of Group Life*. London: Jossey-Bass.

Stern, D. (1985). *The Interpersonal World of the Infant*. New York: Basic Books.

Thornton, C. (2017). Towards a group analytic praxis for working with teams in organisations. *Group Analysis, 50*: 519–36.

Winnicott, D.W. (1949). Hate in the counter-transference. In: *Through Paediatrics to Psychoanalysis*. London: Karnac.

Chapter 10

Discovering the unconscious patterns of a national culture through a large group of psychotherapists and group analysts in Finland

An application of group analysis in an organizational context

Gerhard Wilke

The large group described in this chapter manifests the connections between the individual and collective cultural identity, the social unconscious of the contextual society and its shared traumas, and the sub-divisions of the social system of that society. All of these on the canvas of personal, ethnic, national and international history! This description of my large group work in Finland is also meant to communicate what I regard as the multidisciplinary mindset required to do group-analytically and ethnographically-inspired organizational work (Wilke, 2014).

The social and the psychological dimension and the prehistory of what is enacted in the sphere of a group are not separable. This is true for all social exchanges between humans in any group context. As a facilitator of a large analytic group, I tend to view the large group as a therapeutic, ritualistic and observational socio-psychological event. Consequently, I view the setting and the occasion itself from a group analytic and anthropological standpoint.

Rituals, like regular large groups in the analytic community, are a communicative event in which action, thought and belief are experienced as inseparable and which thereby help the splits and conflicts to be raised and worked upon. For example, group analysts expose themselves to the large group process at their regular symposia at triennial intervals in different locations in order to find out how their community is organized, sub-divided and integrated. In psychoanalytic institutions, a split between active and non-active members is common and boundary disputes between the various committees reporting to the chair and management committee are often so bitter that the attachment to the whole community gets lost: in this context, even three large group sessions, twice a year, have proved to be very useful.

The binary opposition that comes into a shared dialogue in the ritualized encounter of a large group is the conscious level of verbal communication and the unconscious level of fear, anxiety and defence. The conductor's work is to facilitate, widen and deepen the communication at the level of the individual, the subgroup and the group as a whole. Symptoms of dis-ease are not an expression of individual pathology or collective fusion alone, they are also of social significance. Psychic conflict in the large group results from lost connections, disturbed communication patterns and disrupted mourning processes. Disconnectedness has social implications and the recovery of a sense of relatedness between large group members requires a conscious or unconscious act of remembering and engaging with the social rules governing human exchange.

Large Group theory

Lionel Kreeger (1975) outlined three approaches to large group work. One is rooted in the Kleinian tradition of psychoanalytical thought, which in his view focuses on projective processes. Another approach utilizes the counter transference to illuminate the use of the object – be that the conductor or the group. The third approach is based on the writings of Foulkes (1948), who perceived the individual, the subgroup and the whole group as a transpersonal matrix of relatedness. Foulkes overcame the opposition between the individual and the group by stressing the human need to integrate a sense of me and us – and 'not me' and 'not us' – in the self and the whole group.

In my organizational work, I focus on the 'I and We' and 'Us and Them' dynamic very deliberately. As an anthropologist, I know that the dream of overcoming 'us' and 'them' splits between different insider and outsider groups is a vain hope of top leaders, who invoke everyone to be one firm or family in the organization. It is necessary for the leader, supervisor and each section of an organization to learn that the boundaries between team and departments and between top, middle and bottom of the organizaton need to be respected and opened, depending on the context, repeatedly. In fact, in group and individual coaching I focus on leading as 'boundary work'. The overall task is to invest enough time and effort in holding the whole organization together and facilitating the connections that help things to work.

In my experience, forms of regression and defence observable in each large group are pregnant with a longing to connect, to be understood and accepted. The individual member or subgroup of a large group is expressing a need to find a place and a voice to share in a sense of belonging, to develop a shared identity and a shared language. This line of thinking about large groups and communities is based more on the work of Norbert Elias (1994) than it is on that of Freud (2000), Turquet (1975), and Volkan (2004). Elias conceptualized the relationship between the individual and society (the biggest 'large group') as dynamic and more in the tradition of exchange and relatedness. In group analytic terms, large group work amounts to a form of re-socialization, as we think of mental dis-ease as a loss of social ability and our treatment is to work on regaining this capacity. In the large group this means to work with the tendency to defend the belonging group of origin, be it national or ethnic, by pointing the finger at the other, the stranger group. Most importantly, to offer a setting in which large group members could repeatedly experience the sense of self-worth by denigrating the other. So, if one wanted to be idealistic about it, the large group works through exposing the attraction of warlike intergroup dynamics, and thereby gives people something to think about and encourages the need to work on diplomatic approaches to intergroup conflict.

I was socialized as a social anthropologist and tried in my own research in the 1980s, before training as a group analyst, to show how history has the socially habitual, the culturally ritualized and psychologically unconscious power to pre-structure all social interactions. Therefore, I am predisposed to be suspicious of attempts to focus only and simplistically on psychological defences, oedipal dynamics, or emergent bounded chaos in any group process.

Foulkes' communication theory overcame the limitations of the original Freudian model that proposes that group phenomena can be explained through individual psychology alone. Foulkes thought about the psychology of the individual with reference to the social context. For him, each member of a group is a nodal point in a relationship network who communicates on four different levels simultaneously: the conscious level of speech; the unconscious level of neurotic defences; the more disturbed projective level of schizoid and psychotic splitting; and the archetypal and cultural level. This more complex conceptualization of the interaction of the psychological, social and cultural forces in the mind of the individual, as well as in the exchanges between group members, allows a conductor to intervene on several levels. Even more important, the conductor is freed up to be the participant observer in the group, with special responsibility for making the social space in the group safe enough for dialogue. There is no guarantee of success, but the conductor can try to intervene in such a way that the communication flow takes several directions: horizontal (siblings and peers), vertical (parents and children) and external (kinships system and social context), and historical (collective trauma and trans-generational transference). The conductor can, with these thoughts in mind, be free from embodying the master of the group. Instead, the conductor can become the servant of the group and its members when they search for meaning and sense.

This containing posture of the large group conductor creates a transitional space – appropriate to a ritualized setting – in which destructive and creative, healthy and pathological forces begin to interact against the cultural background of the group as an 'as if' world, representing society, culture and human history. In other words, the large group allows conductor, subgroups and members to explore the connections between the primary socialization in the family and the secondary socialization in society and the re-socialization happening during the lived large group ritual. For a group analyst, the dyadic view of the individual and the group in opposition is at best a half-truth about the nature of any social group.

Pat de Maré (1991) claimed that the large group frustrates the satisfaction of libidinal needs of each individual present and therefore causes feelings of hate. Resentment finds a channel for expression in subgroups that contain the hate and are, out of frustration, turned into belonging groups that sections of the larger group can identify with. The subgroups who speak in terms of I as a woman, I as a member of the older generation, I as an English person, etc., feel the need to speak their truth in front of witnesses. Through the exchanges between the subgroups, hate is transformed into dialogue, which is the precondition for thinking, linking, and social cohesion and differentiation. De Maré concluded, therefore, that a large group can build a matrix between differing subgroups and develop the capacity for fellowship (*koinonia*) and fraternity across the subdivisions within a larger social whole. This perspective tallies with my own experience of the struggle of any social system, including a large analytic group, to find enough glue to hold it together. In society that glue is differentiation and mutual interdependence, as it is in an analytic group (Hopper, 2003, 2012; Wilke, 2012).

Discoveries about the Finnish group analysts' and psychotherapists' social unconscious in the large group

In the new millennium I was asked to conduct a series of large groups, spread over several years, to explore the social unconscious of group analysts and psychotherapists in Finland. This invitation was unique in several ways. First, it was planned to work in eight consecutive large group sessions over a weekend. It appeared from the start that the culture of Finland contained a propensity to try out extremes and test boundaries of which, it could be argued, the Finnish people were unconscious. Second, the task enabled me to use the large group as a developmental tool and exploratory laboratory over several years. This was also unusual, because I am usually asked to facilitate large groups in moments of organizational crisis, when it is apparent that only an unconscious understanding of what is happening – in a psychoanalytic institute, for instance – can open up a potential space for an analysis of the situation and the exploration of more adapted forms of communal exchange. Third, the research task for the large group enabled the conductor and the participants to explore the social as well as psychological nature of the intertwined regressive and developmental process in an established large group.

Large group sessions can often help to discover some lost glue to hold the parts of a fragmented social system together. They also offer its members a space in which they can work through the socially unconscious material that they carry on behalf of their parents' generation, the society they were born into, or the organization they have 'chosen' to belong to. This is very apparent in societies that have suffered the trauma of war or dictatorship. In a three-day workshop that included participants from Russia, Ukraine and the former East Germany, the first two days of the dialogue were dominated by mutual accusations by the Russians and Ukrainians that related to repressed memories of the Second World War and the recent conflict in Eastern Ukraine. The Germans were reduced to the role of listeners and witnesses in this drama between perpetrators and victims until the second evening, when an East German announced that he could not come the next day for family reasons. In the morning, I left his chair in the circle, but an elderly East German psychiatrist took it out again. I let her and then put it back in, whereupon she said that in East Germany this would have been unacceptable, a member of a 'collective' who drops out, no longer belongs. I pointed out that we could debate about the chair for a long time, but as we were working on the topic of therapy in post-totalitarian societies I decided that an empty chair could be very significant for the rest of the group. This was followed by a longish silence and then by a rush of stories of deportations, sudden arrests, early morning raids and unmourned war dead in all the families of each group members – explaining, at least in part, why people had ended up in careers in psychiatry and what a powerful signifier an empty chair could be.

In Germany the issue of collective guilt and, by association, the shame of the second-generation descendants of Nazi perpetrators is tangible in most large group settings. In the case of Finland the shared collective aspects of the culture, which were both inside and outside the individuals who spoke, resembled that of a young nation pre-occupied with its own identity, reputation, language, cohesion and coherence. The Finnish large group project aimed to understand itself in the here and now, whilst surfacing, through free association, socially unconscious traumas from history and the shared collective myths that shape the private and collective lives of all Finns.

The conductor of a large group needs to think of himself as embodying three roles in the service of the group: the analyst, the translator and the dynamic administrator. The clarification of these three roles gave me the opportunity to explore some of the elements of the shared Finnish social unconscious. In the dynamic administrator role, I had to take care of the setting and create the conditions for people to meet face to face and take the risk of exposing their innermost feelings. In the case of the Finnish large group this meant linking with the people tasked by the Institute of Group Analysis in Helsinki to organize the event, identifying and hiring a meeting place, and providing the kind of environmental mothering that according to Winnicott (1971), is one of the pre-conditions for analytic work. On a psychological level, the frequent changes of venue created a sense of existential uncertainty, but also a sense of shared identity as nomads or 'marginalized people'. This linked with the socially unconscious wish to re-dramatize the insecure position of Finland in the world, between East and West and at the edge of the world, just below the frozen wilderness. On a social level, the pattern of moving between buildings confronted the group with the past of colonization, ethnic displacement, territorial war and collective repression. The wandering about reminded us all of the very long struggle over many centuries to define nationhood through the ownership of the Finnish language and eventually by having a communal assembly in a settled place in Helsinki. Before this time, the representatives of the Finnish people always met in places chosen by their Swedish or Russian colonial masters or, in secret, in the forest. The dynamic administration process of this large group re-enacted this history and the stages of the journey.

In my role as dynamic administrator, the propensity of the organizers to change places befitted the shared 'we-ideal' of the group and, in the counter transference, left me with a sense of dislocation and helplessness – presumably on their behalf. The nomadic pattern of moving from a Swedish Adult Education Institute, to the ballroom of the Russian Generals, into a Geriatric Community Centre and then into the ex-assembly hall of the Freemasons fitted in with the chosen myth of the Finns as a not-yet-settled community. At the level of the social unconscious they still see themselves as migrants from the wilderness into settled farmsteads, the first step in the civilizing process. Collectively the group seemed to share a sense that they had not quite arrived in towns, as far as their collective we-ideal is concerned. They could only feel safe by not committing to a permanent settlement. My first working hypothesis about the Finnish social unconscious was therefore that those gathered under the national large group tent were still deeply in touch with nature, the wilderness, the undomesticated and the untamed parts of their character and community – in spite of living in a modern industrialized society. The members of the group had a collective sense of being in-between the wilderness of nature and the cultured world of towns, between colonial dependence and national independence, and between autocracy and democracy.

In the Helsinki group, unspoken conflicts centred on the question whether several languages could be spoken and tolerated in the group or whether the members had to submit to a single and foreign tongue. The majority of the members spoke Finnish, a minority spoke Swedish and Finnish and the conductor spoke English. The exploration of sensitive inter-group themes required the construction of a small tower of Babel to lend everyone a voice. It proved hard to construct a multi-lingual universe. The resentment against the imposition of a foreign tongue was acted out through long and passive-aggressive silences. The majority of the large group were forced to speak English, because the authority figure could only work in that language, yet they needed the foreigner to feel safe in each other's presence. The basic pattern of social interaction in this group was condensed in the following scene on the evening of the first large group day. A group member challenged me to say what characterized the Finns. My answer came spontaneously and without thinking: "A Finn is a person who doesn't speak Swedish. A Finn prefers to be silent, if he can't speak his mother tongue."

The group, its 'chosen' challenger and I were caught up in the scenic dramatization of the "chosen trauma" (Volkan, 1997) of the Finns. They sat for lengthy periods in the group with a collective sense of victimhood, as survivors of the sessions with an imagined colonizer, less so as participants. For many centuries, the Finns were ruled by the Swedish crown and the official language of administration was that of the colonial masters. The Swedes were deposed and replaced by the Russians, who defeated them in the nineteenth century. It was the Russians who gave them a parliament and who made Finnish the legitimate first language. National independence was eventually granted to the Finnish people by Lenin's first post-revolutionary government. The person in charge of this act being Joseph Stalin. Enough reasons to insist on Finnish being spoken, enough reasons to feel insecure about the right to insist on it, enough reasons to be reluctant to speak without inhibition, to be proud in a testing and dependent fashion simultaneously.

Although the large groups were announced as being conducted in English, I had deliberately not issued an edict that speaking Finnish in the group was forbidden. Indeed, I had at the beginning invited people to use their mother tongue if they felt the need to do so. What the group heard was that I insisted on the use of English and had taken away their freedom to speak in their own tongue. The misunderstanding rapidly became an implicit group rule, observed compliantly and resentfully. It was this enactment of passive-aggression against the imposition of a foreign language that retold the socially unconscious struggle to give birth to the Finnish nation. We had to repeat the story of the official and dominant language in society and the right to use it. This repetition compulsion made clear to the conductor what the chosen foundation myth of the modern Finnish nation was. The collective identity of the participants centred mostly around this issue. It became the measuring rod for deciding what was right and wrong, good or bad, and who were the real insiders, the marginalized, and the foreigners.

The test of the authority of the conductor was whether he could tolerate Finnish being spoken and whether he would, in response to being excluded from the conversation, become a punitive, colonial master. The scene was enacted in the second year of our joint exploration of the Finnish social unconscious. The group membership had been enlarged by the presence of a whole training course from northern Finland and a Russian visitor from Estonia. Two of the newly arrived Finnish group members had enough and started the first group in Finnish. Very rapidly more members of the group spoke and were suddenly much more animated than in all the previous sessions. Finnish spread like wildfire and it was a pleasure to behold how the energy flowed to and fro and how free people were in speaking to each other. Shortly afterwards, I could see that the large group subdivided into those who were happy to exclude the foreigners from the dialogue, those who wanted to stick to the agreed task of working in English, and a substantial subgroup who fell silent. Resisting the temptation to break the pattern, I waited until a member of the Swedish speaking minority interrupted and reminded the group of the rule that I had introduced in the previous year: "When you feel the need to speak in Finnish you can, the rest of the time we stick to English". This resulted in a collective response of: "It isn't fair!". The outcry of the majority against the descendant of the ex-colonial master, who had taken on the group leadership by reminding everyone of the rule, was also a rebellion against me, as my tolerance of being excluded and the challenge to it meant that the main group had, at least in phantasy, killed me off and made an ethnically 'clean' group. The resultant embarrassment, guilt and shame ended in a very long silence – a scenic dramatization of the preferred collective form of dealing with the potential for real conflict or real intimacy and tolerance of difference.

The quality and the length of the silence I took to be a message from the group that they wanted me to translate what had been acted out into meaningful dialogue. It was a struggle to find the right words, as the group had succeeded in making me feel that it was not safe to make a mistake. My initial, but in the end unexpressed, thoughts were the following: should I mirror back to the group how my original rule had finally been heard, how they had found a new and powerful way of holding each other to account, and how the group had then split into distinct subgroups? Should I highlight the remarkable energy released by their speaking without fear in Finnish? Should I go on to say how this newly found freedom had tipped the group, on a social level, into the dramatization of an insider-outsider- and silent subgroup gestalt. To paraphrase my internal translation effort, I also thought of pointing out that this was perhaps related to the faultlines in the social structure of Finland: the majority of Protestant Finns, the minority of Swedish speaking descendants of the ex-colonial masters and the silent, dislocated and displaced descendants of refugees from Karelia, an area of Finland lost to the Soviets, who were Orthodox Christians. Should I point out that their distinct and perhaps divided relationship to the shared Finnish language, mirrors their ambivalent relationship to a nation that is both subdivided and united?

Should I go on to say that in all nations, most subcultures require of the insider group that they find a way of engaging with those excluded from the majority and its language and customs? Should I say that the group unconsciously was asking me to translate the binary opposition between majority and minority into the nagging question of who are the real Finns and who is the enemy within? Who is the best scapegoat, to unite us as a group into a sense of oneness? Should I frame my observations simply in terms of whether we can find a shared language in this group between the English speaking conductor, the Swedish speaking minority and the Finnish majority? Should I point out the repeated pattern of defining the Finnish we-identity in terms of: we are what we don't want to speak?

When I finally spoke, I made the following intervention: As the subgroups did not link and no effort was made to translate what was said for the conductor and the foreign visitor, I would be interested in exploring what it meant to you and what the behaviour expressed signified about the shared sense of identity of the majority and its perception of each minority? The group responded and it became apparent that a shared language for communication, not simply for identification, was needed to construct a shared sense of belonging, togetherness and identity within a secure boundary – a textbook answer, perhaps. Nevertheless, language is the means to a bigger end, not the end in itself. It was clear after the exploration of the silence that each group member who spoke had a unique and personal way of answering the question posed and also used the mother tongue that way. The basic law of groups is that together group members form the implicit behaviour norms of the group from which they individually deviate over time. The fear of handing the conductor role to an outsider from England, in order to avoid confidences being broken, made it practically impossible to sit in a large group that could work in the mother tongue. The result was that the group started with binary opposition: authority belongs to the outsider, compliance and rebellion to the insiders. The basic law of a group was inverted, the group placed a deviant from the Finnish norm in the power position and set the majority up in the role of having to test the authority and the security of the group boundary. The re-enactment of the shared fear of being re-colonized and losing the status of an independent person and community was unconsciously set up. This dilemma was felt very strongly and believed to be unique to Finland. It lent the majority in the group a sense of collective singularity that, so it was felt, distinguished the Finns from all their neighbouring nations.

This sense of a divided we-ideal, of being too proud and too unsure is typical of all young nations. The price is a reactive and defensive culture and a propensity to split the world into us: good, them: bad. My feeling after these explorations around language, identity and group cohesion and coherence was that the group was in transition from a self-referential to a more open-minded culture. However, too much civilized and tolerant thought and behaviour was threatening the insecure identity of a young nation and its members, still wedded to a victim story, still clinging to a we-ideal – that our story is so unique that no foreigner can understand it or really identify with us. The secondary gain of the phase of the large group process in Finland was that it became clear to the majority, the minorities and the conductor, that we were not simply dealing with oedipal struggles in the group. We were facing up to the connection between psychological group defences against the fear of contact with the stranger within and without and the dependency on an 'in-between' being – a foreign conductor, or shaman – who could mediate the common search for the social glue between minority, majority and whole belonging group under one 'large-group tent' (Volkan, 1997).

The recounting of this critical incident relating to the struggle for a shared language and polyphonic communication in the group leads me to my second working hypothesis about the Finnish social unconscious. As a young nation, its majority members felt the need to make the former insiders (Swedish descendants of the former colonial rulers) experience what it felt like to be regarded as an outsider in one's own country. This was the dynamic between the indigenous majority and the Swedish minority in the group, but also in relation to the Russian visitor and the German conductor, imagined as English. Everyone embodied and was sucked into an unconsciously delegated role within the group. The Russians were modernizers, enemies, neighbours, and trading partners. The Swedes were colonizers, dominant minority and second language representatives. All Finnish children have to learn Finnish and Swedish, plus a third language, at school. All the Finns in the group had resented having to learn Swedish when they were young and the Finnish Swedes had resented having to learn Finnish. Most malignant mirroring processes in this large group were always linked to this issue. A confident nation with a long history of being proud of itself and secure in its sense of collective identity is able to resist invoking a sense of victimhood and deprivation and can be more tolerant of difference and self-confident in the presence of strangers – in relatively normal times at least. A younger and more insecure nation needs to push the strangers into the role of having to tolerate the majority's need to assert itself and feel accepted. My sense was that the Finnish social unconscious is still predominantly marked by a sense of hurt due to the long centuries of domination, and that our work in the large group was a search for a kinder relationship to the collective and individual sense of identity.

Inside the Finnish large group, the psychological need of the majority to be accepted and recognized came over as overly insistent and demanding and, in response, led to the inversion of the insider–outsider dynamic between the Finnish and the Swedish Finns. The very opposite of what was wished for by the majority group – looking for a sense of affirmation from the descendants of their former oppressors – was repeatedly re-enacted. Instead of being accepted as Swedish Finns, members of the minority got irritated by the majority's demand for repentance and humility. The Swedish minority defended itself by telling the majority group to get on with growing up and refraining from protesting too much. Exchanges that ended up putting the Swedish Finns back in the superior position and made the majority of indigenous Finns feel as outsiders in their own country. The way the majority defended against what they feared, became a self-fulfilling prophecy. What followed was always a retreat into long silence – the familiar place of self-reassurance.

The frequent and long silences were the identity badge of the Finnish large group. In the role of the analyst I was repeatedly put in the position of having to tolerate long silences of up to forty minutes. It was a unique experience to learn that silence could function as social glue through an unconscious pact – that it is the duty of every Finn to be proud by avoiding being shamed. The superego of many group members urged them on, to demonstrate to the community that they did not need to be dependent and could do without social chat and help. It was shameful to make yourself feel at ease through a sense of belonging achieved through an open exchange of feelings and thoughts in the service of a sense of communion. On the psychological level, the frequent silences, at least in my interpretation, were related to a fear of being envied and the repression of the wish to be seen as superior in the eyes of your neighbour. In this way, silence functioned in this large group as a ritual of communion, where oneness without social division and beyond language and power differences could be held and maintained.

This insight came to me in a group session in which some members were praised for having just published a book. The response to the public praise was that those who had received it felt, in their words, "naked and exposed". When I made an interpretation, saying that the fear of envy was perhaps linked in the social unconscious with the painful struggle to win the right to speak in the mother tongue, I was interrupted by a woman, who spontaneously said: "Our whole history is marked by periods of long silence and short periods of speaking up." In response, I asked: "Can we explore which historical events you have in mind, and how they might live on in you individually and collectively?". This was followed by yet another silence. To raise the collectively lowered heads, I said: "Obviously you think that the wish to remain silent in the face of the enormity of history and what humans are capable of is something unique to Finns. You feel the odd one out amongst the Scandinavians, you feel culturally trapped between East and West – politically and religiously. It is hard for you to see that your collective difficulties are also a universal human problem. If you could accept that you are one among many nations with different but also similar stories, it might be possible to open up a space in the group to explore some of the key events in history that burden your minds." "Universal, in what sense?" someone asked. Again I waited for the group, but no one spoke on my behalf. Realizing that I needed to model more open-minded talk, I added:"I was thinking of the literary work of Samuel Beckett (Parkin and Wilke, 1975). His plays demonstrate how inventive humans are in creating interaction rituals and modes of speech that serve the purpose of not communicating, not connecting, and avoiding any kind of social and psychological truth between those who relate to each other, in a habitual rather than connected way".

This perhaps overly long interpretation was followed by a very short silence. Progress, I thought. As I began to wonder what had shifted, someone began to list the historical events that weighed on her conscience and hovered, in her view, beneath the surface of the collective memory. She said: "The Bolsheviks finally gave us national independence, afterwards we were overtaken by a terrible civil war and then we were invaded by the Soviets. We gave them a bloody nose and to prevent it happening again, we forged an alliance with the Nazis. In the first half of the Second World War we fought with the Nazis against the Russians and in the middle of that war, we switched sides and joined the Allies against the Germans. When the war ended, Stalin took his revenge and annexed parts of Finland and expelled most of the ethnic minority that lived between Saint Petersburg and Helsinki".

Someone else then said: "In my family the social trauma which weighs down on at least three generations is the evacuation of about 75,000 Finnish children to Sweden, in order to protect them from the raging war." This was the decisive moment in the group, when its members began to trust each other enough to honestly explore the social unconscious of the Finns, and which chosen traumas and foundation myths were used to construct a coherent story for the national narrative. After this point, it could be worked out what the unifying story was that the Finns, the Swedes and the Karelians subscribed to in order to integrate their I- and we-ideal. The critical incident of rebelling against the English language, taking the right to speak in Finnish and the working through of the us and them dynamic with the shared belonging group enabled the participants to end their work with me. At the end of our joint exploration, the group arrived at a consensus, that future large groups would be facilitated by one of their own group analysts in Finnish: they would risk trusting each other and shift the dynamic between engagement and distance more in favour of engagement.

As a result of this work, the sense of community connection, interdependence and shared culture – "the way we do things around here in the Finnish IGA" – was seen by the members as part of the critical work of leading and developing the organizations. Participants learnt that community development work, with the help of large group sessions, is not a luxury or an expedient when there is a problem, but a precondition of performance and productive cooperation between the various bodies managing the organization. Through the large group work, the organizations' leaders and members learnt, in good time, what it means to work *in* and *with* their organizations as a living community. At the core of large group work, in relation to being more effective as an organization, is the art of naming things. Naming things for what they are is a powerful and important process in enabling a community to stick together and cooperate beyond their functional and specialist divisions. Naming things aloud and in front of others amounts to a way of ordering and reordering the world we find ourselves in externally, and the world we belong to and identify with internally. The symbolic naming of how we see things does not in itself define the meaning of what is being perceived and said, but it allows members of a group and community to confirm or adapt the meaning of who they are, what they stand for, why they do what they do, and who is meant to benefit by their joined-up efforts.

Conclusion

This large group work in Finland illustrates why I tend to conceptualize organizations as 'living communities', rather than an emergent order or a system. Instead of a static social system, I think in terms of three generations and continuity of social structures in space and time existing beyond the limits of an individual life. In an organizational setting the large group conductor can intervene in such a way that the communication flow takes a horizontal (siblings and peers) direction, a vertical (parents and children) and external (kinships system and social context), and a historical (collective trauma and trans-generational transference) direction. This makes clear to participants that their division of labour, their hierarchical status differences both divide them, but also make them interdependent and provide the minimum of "social glue" to hold their organization together. The conductor can, with this in mind, model how leadership can be conceptualized as boundary work and be understood as a communal effort, and is not, as is the current myth, all up to the heroic person at the top.

The process of free association makes it abundantly clear that what appears to be set and timeless is in fact in flux and subject to negotiation, confirmation and adjustment – always in the light of external circumstances. Like in a tribal initiation ritual, a large group session in an organizational setting will confront its members with the interdependence of past, present and future and with the relatedness of forces that tend towards integration and fragmentation. This is especially true in current organizations that have been subjected to 'serial' restructuring processes and are therefore subject to a shared sense of incomplete mourning and communal fragmentation and competition for scarce resources. In short, in today's organization, its members are struggling with existential insecurity and survival. This contextual reality implies for me that a conductor intervenes on the group as a whole, the subgroup, the individual and on the socio-historical level.

The use of the large group ritual in an organizational process is, for me, an investment in the social capital of the organization and enhances the capacity of its leaders at various levels to hold the whole community and its resources in mind. This way of seeing the organization is useful during change processes, which from a group analytic perspective, are always about more continuity than change. In my experience during periods of transition, organizations that have a tradition of joint sense making in forums that allow a free-floating conversation – or free group association, as group analysts would call it – have more internal capacity to hold themselves together individually and collectively in crisis situations. Organizations reflect their history, they do not have a culture but live in one. Any culture is not an object that its social members possess but is both within them and without them as a symbolic frame of reference that gives meaning to their actions and lends them a sense of shared identity, especially when they interact in a ritualized social context like a meeting, a complex operation in a hospital, or in supervision or reflective practice sessions. The group analyst leading an organizational large group needs to pay attention to being a master of exchange ceremonies, the witness of history, and the analyst of the dynamic process. As well as seeing projection, splitting, projective identification and similar phenomena simply as defences against anxiety, we need to learn to see them as an attempt to communicate and seek exchange and some kind of social structure.

References

de Maré, P. et al. (1991). *Koinonia: From Hate, through Dialogue, to Culture in the Larger Group.* London: Karnac.

Elias, N. (1904). *Die Gesellschaft der Individuen.* Frankfurt: Suhrkamp.

Foulkes, S.H. (1948). *Introduction to Group-Analytic Psychotherapy.* London: Heinemann.

Freud, S. (2000). Massenpsychologie und Ich Analyse. In: *Studienausgabe. Fragen der Gesellschaft: Ursprüng der Religion* (pp.61–125). Frankfurt: Fischer Suhrkamp Wissenschaft.

Hopper, E. (2003). *Traumatic Experience in the Unconscious Life of Groups.* London: Jessica Kingsley.

Hopper, E. (Ed.) (2012). *Trauma and Organisations.* London: Karnac.

Kreeger, L. (Ed.) (1975). *The Large Group, Dynamics and Therapy.* London: Constable.

Parkin, E. and Wilke, G. (1975). Schluß mit Warten. In: H. Mayer and U. Johnson (Eds) *Das Werk von Samuel Beckett* (pp.87–132). *Berliner Colloquium.* Frankfurt: Suhrkamp.

Turquet, P. (1975). Threats to identity in the large group. In: L. Kreeger (Ed.) *The Large Group, Dynamics and Therapy* (pp.87–144). London: Constable.

Volkan, V. (1997). *Bloodlines: From Ethnic Pride to Ethnic Terrorism.* New York: Farrar, Straus and Giroux.

Volkan, V. (2004). *Blind Trust: Large Groups and Their Leaders in Times of Crisis and Terror.* Charlottesville: Pitchstone Publishing.

Wilke, G. (2012). Leaders and groups in traumatized and traumatizing organizations: a matter of everyday survival. In: E. Hopper (Ed.), *Trauma and Organizations*. London: Karnac.

Wilke, G. (2014). *The Art of Group Analysis in Organisations: The Use of Intuitive and Experiential Knowledge*. London: Karnac.

Winnicott. D.W. (1971). *Playing and Reality*. London: Tavistock.

Part III

The group as a whole, the individual in the group and the group in the individual

Aleksandra Novakovic

In this chapter I will discuss the dynamics in a team group as a whole, the experience of individuals in the group and the 'group' in the mind of an individual. Although I will be considering a particular level – a group, an individual in the group, or a group in the individual – these levels are fundamentally interconnected and mutually dependant and continuously influence each other.

In order to present the dynamics at these different levels, I will discuss the material from staff groups that I facilitated with two staff teams in two different organizations.[1] One of the aims of a staff group based on group analytic principles is to facilitate development of a free-floating communication in the group. In order to enable participants to associate more freely, the staff group is not structured, or if there is a structure or an agenda, it is usually minimal. The staff group facilitator shifts attention between the foreground and the background in a given constellation and changes the level of observation. For example, the focus can change from the individual and his or her experience in the group to the dynamics in the whole team (or to the dynamics in the patient or client group) to the wider organization and the social, cultural, or political context.

This chapter is divided into two sections. In the first section, 'The group as a whole', I present a staff group with a palliative care staff team and I specifically focus on the team group *as a whole*. I explore staffs' shared anxieties in their work with dying patients and collectively exerted and sustained defences in the team group against these anxieties. In the second section, I present material from a staff group with a psychiatric inpatient rehabilitation unit and I consider the *individual in the group* and the *group in the individual*. I found that psychotic experiences and confusional states are characterized by co-existing, split and conflicting feelings that stem from a psychotic person's contemporaneous relationships with different internal and external figures, or, as I phrase it, the subject's 'internal group relations'. I suggest that this state of confusion – manifest in the patient's different co-existing feelings, resonated with the experiences in the group and that these two levels were interrelated. I also suggest that internal group relations are a universal phenomenon, apparent in dreams and in the experience of any individual in a group, when very primitive feelings are unleashed and psychotic processes predominate.

The group as a whole

Inevitably, most, if not all, people are confronted with anxieties about dying and death and Jaques (1965) describes the unconscious links between the experience of life and death. His view is that the intensity of persecutory anxieties about loss and death depend on the balance between a person's ability to acknowledge the loss and to mourn and accept it, and the feelings of frustration, hatred, persecution and guilt aroused by the loss.

In the next section, I shall discuss staffs' anxieties and defences in work with dying patients and how these are reflected in the dynamics of the palliative care team group as a whole.

Preliminary meeting with the manager

I met the manager of the palliative care team for the elderly at a meeting for health professionals and she expressed an interest in a staff group for her team. My department was able to offer only short-term work to services in other municipalities and we discussed the possibility of a fortnightly staff group for a duration of three months. This would be an opportunity for the team to have an experience of having time to reflect together, and also to think about whether the staff group might contribute to teamwork if they were to consider this kind of work in the future.

Preliminary meeting with the team

The team consisted of 13 members from three different professions: nurses, doctors and social workers. In the preliminary meeting, the staff appeared to be interested in the prospect of the group, yet at the same time they seemed keen to return to their work as soon as possible. They quickly decided they wanted to go ahead with the staff group and agreed with my suggestion that they take turns in a ten-minute case presentation at the start of the group and use the remaining time to reflect on the presented material and other relevant issues for the team. Concern was expressed about the short duration of the staff group, there were worries about 'things' being exposed and how these issues might be left unresolved. Staff members debated whether the group should be compulsory for the whole team, and after contemplating the alternatives, they decided that all should attend. They thought that the benefits of being together as a whole team, with no-one left out, counteracted the pressure to attend, and that compulsory attendance was a minor problem compared with the consequences if someone was left out.

The staff group quickly decided to go ahead, demonstrating how, in a short space of time, they could make decisions. It would seem as if the limited time their patients had left to live compelled them to be very efficient and they came across as busy, competent and brisk. I thought that they took me energetically and reassuringly through this first meeting, perhaps a reflection of how they met their patients and their families.

First staff group

Members of the team gathered in a quick, enthusiastic, and somewhat expect-ant manner. When they quickly settled down with coffees and teas, the manager, Stefania, made a joke, asking whether we should have a prayer. Everybody laughed. Nina, one of the team's doctors, presented her patient, a 79-year-old woman, who was refusing to be examined by her or treated by anyone else from the team. Nina remembered similar situations when patients would not allow her to touch them or refused to let her into their rooms. When I asked Nina how she felt about this she said that being unable to help a patient left her feeling useless.

Sonia said that it seemed pointless to insist on helping someone when they declined help. They explained that there was a professional dilemma: How much responsibility could be taken? Should they insist? Anna said it could be difficult when a patient refused help and everybody agreed that it made them feel angry when they did not have the satisfaction of helping people. Tania said professional satisfaction was important in their work. She thought their feelings depended on the people they were working with: it was not like working with paper in a bank – being rejected by a patient made her feel bad. She added bluntly that in the end some patients liked you and others did not. Everybody agreed. I asked how they felt when a patient liked one staff member and disliked another.

After a brief silence, Maksim said it could be particularly difficult if a patient complained to one of them about another member of staff. Nina thought that in the case she had presented, the patient had rejected them all: they felt like a close group when they later discussed this among themselves. They concluded that it was helpful if they all experienced the same difficulty, as it brought them closer together. I wondered what the implications might be when a patient liked one member and rejected another member of the team. Maksim said he did not feel good in this situation and jokingly went on to say that a patient might complain to him about X and he might say to the patient that he had suspected something dreadful like that about his colleague all the time. They all laughed, agreeing that it was crucial that such situations were brought back to the team. If they could openly discuss things together there would no longer be a problem. They gave examples of similar situations.

The staff thought that some difficulties they experienced with patients stemmed from their own differences, but also in some instances there was the difference between the temperament of the staff member and the patient, and that they took into consideration the temperament of the patients and staff members. Marina, Mira and Tania discussed in a lively manner how some staff members sometimes became attached to some patients. Tania said it might be regarded as possessiveness to have a special relationship with a patient and that such possessiveness was not helpful. Marina said that when she realized that she was becoming quite attached to a certain patient, she felt something like a light being switched on in her mind, warning her of how dangerous it might be.

When patients refused their help, the meaning of their work, of helping in some way, was brought into question, reinforcing their doubts about what help they were able to give and how they could help when their patients died. In discussing feelings about being rejected by a patient, they generalized and their individual experiences became something that happened to everybody in the team. Even when they acknowledged their differences, as far as their patients' welfare was concerned, they were united in their agreement on matching a staff member's 'temperament' with that of the patient. If everybody wanted the same thing, or if everybody experienced and thought in the same way, for instance, about a patient's rejection of help, this was explicitly stated to be 'bonding'.

I think that the denial of their differences and the defensive way in which they united was directly linked to the nature of their work – their conscious experiences of their dying patients, as well as their own unconscious phantasies and fears about dying and death. It seemed necessary to collude in not allowing 'something' to happen or be experienced. I think that the pressure in the team group for holding together was a defence against an unconscious dread about feeling left out, forever separated and abandoned in the process of dying. After all, how unbearable it would be if one was left to die alone, isolated from everybody, and cut off from everything.

However, team members acknowledged a need to discuss difficulties openly, such as patients' criticism and rejection of staff, and they appeared to feel supported by the team. The issues of trust were raised humorously and openly and they talked about how destructive it could be to side with a patient against a colleague.

Second staff group

The group discussed how staff changes created problems, and this related particularly to junior doctors, who changed jobs on a six-monthly basis. It was acknowledged that when rooms were shared according to their professions, it felt divisive, but Sonia thought it was good for doctors to share a room, since they could learn from each other. They noted how it was not easy for doctors, as they were burdened and rushed, and someone pointed out that doctors were usually late for their Continuous Professional Development Meeting.

They thought about how they did not work in a rigid way. For example, they could not 'cut off' a patient in the middle of a telephone conversation and patients could delay them. Their profession was not one in which they could interrupt work with a patient at a moment's notice. Stefania said that she herself was not a 'watch' person and pulled up her sleeve to show that she was not wearing a wristwatch.

Discussion reverted to the Tuesday meeting and near the end of the staff group the team agreed to change the time, as 4pm was not ideal at the end of their working day. There was some puzzlement when they realized that this meeting was organized just for them and they wondered why they did not attend this and agreed to make full use of it.

The group was concerned about staff becoming divided into different professionals and cut off in their respective 'professional' rooms. Their description of the junior doctors as an unstable, changeable, hard-to-assimilate subgroup reflected the team's continuous emphasis on the strength of the team as a whole and their need to feel united.

In contrast to patients, staff were not in a position to refuse my help, since they had agreed to compulsory attendance for all team members. There were suspicions about my capacity as a newcomer to understand them and there was a resentment of the disruption caused by my 'coming and going'.

The staff seemed unable to extricate themselves from their commitments to patients. Team members experienced their patients on the telephone as being on a life-line that they could not sever by ending the conversation at a given time. It seemed that it was unmanageable, even cruel, to define boundaries and set limits. Their manic defences were used to deny various aspects of reality: team members were unwilling to acknowledge watches and time; they avoided a deeper engagement; and they were immersed in what seemed a perpetual state of urgency and warding off of disturbing feelings.

Third staff group

The group discussed the changes in the team, but agreed there had been an improvement recently, when nurses ceased to wear uniforms. Commenting on how a uniform made a distinction between the professions, I asked what this meant to them. But they were reluctant to consider this.

A discussion ensued about routine practices in multidisciplinary work. Staff felt that routine visits to a patient were stressful, when a telephone call to the patient might be enough. They agreed that their approach to patients should be holistic, that it was artificial to make differences between the roles of team members and for different professionals to have to make regular appointments with a patient. The requirement that every patient had to be seen by a nurse, a doctor and a social worker, might be too rigid; it might not meet the patient's needs and patients could become frustrated. Staff agreed that they needed to discuss this. But they never had time for a meeting. So the months passed.

It seemed impossible for the staff to sustain the unifying experience of non-differentiation in the team, and at the same time to think about the necessary differentiation in their multidisciplinary work. They therefore postponed meeting and avoided thinking about their different professional capacities in connection to patients' diverse needs. Such thoughts would bring recognition of differences between them, and recognition, too, that they were not interchangeable, nor could they all be equally involved with all the patients all the time.

Fourth staff group

As I came into the room I found the group enjoying themselves, laughing and appearing to be somewhat excited. Maksim put his bleeper down on his shoe and the others enquired what that meant. He said it was a new style and they all laughed. Maksim said that he was actually very surprised to receive a Christmas gift from the team, on which he was called a sexual maniac, or something of the kind. His children had found it very entertaining. Everybody laughed heartily. Tania was laughing so much she had to go out of the room to collect herself. I wondered about the laughter and about two members who were leaving and added whether they were afraid of spoiling things. Marina joyfully said they usually have a party when somebody leaves. I suggested that perhaps a party had started for me because this was our penultimate meeting.

Marko seriously suggested that it might be better if they had a party when somebody joined the team. They all agreed that it could feel a bit strange to have a party when somebody was leaving. Stefania critically considered how there was always a farewell party when somebody left: one would almost think people were pleased that someone was leaving. I said that perhaps they had certain ways of dealing with separation. Tania thought that in their case, working with elderly patients, the endings were final because the patients died; in that sense, perhaps, they had learned to become resigned to people leaving and accepted it quite well. She said that they were used to experiencing loss. Maksim added that perhaps it was connected with expecting less from people.

The group agreed how vital it was for the team to feel supported and how having support was one of the important aspects of their work together. They discussed how they might feel let down and how difficult it was to explain this to other people. Stefania said it was helpful if one knew why someone was leaving and they thought how difficult it was to experience misplaced trust. I commented that perhaps separation was difficult, and that they were facing separation all the time, when patients died, or when staff members left.

And now this group was going to end. So perhaps they had various feelings about this. Marko agreed and said he thought they had difficulty in confronting each other.

The use of the word, 'vital', is interesting, with connotations of something essential, like 'life', 'life-giving', and 'sustaining', and there was tremendous significance attached to something being vital. It is likely that patients projected strength, energy and vigour on to staff, while the patients could be left with all the losses and with the ultimate loss – of life itself.

Manic defences, with exciting, erotic, light and quick interactions were more prominent than usual, and were, I thought, also related to the ending of our work. Feelings about my impending departure were mixed. There was relief, even some triumph, as they prepared to celebrate with a party. Then they became suddenly concerned about having farewell parties and proposed a 'welcoming a new person' party instead. This might also be indicative of their apprehension about feeling relieved when a terminally ill patient died. De Hennezel (1989) pointed out that anybody involved in work with dying patients would inevitably, at some point, become impatient and irritated with the time the patient is taking to die and with their clinging to life, when all the signs of imminent death are present.

They spoke briefly about how important it was for them to have 'support', but this recognition was mixed with doubts about the possible reasons for my leaving, and it is likely that 'misplaced trust' and disappointment were related to the oncoming ending of our work. It may be that the experience of having had something, in this instance, an opportunity to think and talk to each other, was spoiled, because it did not last. I think that a particularly disturbing experience for staff was a shared anxiety that they gave nothing worthwhile to their patients. They were worried that patients would experience them as disappointing and abandoning, since whatever patients had received from them could not last, nor could it change the course of their physical decline and death.

But there was another dimension in their appraisal of our work and likewise of their work with patients: the reality of how limited it was in various ways. I think the resignation that was expressed conveyed two distinct experiences: a bitterness and disdain about the inevitable loss and 'nothingness', and an acknowledgement of a harsh and painful experience of the reality of limitations and losses – just as it is in life and in their work.

Sixth staff group

In the last meeting, the separation and ending were denied. At times the group seemed oblivious of my presence: they did not discuss the ending of the group, though it was remarked upon in a matter-of-fact way. They thanked me quickly and somewhat dismissively. At some point in the group, I felt isolated, forgotten and buried with the past. The present did not exist: it was either the already-gone-past, or it was the future that I would not share with them.

After the group, I walked away in a pessimistic mood, questioning the meaning of staff group work. Then, gradually, I had a sense of loss. I was left feeling sad that I would not be seeing this team again. I also felt sorry about the people who were dying and about staff staying on to care for them, and guilty for leaving. And, finally, I, too, did not want these thoughts to linger, when there was no future for our joint work and I did not find time to write up this last meeting.

There were mixed and difficult feelings in the face of separation and loss, and uneasy doubts about the meaning of our work. But I also thought that the staff evoked in me feelings similar to the feelings evoked in their work with dying patients, about surviving, being alive, having a future and a life yet to come, and guilt about being able to leave and live.

Dynamics in the palliative-care team group

Death means being subject to some external reality, and we, in each and every moment of our lives, *are both a reflection* and *an effect* of what surrounds us.

Pessoa, *The Book of Disquiet First Phase*, p.138 (italics added)

Pessoa (2017) reminds us that awareness of death is always present somewhere in the mind, and is continuously *reflected into* and has an *effect on* each of us, and in this particular unit, the feelings about dying affected all, staff and patients alike.

In this section, I explored how the experience of death and dying manifested on one particular level in the team group as a whole. The team used manic defences against depressive anxieties, and the disturbing feelings arising from their patients' nearness to death were denied by their quick and tireless involvement. It seemed as if it was necessary not to allow time to think. They were rushed, as if their work required them to act as one and to be in two places at once. The team culture, apparently supported by staff, promoted the denial of time and perpetual manic engagement.

In addition to the more universal anxieties around death and dying, such as staff's unconscious anxieties about their own death and the death of their loved ones, it is most likely that both patients and staff projected their feelings into each other: staff projecting into patients how they would feel if they thought they were dying and the patients projecting their feelings about dying, their anquish and fears, onto the staff.

Team members avoided experiencing differences, separateness and limitations. They held themselves together by collectively exerting and sustaining a defensive lack of differentiation and maintained this state of being everywhere and nowhere in particular. This way of 'holding together' could spare the team members the envy, rivalry and potential conflicts that personal and professional differences could otherwise bring out between them. Separate relationships between members of the team, between the same professionals in their own rooms, and between patients and staff, would not be supported. Such relationships could be seen as exclusive, disturbing, and even destructive – like the 'special possessiveness' to which they referred. Holding together was a defence against their own depressing feelings, as well as their anxieties about the patients' envy or resentment for being left out of a relationship enjoyed by others and cut off from love and the source of life. Some patients facing death might have had just such feelings about being excluded from life and a future they could not participate in.

In feeling united, staff were protected from the difficult experiences that could be very difficult to endure alone, especially when they are more deeply involved with a patient. I think that the emphasis on their absolute availability reflected a collective pressure to provide some kind of ideal care and that they were caught up in a manic reparation defending against their own guilt, resentment and feelings of hopelessness that 'things cannot be put right'.

Staff caring for terminally ill patients are faced with a difficult job and it is inevitable that professionals in this work will experience tensions about how emotionally involved they can bear to be, and how uninvolved they can bear to remain.

The individual in the group and the group in the individual

In this section, I consider the *individual in the group* and the *group in the* individual, or the group in the mind of the individual, although I also make a few brief references to other levels, such as, the social issues of class and race, a management and organizational issue manifest in the inherent tension in one of the team's primary tasks, and the hatred and fear of madness in the wider social context.

In order to explore the experience of an individual in a group and the group in the mind of an individual, I will present the incidents that occurred on the outings as recounted by the nurses in the course of a staff group.

I facilitated a staff group on a psychiatric inpatient rehabilitation unit during the period of one year. The unit consisted of 12 patients and 16 full-time nurses and nursing assistants; the occupational therapist, clinical psychologist and a psychiatrist provided approximately one session per week and were not able to take part in the staff group. All patients suffered from a chronic psychotic illness, most with a diagnosis of schizophrenia, and were between 30 and 50 years old. The patients had 'challenging behaviour' and this meant that they were more difficult to work with and had a greater propensity to become violent. These were important factors that contributed to the problems around their discharge. The aim of the unit was to engage the patients in rehabilitation, to support the development of the skills they would need to lead a more independent life, and to facilitate their move into the community. Outings were, therefore, an important part of the work. Patients and nurses would go on outings to different places, such as restaurants, shops and the cinema, as part of the programme.

In the course of our work it became clear that nurses, as well as patients, were not only aware that there was greater scope for patients' acting out when they were on outings, but that this impacted on the nurses' anxieties concerning the risk to the patient and to others, and their legal liability. This in turn affected the emotional state of patients. The outings were experienced by patients and staff as a test of how patients might manage living in the community and it became apparent that patients had mixed feelings about this move. The outings were a complex work task, since the nurses had diverse responsibilities and they needed to:

Promote a particular model of patient care that involves taking the patients on outings.

Monitor at all times the patients' tendency to act out on outings, while being mindful of being over protective and thus provoking the patients.

Protect the patients from the consequences of their disturbing behaviour when they acted out.

Protect the patients from the disturbing impact that members of the public or other patients could have on them.

Protect members of the public from the patients.

Considering all the points above and the patients' propensity to act out on outings, it seems likely that at some point the nurses would feel they were failing in some respect the patients, the members of the public, or the task of implementing the outings.

During our work, the nurses became interested in thinking about the patients' tendency to act out and create incidents on the outings in the community. The staffs' openness to their own experiences and those of their patients in the 'situations of disarray', was important in helping them gain a greater understanding, both of their patients and their own feelings, and particularly the dynamic meanings that underlie rehabilitation work.

I will focus here on the parallels between the psychotic patients' experiences and experiences in the group on outings and consider the impact of patients' acting out on others in a group, specifically on the nurses. I refer to a *group* or a *group situation* when a number of individuals (patients, nurses and members of the public) participate in the event precipitated by the patient's acting out and are involved, in one way or another, in jointly creating or sharing experiences in the given situation. Such a group is highly specific: it is very short-lived; some participants will not have met before and will never meet again.

Patient's seizure

A female nurse went on an outing with a male patient who was known to be able to produce pseudo fits that had all the appearance of dangerously uncontrollable behaviour. The patient would start to shake violently, would then lose coordination and throw himself onto the floor. When this happened in the unit, if he was ignored, he would eventually stop. However, on outings this behaviour was much more difficult to manage. The patient started trembling in a shop and falling all over the place. The nurse said that there were many customers and shop assistants around, but she felt quite alone with him. Although she was familiar with this behaviour, in this particular context it nevertheless made her feel very anxious. She did not know when he would stop, how far the fit would escalate, and to what extent he might become uninhibited and unrestrainable. At the same time, she felt that he was doing it on purpose, to gain control of the situation. People in the shop were disturbed and quickly moved away, forming a circle at a safe distance. The nurse felt very uncomfortable, thinking that she must appear uncaring or even cruel, in allowing the patient to terrorize other people.

She could not restrain the patient and take him back to the unit and so was forced to wait, as it seemed, indefinitely, her anxiety escalating. As her repeated attempts to make contact with the patient failed, she was finding it almost unbearable to be so helpless. She said she felt more and more trapped and this in turn made her feel increasingly angry with the patient and also quite resentful towards the onlookers. At the same time, she thought that the others were watching her from a distance to see how she treated the patient. She thought that they were angry with her for not 'doing' something.

The patient's behaviour stirred uncomfortable feelings in the group. By creating this upheaval, according to the nurse, the patient was able to evoke fear and resentment in the group of onlookers. In the midst of all the disarray provoked by the patient, it was impossible for the nurse to contain him; she felt trapped and paralysed. It seemed that all the participants shared the same experience – 'no one to turn to', no one who could help. The onlookers could not, or would not, step in to help the nurse, and the nurse did not, or could not, alleviate the tension in the group by doing something. In many ways the shared experience in the group reflected a state of mind that was familiar to the patient, that is, being in the grip of an overwhelming experience, without any containment, without any support internally or externally.

Furthermore, there was a sense of confusion with mixed if not conflicting feelings. The nurse thought that the patient's behaviour was experienced by other people as increasingly unrestrained and persecuting. Simultaneously, the patient also appeared to feel increasingly persecuted. By becoming more uncontrollable, the patient was also forcing others to experience something that was out of control. So all participants were caught up in a mutually reinforcing cycle of fearing something dangerous, which in turn made the patient become increasingly disturbed.

The nurse said she felt angry with the patient for making her feel so anxious and helpless. She was also angry with the other people in the shop because she thought that they blamed her for allowing the patient to 'fall all over the place'. Or even worse, she felt harshly scrutinized and imagined that the bystanders thought that she had provoked the patient into a fit of uninhibited rage by mal-treating him.

She also thought that the patient was deliberately tormenting her, that he was triumphing in the chaos he had created and even in her suffering. The nurse was unable to make contact with the patient; she felt anxious and uncontained her-self and this may have further fuelled his acting out. Although it appeared as if the patient forcefully seized control, he ended up feeling quite uncontained and uncontrollable. When the patient became unreachable while fear and hostility were circulating through the group, everyone, including the patient, could believe that this confirmed that he was, after all, dangerously insane. The more painful feelings arising from witnessing an unstoppable regression towards disintegra-tion were denied. There was fear, resentment and anger in the group, but all par-ticipants seemed to manage the turmoil by locating the blame elsewhere, in the patient, the nurse, or the people in the shop.

I would like to point out that the nurse's concern that others would think she was abusive to the patient is one that is frequently voiced by nurses working with psychotic patients. I have observed in other staff teams that staff often express a worry that patients, their families, colleagues, or management see them as being abusive to the patients (Novakovic, 2002, Novakovic, 2011). This tends to become a preoccupation when the nurses feel attacked and provoked by patients, and when in turn they feel resentful towards patients, particularly because of the disturbing feelings that they are made to experience, including a wish to retaliate. The nurses may defend themselves against their vengeful feelings, persecutory guilt and fear of being found out to be harsh, by appeasing and inviting patients to control them in a cruel way.

It also needs to be noted that some patients are peculiarly sensitive to being receptacles for what others have projected onto them, and that they can collude with these projections. These patients lend themselves to this process: sometimes they seem to act out the (others') madness, and sometimes even to *act* it. In such situations, the public, family members, or nursing staff can feel compelled to use and abuse the patient as a depository for badness and madness. This has a broader reference – particularly in families where the patient acts as a kind of container for all the madness in the family, but also in institutions where similar dynamics can pertain.

Responses from the public

The nurses thought that, apart from the patients' propensity to engage in poten-tially disturbing interactions with members of the public, members of the public also sometimes interacted with the patients in a disturbing way. The nurses said they found it particularly frustrating when people related to the patients in a negative way 'for no apparent reason'.

> One nurse remembered a group outing to the large department store, Harrods. On this occasion the shoppers' attitude to the patients affected all the patients, provoking one to make an offensive statement. The patients had not engaged in any particular behaviour that was disturbing, yet the people in the store behaved in a strange way, eyes were cast downwards or averted, as if they did not want to know about the patients' existence in the store or were pretending that they were not there; they seemed to move away from the patients and the nurses thought that they feared being 'infected'. The nurse said that, as she walked through the store, she experienced rising anger towards the public; she also noted that the patients seemed quite uncomfortable, walking in silence and keeping unusually close to each other and to the nurses. Suddenly a female patient raised her arm and announced loudly that she wanted to go to the toilet. What felt like a terrible silence fell and although it seemed as though no one paid any attention to the patient, the situation felt extremely humiliating. When they found out that they had to pay a pound to use the toilet, the patient proclaimed very loudly, "A pound for a shit!", and the words seemed to reverberate through the store.

The nurse said she perceived in the public an anxiety about some kind of contamination or intrusion of something noxious from the patients, and this perhaps contributed to the patient's need to go to the toilet. The patient might have been additionally stirred by the discomfort and embarrassment the staff felt. All the patients seemed to feel quite intimidated and were unusually silent.

The other shoppers in the store ignored the patients and the patients must have seen that nobody wanted to look at them and so were affected and provoked by the disturbing impact they appeared to have on others. They probably felt both humiliated and angry. It is very likely that in addition to the manner in which the patients walked, their peculiar expressions and their odd attire combined to make them particularly conspicuous. The patient's sudden mentioning of her need to defecate was most likely an angry or envious attempt to soil this pristine and enviable place, with its seemingly infinite plenitude. In different circumstances her comment 'a pound for a shit' might have been thought of as a ridicule of the toilet money and wealth connection, a parody on the extravagant and 'filthy' prices in the store, a mockery and denigration of consumerism, etc. However, in this particular context, I think that the patient felt compelled to attack the customers and shopkeepers in order to manage the experience of being made to feel like 'shit' – dirty or worthless.

The nurses argued that the patients were well behaved prior to the incident and that the people in the store were hostile towards the patients 'for no apparent reason', and it would seem that the nurses alluded to what Hedges (1994) argues when he states, "Throughout all time and in all cultures people have developed a variety of ideas and prejudices about madness", and that there is a general tendency "to externalize and then to persecute our own sense of fear and uncertainty – our own private madness" (p.12). Looked at it in this way, the customers projected something intolerable (their own fears of madness in themselves) onto the patients and the nurses, and so the nurses' experience in the store mirrored something essential about the general fear and hatred of madness. However, being in the vicinity of people who could become uncontrollable, violent, or unpredictably provocative is understandably in itself very unsettling.

Apart from the ordinary universal fear of madness, class and racial differences make their contribution to understanding this incident. There was a tension between the affluence of Harrods' customers and the patients: the customers and shop assistants were mostly white, the patients and nurses were mostly black. The all too apparent social and financial superiority of the customers and shop assistants in this vignette may have brought the nurses and patients closer together.

In this example, social class and racial differences are particularly striking – other vignettes present situations in the ethnically mixed and deprived inner city areas where class and racial differences between patients and public were much less marked. The nurses' choice of Harrods is interesting. It was probably predictable that the differences between the patients and the members of the public would be quite significant in this particular setting and therefore likely to provoke a reaction in all parties. However, it did not seem to me that the nurses were guided by a need to punish or attack their patients and themselves, or the members of the public, although such deeper motives cannot be ruled out. The ethos of the team was to help the patients to 'go back' into society. The patients liked going to these shops and although this outing proved to be one of those 'difficult' situations, the nurses thought that the patients would enjoy and benefit from the visit to this famous and opulent store.

Patient's exposure

A female nurse and a female patient went on an outing. In a queue for the bus, the patient started struggling – she did not want to get on the bus, but the nurse insisted. This made matters worse. The patient became more restless and quite suddenly she pulled up her blouse and exposed her bare breasts. There were a lot of people in the immediate vicinity and at first the nurse was stunned. She reported that the patient had done this with considerable pride yet also with a shocking mockery. The patient then started running down the street, exposing herself to a person who happened to be near her. She then ran towards other people, repeating this sequence.

The nurse felt profound shame and humiliation as she followed the patient helplessly. She explained that it was not only humiliating that the patient was partly naked, she was sexually provocative to bystanders, looking directly at each person and offering them her breasts and they, in turn, watched the display with awe, turning their heads as if to follow with interest what might happen next, and an element of excitement was unmistakeable. She was very worried about what these onlookers would think of the patient, but, over and above this, very concerned about what they might think of her, imagining that it was apparent to all that it was she who was responsible for allowing this disorder to occur.

It is hard to say why the patient decided that she did not want to get on the bus, but her manner conveyed some sense that she was driven to act in this way. She was ecstatic and uncontrollable and the nurse, until she recovered, felt trapped and helpless, but also ashamed and angry. The patient seemingly ignored the nurse, but while she engaged with the members of public in this unpredictable and arousing manner, she was making the nurse a witness to what looked like a bizarre mixture of seductive teasing, triumphant denigration and some kind of insatiable and greedy pursuit. It was as if the nurse was forced to be an accomplice in these different scenarios, and felt that she was silently blamed by onlookers for allowing this outrage to happen. This led to the patient feeling increasingly powerful and exalted, while the nurse felt increasingly helpless, and as she put it, 'destroyed'.

This episode seems thus to condense a number of different inner scenarios. The profound embarrassment and humiliation felt by the nurse which may well have been, in part, a projection of the patient's own experience of herself: as being bad, wishing she could disappear from reproachful and accusing eyes (as the nurse had described her own experience). On the other hand, the patient expressed other aspects of her relationships between her internal figures, for she also subjected the public to this exposure, which on some level, both violated those around her and swept them up in uncontrollable and reckless excitement.

One important source of this enactment derives from the fact that the patient was now 'outside', no longer in the more secure (and controlled) space provided by the ward and so she, in her turn, may have felt she was enticed or even forced into a confrontation with this different, exciting and dangerous world outside. The manner of the patient's exposure, as if she was offering those around a glimpse of a boundless sensuous experience, might reflect a denigration of the poor provisions that were offered her by the nurse/mother/breast. The patient could be seen as showing that *she* did not need the nurse, *she* was not dependent on her for *she had it all* and was *totally free*. Further, it was now the nurse who depended on her (for relief from this disturbance).

Dynamics of psychotic experience

In the situations of disarray on the outings, the nurses experienced a transient breakdown in their ability to think: they referred to feeling crushed, shattered, or destroyed. There are important parallels between the patients' experiences of being confused, split, fragmented, and the blurring of the individual boundaries that can arise between self and others in the group, as I will show. The vignettes in the previous section describe episodes of acting out that occurred in transitory groups composed of patient(s), nurse(s), and the onlookers in the shops or in the street.

A group perspective provides a framework for considering the patients' relationships in terms of the *effects* that they had on other individuals, specifically, the nurses in the context of the groups on the outings. This was manifest, for example, in the nurses' dismay which seemed to arise from having to bear a combination of very different feelings, all of which were felt intensely – not only the feelings stirred up by the patients, but also the very divided feelings they had regarding the members of the public. Although it was the patients who acted out in disturbing ways, the nurses and members of the public all contributed to the experiences felt in the group. Foulkes' (1990(1971)), concept of 'transpersonal processes', though referring to a different context, is helpful here:

> To do justice to the fact that this mental field of operation very much includes the individual but also transgresses him, I have used the term 'transpersonal processes'. These processes pass through the individual, though each individual elaborates them and contributes to them and modifies them in his own way. Nevertheless, they go through all the individuals – similar to X-rays in the physical sphere.
>
> (Foulkes [1971]1990, p.229)

The upheavals that occurred on the outings created a sense of confusion as to who was the victim, who was being humiliated, hurt, controlled, or terrorized – and who was responsible and thus guilty of stirring up these feelings. This recalls the experiences described by Coleridge ([1816]1996):

> . . . A lurid light, and trampling throng
> Sense of intolerable wrong,
> And whom I scorned, those only strong!
> Thirst of revenge, the powerless will
> Still baffled, and yet burning still!
> Desire with loathing strangely mixed
> On wild or hateful objects fixed.
> Fantastic passions! maddening brawl!
> And shame and terror over all!
> Deeds to be hid which were not hid,
> Which all confused I could not know,
> Whether I suffered, or I did:
> For all seemed guilt, remorse or woe,
> My own or others still the same
> Life-stifling fear, soul-stifling shame . . .
> Coleridge, 'The Pains of Sleep'

What is so vividly conveyed here is the tormenting persecution, "Thirst of revenge", "Sense of intolerable wrong" and "Life-stifling fear", but also "Desire with loathing strangely mixed", disconcerting and "Fantastic passions". Most of us can identify to some extent with the unsettling experience that Coleridge describes, understand the madness conveyed in the poem, the fleeting experience of non-differentiation between self and other: "Deeds . . . Which all confused I could not know/Whether I suffered, or I did". Yet there is also something quite unthinkable about the experience of madness.

What I want to suggest here is that the difficulties professionals face in work with these patients arise not only from the difficulty of being in touch with such intense or unbearable feelings and the disturbances in thinking they cause, but from the fact that when psychotic processes predominate, they produce *simultaneously* bizarre internal and external relationships that are in conflict with each other. It is the (inevitably failed) attempt to hold such different or opposing feelings and ideas together in the mind at the same time that I think evokes the profound difficulty in thinking, and that this results in subject feeling a disabling limitation and anxiety, culminating in the experience of feeling incapacitated, 'shattered' or 'crushed'.

Bion (1967) in his 'Commentary' at the end of *Second Thoughts*, describes a disturbing experience that can arise in work with psychotic patients. He refers to a "complex situation" in the "field of emotional force", where individuals lose their "boundaries as individuals":

> The psychotic patient is subject to powerful emotions and is able to arouse them in others; so at least it appears until the situation is examined more closely. The psycho-analysis of such a patient soon reveals a complex 'situation' rather than a complex patient. There is a field of emotional force in which the individuals seem to lose their boundaries as individuals and become 'areas' around and through which emotions play at will. Psychoanalyst and patient cannot exempt themselves from the emotional field. The psycho-analyst must be capable of more detachment than others because he cannot be a psycho-analyst and dissociate himself from the state of mind he is supposed to analyse. The analysand cannot dissociate himself from the state of mind he needs to have analysed. That state of mind is easier to understand if it is regarded as *the state of mind of a group* rather than of an individual but transcending the boundaries we usually regard as proper to groups or individuals.
>
> (Bion, 1967, p.146, my emphasis in italic).

Bion suggests here that within the "emotional field" that surrounds a psychotic patient, individuals are compelled to share intense and extreme experiences in a particular manner, and that in doing so, they transcend their individual boundaries. In the situations of disarray I have described, the nurses were in "the state of mind of a group". The nurses were profoundly affected through the patients' particular use of projective identification and they were 'forced to partake' in the patients' experience. However, introjective identification also plays a key role in generating the experience of loss of the individual's boundaries – I agree with Rosenfeld ([1952]1965; 1987) when he unambiguously states that the confusion in psychotic patients can result from patients having phantasies of being inside the object and phantasies of having the object inside the self at the same time:

> I took the view that identification by introjection and by projection usually occurs simultaneously and emphasized that narcissistic omnipotent object relations are partly defensive against the recognition of the separateness of self and object.
>
> (Rosenfeld, 1987, p.21)

Psychotic patients have difficulty in bringing together different and split experiences of their objects. This creates a paradoxical situation of having two irreconcilable experiences at the same time, or being in two mutually exclusive 'locations' in relation to the object, so that in phantasy the patient can experience entering/being inside the object *and* engulfing/incorporating the object inside the self. Thus, these patients feel both invaded and invading, controlled and controlling, etc. Their capacity to provoke others into enacting different facets of their own experiences can be observed in the different psychiatric inpatient and outpatient units, when some team members can feel that they are controlled by the patient, while others could feel that they are controlling the patient.

The opportunity to think about the nurses' accounts of their experiences in the situation of an upheaval in a group situation on the outings provided a striking insight that at one level all the nurses had a very similar experience. They felt they were subjected to merciless control, but also, simultaneously, they felt that they themselves were cruelly controlling in subjecting 'someone' to endure 'something' that was unbearable.

Furthermore, in the group the feelings *changed locations*. In the Harrods store the nurse experienced the customers' averted gaze and fears about being contaminated by the patients as attacking/intimidating/hateful; the nurse thought that patients felt attacked/intimidated/hated; the patient made the attacking/intimidating/hateful statement and this left the nurses (and probably the public) feeling attacked/intimidated/hated.

In addition to feelings moving around, that is, circulating in the group between different individuals, different feelings simultaneously occurred in *the same location* or in a single individual. In the example of the patient who had a seizure, the nurse simultaneously felt *anxious*, about what the patient might do and about how onlookers might perceive her, *angry* with the patient and with onlookers, *punished* by the patient, *punishing* to the patient and onlookers, *trapped* by the patient, as though she was *entrapping* the onlookers, and *guilty* vis-à-vis the onlookers and the patient. The nurse felt divided, experiencing different aspects of herself in relation to the patient and the onlookers.

Similarly, in the example of the patient who exposed herself, it seemed that while the patient was acting out her conscious desires or unconscious phantasies, perhaps pertaining to an early oedipal scene or an infantile feeding situation, the nurse struggled with feelings she could not reconcile; she felt simultaneously anxious, angry, humiliated, persecuted and guilty towards the patient. As well as being 'fragmented' in her experience of the patient, the nurse was 'fragmented' in her experience of other people. She was anxious that members of the public would accuse her of allowing them to be violated; she was angry with them for looking at the patient in a particular way that acted to fuel the patient's excitement, and she felt guilty that she had been unable to prevent the disaster.

All the nurses agreed that at some point on the outings they felt crushed or in some way disabled. I think that the nurses felt profoundly disturbed because they were 'forced' to endure irreconcilable, *concurrently diverse*, and even opposing feelings that were impossible to contain.

The group perspective: some further theoretical implications

Examining the processes described here from a 'group perspective' brings several considerations to the fore. First, there are the experiences that occurred in the group. Second, the nurses' experience of being in 'the state of mind of a group'. Third, as I will present below, there is what one might call the individual's *internal group relations*, that is, the phantasies of different internal figures and relations between these figures.

1. Context of the observation: observation of psychotic processes in a group

Patients, and people in general, can project different aspects of themselves into different individuals in a group. However, what was particularly highlighted here was the impact of a patient's acting out on one individual *within a group*. The perspective of observation of an individual's experience in a group – in this instance a nurse's experience – provided an opportunity for thinking about how an individual could become 'split' by having irreconcilable but simultaneous feelings concerning different participants in the group. Thus, for instance, the nurses were able to feel *at the same time* that they were *mercilessly controlled* and *cruelly controlling* someone in the group on outings. It was relevant that nurses presented the feelings *they had in the group*, since the simultaneity of their diverse and split feelings towards different participants, both patients and the members of the public, became apparent, perhaps only because it was possible to reflect on the experiences that the nurses had in the context of a group.

2. 'The state of mind of a group'

The nurses' confusion, in the situations of disarray on the outings, can also be understood as arising from being in 'the state of mind of a group' (Bion, 1967). That is, the nurses were compelled to share intense feelings within the 'emotional field' that surrounds a psychotic patient, resulting in their confusion as to *who did what to whom*, aptly described by Coleridge as: "Deeds . . . Which all confused I could not know,/Whether I suffered, or I did" (p.202).

3. The individual's 'internal group relations'

Bion ([1975]1991), in his trilogy, *A Memoir of the Future*, makes use of a group 'perspective' to express complex relationships between parts of the self. I think that in this book Bion revisited his interest in groups. In this work, different protagonists are relating with each other, such as, 'Bion', 'Myself', 'Twenty Years', 'Mind', 'Body', 'Girl', 'Boy', etc. These protagonists could be seen to represent a group of different internal and external figures, and like in any group, these figures are in a relationship with each other. My understanding is that Bion is drawing attention to the relationship between internal figures and that he is describing an internal group or group in the mind. Meltzer (1994) makes a similar point, seeing the trilogy as ". . . the dismembering of the universal preconception of the unity of the mind . . ." (p.521), and an investigation of ". . . the individual as a 'group' with only the tools of analogy, reversible perspectives, multiplication of vertices, and negative capability as our equipment" (p.532–33). Further on, he suggests, "The group, however, is not only external, but internal as well . . . [with] . . . different parts of the personality separated from one another, incommunicado" (p.529), that is, an *internal group* composed of different internal figures.

However, in my view, an important further feature of the trilogy is the *dynamic* aspect, that is, the nature of relationships *between* different internal figures, and the overall *emotional tone of the internal group constellation as a 'whole'*. I think Foulkes ([1977]1990) indicates the individual's internal group relations when he describes the mind as a network of continuous interactions, in a continuous interchange on various levels with various 'others', and that a group with its multi-layered, multi-personal simultaneous relating closely mirrors this multi-layered interactive dimension of the psyche.

Consideration of the relationships between the internal figures or an internal group can be compared to the simultaneously occurring relationships in dreams, what can be thought of as a 'dream group'. Resnik (1995) asks how it is possible that the different characters in a dream can reflect and contain the dreamer. He makes use of Matte-Blanco's concept of "multiple dimensions" to provide a structure for understanding these otherwise chaotic and incomprehensible phenomena (the coexistence of part and whole object relations, the potential in dreams for thoughts or feelings to occupy simultaneously the whole ego and only a part of the ego). Resnik points out:

When we dream, we become multiple personalities, experiencing our adventures in time and space simultaneously through each of the protagonists.
(Resnik, 1995, p.10)

The relationships depicted in dreams reveal the relationships between the *parts* and the *whole*, the interplay between the part object relations, whole object relations, and also the dynamics of the dream group as a whole. A common feature of all group constellations, whether a group composed of different individuals, a dream group, or an internal group, is the existence of different, but concurrent relations between different 'parts' within a 'whole'. The universal phenomenon of a dream group and the particular phenomenon described here, where very disturbed patients both suffer and evoke in others concurrent experiences, can then perhaps be best understood as all deriving, at some fundamental level, from relationship between different internal figures, i.e., from internal group relations or 'group' in the individual's mind.

A parallel is drawn here between the concurrent relations in a psychotic state of mind and the more ordinary dream group experience. Both dynamic scenarios can be conceptualized as the individual's internal group relations.

Conclusion

The aim of this chapter was to present different levels: the dynamics in a group as a whole, the individual in the group, and the group in the individual. In the first part of the chapter I looked at the dynamics of the team group *as a whole*. The style of patient care in the palliative care team indicates that the staff team felt they had to protect their patients from the physical and mental pain of dying. The team group dealt with persecutory and depressive anxieties by holding together defensively, as if they were united in hope of being protected from despair, anxiety and guilt that they would otherwise endure alone, when they were individually and more deeply involved with a dying patient. Manic defences were employed against depressive and persecutory feelings. By non-differentiating and merging, staff, as a group, defended themselves not only from the possible conflicts in the team, but more relevantly from the disturbing feelings evoked in their work with patients who were dying. The dynamic of the team group as a whole, reflected something essential about the individual experiences of all involved.

In the second part of the chapter I focused on the *individual in a group*, or the individual's experience in a group, and I also explored the coexistence of different internal relations and figures, that is, the *group in the individual*, or as I phrase it, the *internal group relations*. I suggest that the disturbing feelings that the nurses experienced in their work mirrored the patients' experiences. The very primitive processes generated or unleashed in a group when the patients act out, create a bizarre shared experience of persecution and excitement, blurring of the boundaries between the individuals and confusion about *what belongs to whom*.

The nurses' capacity to reflect on their feelings suggested a parallel between 'the state of mind of a group' experience that they endured and the patients' state of mind.

The observation of the different and multiple effects that the patients can have on one participant in a context of a group, for example, on a nurse, also provided an opportunity for thinking about the phenomenon of concurrent relations, which I have suggested is characteristic of psychotic states of mind. It was the individual's, that is, the nurse's reflections in a *staff group* about their experience of feeling shattered while having conflicting and contemporaneous feelings about patients and members of the public in a *group on the outings*, that led me to think that the nurses' experiences reflected the psychotic patients' unconscious enactments of their *internal group relations*. I think that the phenomenon of internal group relations is not only characteristic for psychotic states of mind, but is also an aspect of the universal mental functioning that becomes apparent in dreams, or dream group, as well as in the experience that can be evoked in individuals, in any group situation when very primitive and psychotic processes predominate.

Obholzer (1994) states how in addition to primitive anxieties that are ever present, all pervasive, and that beset the whole of mankind, there are personal anxieties of staff and particular anxieties that arise from the nature of the work. In this chapter, I presented different anxieties and defences evoked in work with two different patient groups. Halton (1994) points out that in the institution, the client group could also be regarded as the originator of projections and the staff group could be recipients, and in such a situation staff may come to represent different and possibly conflicting emotional aspects of the psychological state of the client group. I looked at the various 'impacts' that terminally ill and psychotic patients 'make', the anxieties these impacts evoked in staff, and the defences employed against these anxieties. Yet, the situation is far more complex since staff 'make impacts' on each other, on the patients, and on the organization, while at the same time, both staff and patients are affected by the wider organizational and social context. These different levels are mutually interdependent and coexist, and they continuously influence and constitute each other. I think Foulkes ([1977]1990) poignantly describes this:

> In the group-analytic group individuals not only resonate on a large scale to each other, simultaneously and reciprocally but also to the group as a whole . . . It is as if all the events were specifically interrelated with each other in their *vital* meaning and showed this interrelationship by resonating.
>
> (Foulkes[1977]1990, pp.299, 300)

Note

1   In this chapter I use material from A. Novakovic (2001) 'Work with dying patients: team dynamic and team work', *Journal of Psychoanalytic Psychotherapy*, *15* (3): 279–94, and 'Psychotic processes: a group perspective', in: D. Bell and A Novakovic (Eds), *Living on the Border: Psychotic Processes and the Individual, the Couple and the Group*. Tavistock Clinic Series, Karnac Books, 2013.

References

Bion, W.R. (1967). Commentary. In: *Second Thoughts: Selected Papers on Psycho-Analysis* (pp.120–66). London: Heinemann.

Bion, W.R. ([1975]1991). *A Memoir of the Future*. London: Karnac.

Coleridge, S.T. ([1816]1996). 'The Pains of Sleep'. In: *Samuel Taylor Coleridge: Selected Poems* (p.202). London: Penguin.

De Hennezel, M. (1989). Denial and imminent death. *Journal of Palliative Care, 5* (3): 27–31.

Foulkes, S.H. ([1971]1990). The group as matrix of the individual's mental life. In: *Selected Papers: Psychoanalysis and Group Analysis* (pp.223–33). London: Karnac.

Foulkes, S.H. ([1977]1990). Notes on the concept of resonance. In: *Selected Papers: Psychoanalysis and Group Analysis* (pp.297–305). London: Karnac.

Halton, W. (1994). Some unconscious aspects of organisational life: contributions from psychoanalysis. In: A. Obholzer and V.Z. Roberts (Eds), *The Unconscious at Work: Individual and Organisational Stress in the Human Services*. London and New York: Routledge.

Hedges, L.E. (1994). A Shattered Self. In: *Working the Organizing Experience: Transforming Psychotic, Schizoid, and Autistic States* (pp.3–22). New Jersey: Jason Aronson.

Jaques, E. ([1965]1988). Death and the mid-life crisis. In: E. Bott Spillius (Ed.), *Melanie Klein Today: Developments in Theory and Practice: Volume 2: Mainly Practice* (pp.226–48). London: Routledge.

Meltzer, D. (1994). Three lectures on W.R. Bion's *A Memoir of the Future*. In: A. Hahn (Ed.), *Sincerity and Other Works: Collected Papers of Donald Meltzer* (pp.520–50). London: Karnac.

Novakovic, A. (2001). Work with dying patients: team dynamic and team work. *Journal of Psychoanalytical Psychotherapy, 15* (3): 279–94.

Novakovic, A. (2002). Work with psychotic patients in a rehabilitation unit: a short-term staff support group with a nursing team. *Group Analysis, 35* (4), 560–73.

Novakovic, A. (2011). Community meetings on acute psychiatric wards: rationale for group specialist input for staff teams in the acute care services. *Group Analysis, 44* (1): 52–67.

Novakovic, A. (2013). Psychotic processes: a group perspective. In: D. Bell and A. Novakovic (Eds), *Living on the Border: Psychotic Processes and the Individual, the Couple and the Group* (pp.108–31). Tavistock Clinic Series, Karnac, 2013.

Obholzer, A. (1994). Authority, power and leadership: contributions from group relations training. In: A. Obholzer and V.Z. Roberts (Eds), *The Unconscious at Work: Individual and Organisational Stress in the Human Services*. London and New York: Routledge.

Pessoa, F. (2017). The Book of Disquiet First Phase. In: *The Book of Disquiet.* London: Serpent's Tail.

Resnik, S. (1995). Introduction. In: *Mental Space* (pp.1–11). London: Karnac.

Rosenfeld, H.A. ([1952]1965). Notes on the psycho-analysis of the superego conflict in an acute schizophrenic patient. In: *Psychotic States: A Psychoanalytical Approach* (pp.63–103). London: Maresfield Reprints.

Rosenfeld, H.A. (1987). A psychoanalytic approach to the treatment of psychosis. In: *Impasse and Interpretation* (pp.3–27). London: Routledge.

Index